OXFORD MONOGRAPHS IN
INTERNATIONAL LAW

General Editor: Professor Ian Brownlie QC, DCL, FBA
*Chichele Professor of Public International Law in the University of
Oxford and Fellow of All Souls College, Oxford.*

THE SHATT-AL-ARAB BOUNDARY QUESTION

OXFORD MONOGRAPHS IN INTERNATIONAL LAW

This new series of monographs will publish important and original pieces of research on all aspects of public international law. Topics which will be given particular prominence are those which, while of interest to the academic lawyer, also have important bearing on issues which touch the actual conduct of international relations. None the less the series is intended to be wide in scope and thus will include the history and philosophical foundations of international law.

ALSO IN THIS SERIES

The Juridical Bay
GAYL WESTERMAN

The Exclusive Economic Zone
DAVID ATTARD

Judicial Remedies in International Law
CHRISTINE GRAY

Occupation, Resistance and Law
ADAM ROBERTS

The Legality of Non-Forcible Counter-Measures in International Law
OMER ELAGAB

State Responsibility and the Marine Environment
BRIAN D. SMITH

The Shatt-al-Arab Boundary Question

A LEGAL REAPPRAISAL

KAIYAN HOMI KAIKOBAD

CLARENDON PRESS · OXFORD
1988

Oxford University Press, Walton Street, Oxford OX2 6DP
Oxford   New York   Toronto
Delhi   Bombay   Calcutta   Madras   Karachi
Petaling Jaya   Singapore   Hong Kong   Tokyo
Nairobi   Dar es Salaam   Cape Town
Melbourne   Auckland

and associated companies in
Berlin Ibadan

Oxford is a trade mark of Oxford University Press

Published in the United States
by Oxford University Press, New York

© Kaiyan H Kaikobad 1988

All rights reserved. No part of this publication may be reproduced,
stored in a retrieval system, or transmitted, in any form or by any means,
electronic, mechanical, photocopying, recording, or otherwise, without
the prior permission of Oxford University Press

British Library Cataloguing in Publication Data
Kaikobad, Kaiyan Homi
The Shatt-al-Arab Boundary question : a
legal reappraisal.—(Oxford monographs
in international law).
1. Shatt-al-Arab (Iraq and Iran)—
International status
I. Title
341.4'2   JX4084.S4/
ISBN 0-19-825591-8

Library of Congress Cataloging in Publication Data
Kaikobad, Kaiyan Homi
The Shatt-al-Arab boundary question: a legal reappraisal/Kaiyan
Homi Kaikobad.
p. cm.—(Oxford monographs in international law)
Bibliography: p. Includes index.
1. Iran—Boundaries—Iraq.   2. Iraq—Boundaries—Iran.   3. Shatt
al-Arab (Iraq and Iran)—International status.   I. Title.
II. Series.
DS274.2.I57K35 1988   341.4'2'02685505—dc19   87-31329   CIP
ISBN 0-19-825591-8

Set by
Promenade Graphics Ltd, Cheltenham
Printed and bound in Great Britain by
Biddles Ltd, Guildford and King's Lynn

Editor's Preface

The problems presented by territorial disputes are persistent and are among the most important of our time. The 'Falklands war' and the war between Iran and Iraq are but recent illustrations of the potential for mischief which attaches to issues concerning boundaries and the validity of title to territory (including maritime rights). The significance of these issues is in inverse proportion to the level of understanding exhibited by the media and by political scientists. For the most part, it has been left to lawyers and geographers, with the occasional historian, to study particular disputes. Those professing a generalized interest in 'peace' and so forth tend to be pathetically ignorant of actual disputes and the related diplomacy.

The proper study of a boundary dispute calls for the careful teasing out of the strands of history, politics, diplomacy, and law which go to make up the special universe of each boundary dispute. Dr Kaikobad has brought the necessary qualities of patience and scholarship to his task, and he has used an impressive variety of sources. The result is not only a major work on the background to the Gulf War but a contribution of quality at once to the literature on territorial disputes, to the development of a typology of disputes, and to diplomatic history.

Oxford   IAN BROWNLIE

Acknowledgements

My attention was first drawn to the potential existing in the field of the international law relating to boundaries and frontiers in January 1978 by Ian Brownlie, QC, DCL, FBA, Chichele Professor of International Law, University of Oxford, then Professor of International Law, University of London, at the London School of Economics, when I was committed to securing the degree of Doctor of Philosophy under his supervision. The degree was secured, but my interest in the field of title to territory in general and frontiers in particular, inspired no doubt by Professor Brownlie's significant contribution in the same area, both as practitioner and academician, continues unabated. It is this interest which has compelled the writing of this book on the Shatt-al-Arab boundary question, and in this regard I am greatly indebted to him. His invaluable suggestions and observations have considerably enhanced the quality of the work. I am also grateful to D. W. Bowett, CBE, QC, Whewell Professor of International Law, University of Cambridge, who helped me to avoid certain pitfalls and commented upon an earlier draft of this work. The responsibility, nevertheless, of the endeavour rests squarely on my shoulders.

I would also like to extend my sincere gratitude to the President and Committee of the Zoroastrian Trust Funds of Europe, who, over the period 1982–4, permitted me to draw on their charitable financial resources in the way of maintenance. My gratitude also extends to Mrs Susan Hunt of the London School of Economics for typing and retyping several times over certain sections of the book with an extraordinary degree of patience, good humour, and, above all, efficiency.

I must take this opportunity and record a special word of appreciation for the staff of the Library of the Institute of Advanced Legal Studies, Russell Square, London, whose members were, over a long period of time, extremely kind and co-operative in the face of tiresome enquiries and repeated requests for favours. I would also like to thank the staff at the India Office Library and Records for their help and assistance over the years. I am also extremely thankful to Mr Ali Khadr of the London School of Economics and Policital Science who translated many of the French language documents which I came across in the course of my research in the India Office Library and Records.

Finally, I am beholden to my father, my late mother, and members of my family for providing me with not only the opportunity of an education abroad, but also for faithfully enduring long absences from home, and for fostering an abiding respect for scholarship.

Bloomsbury
London K.H.K.

TO MY PARENTS

'It is part of the mystique of the notion of territory that boundary lines are, even by the most cynical, strongly associated with the idea of legal rights. Governments, even when they are being unreasonable are always intensely legalistic about the boundaries of their territory.'

Sir Robert Jennings, General Course on International Law, Recueil des Cours, vol. 121, p. 429.

Contents

Abbreviations
List of Figures
Table of Cases
Introduction

1. The History
  I. Geographical Description of the Region   5
  II. A General Historical and Political Provenance to the Boundary Problem   6
    1. The location and description of the boundary   6
    2. Early history of the boundary question   7
    3. The questions of tribal allegiance and traditional control   8
      (a) Tribal allegiance   9
      (b) Traditional limits of control   12
    4. The development of the frontier question after 1843   16
      (a) The Conferences and Treaty of Erzeroum, 31 May 1847   16
      (b) Demarcation attempts: 1850–1852   18
      (c) The Indentic Map and the Agreement of 1869: further attempts at demarcation   22
      (d) The Tehran Protocol of 1911 and the Boundary Protocol of 1913   23
      (e) Boundary demarcation proceedings, 1914   51
      (f) The Treaty of 1937   52
      (g) The Algiers Protocol and Baghdad Treaty of 1975   64

2. The Legal Analysis
  I. The Legal Regime of the Boundary before 1975   68
    1. General   68
    2. Specific Issues   75
      (a) Mid-line or Thalweg in the Shatt   75
      (b) The abrogation of the Treaty of 1937   85
      (c) General conclusions   92
  II. The Legal Regime of the Boundary after 1975   93
  III. War and the Baghdad Treaty of 1975   99

Conclusion   116

Contents

Annexes 119
1. Second Treaty of Erzeroum, 31 May 1847 — 119
2. Agreement Relative to Frontier Delimitation between Persia and Turkey, signed at Tehran, 21 December 1911 — 121
3. Protocol signed at Constantinople, 17 November 1913 — 122
4. Boundary Treaty between The Kingdom of Irak and The Empire of Iran. Signed at Teheran, 4 July 1937 — 130
5. Joint Iranian-Iraqi Communiqué: [The Algiers Protocol] of 6 March 1975. — 134
6. Treaty *Concerning the State Frontier and Neighbourly Relations* between Iran and Iraq signed at Baghdad on 13 June 1975 — 136
7. Protocol Concerning the Delimitation of the River Frontier between Iran and Iraq, Baghdad, 13 June 1975. — 139

Bibliography 143

Index 154

Abbreviations

AJIL	*American Journal of International Law*
APOC	Anglo-Persian Oil Company
Baxter Memorandum	Memorandum on relations between Persia and Iraq: Baxter, 4 June 1928, FO PCP 2936/29/65, Reg. P3641, 1928, in L/P&S/10/1229
BFSP	*British and Foreign State Papers*
BYIL	*British Yearbook of International Law*
CO	Colonial Office
DO	Demi-Official
Eastern Department Memorandum	Memorandum on the frontier between Persia and Turkey, and Persia and Iraq, 1639–1934: Eastern Department, FO, 8 January 1935. PCP E171/32/34 at PZ462, 1935, in L/P&S/12/2869
FO	Foreign Office
ICLQ	*International and Comparative Law Quarterly*
IO	India Office
L/P&S	Letters Political and Secret
Parker Memorandum	Memorandum respecting the frontier between Mohammara and Turkey, 3 April 1912: A. Parker, FO PCP 14638, Reg. 1595, 24 March 1912, in L/P&S/10/266
PCP	Persia Confidential Print
Rawlinson Memorandum	Enclosure: Letter from British Minister, Tehran to Secretary of State for Foreign Affairs, 3 February 1844 PCP 10021, P1916, 1912 in L/P&S/11/16.
Reg. No.	Register Number: Refers to the India Office file/register and distinguishes it from Foreign Office and individual documentation.
Research Department Memorandum	Memorandum on the Persian frontier: FO Research Department, 31 January 1947, PCP E10136/4029/34, Ext. 1133 in L/P&S/12/1201

RIAA	*Reports of International Arbitral Awards*
UNTS	*United Nations Treaty Series*
YILC	*Yearbook of the International Law Commission*

List of Figures

1. Turkish, Persian, and Mediating Commissioners' claim lines in 1850 21
   From file L/P&S/10/266, India Office Library, London
2. Sketch showing approximate Turco-Persian frontier 24–5
   From file L/P&S/10/267, India Office Library, London
3. Lt. Wilson's map compiled from Plane Table Surveys in 1909 27
   From file L/P&S/10/266, India Office Library, London
4. Sketch showing Turco-Persian frontier west and south of Hawizeh; delimited in 1913 32–3
   From file L/P&S/10/430, India Office Library, London
5. Sketch of Mohammarah to indicate the Turco-Persian boundary; delimited in 1913 36–7
   From file L/P&S/10/430, India Office Library, London
6. The Shatt-al-Arab and [Bamishere]; delimited in 1913 Foldout*
   From file L/P&S/10/430, India Office Library, London
7. The Shatt-al-Arab and [Bamishere] up to the sea 38–9
   From file L/P&S/10/430
8. Sketch of the province of Zohab Foldout*
   From file L/P&S/10/430, India Office Library, London
9. Sketch of the province of Zohab showing the Soane–Orlof proposals 44–5
   From file L/P&S/10/267, India Office Library, London
10. The Shatt-al-Arab portion of the Perso-Iraqi frontier as fixed in 1913–14 and amended in 1937 60–1
    From the files of the Research Department, Foreign Office, London (dated March 1945)

* Figs 6 and 8 appear as foldout maps between pp 40 and 41

The figures are reproduced by permission of the Controller of Her Majesty's Stationery Office.

Table of Cases

Alaska Boundary Arbitration
15 *RIAA* p. 491 78
   (a) *Argument of the United States Before the [Alaska Boundary Tribunal]* Washington, 1903 79
   (b) *Alaska Boundary Tribunal, Minutes of Proceedings*, [London] 1903 79
Appeal Relating to the Jurisdiction of ICAO Council, Judgment.
ICJ Reports 1972, p. 46
ICJ Pleadings, Appeal Relating to the Jurisdiction of the ICAO Council, Indian Memorial 88
Arbitral Award of the King of Spain
ICJ Reports 1960, p. 192 72
Arkansas *v*. Mississippi
250 US 39 .... 79, 80
Arkansas *v*. Tennessee
246 US 158 .... 79, 80
Barotse Kingdom Boundary Arbitration
Brownlie, *African Boundaries: A Legal and Diplomatic Encyclopaedia* (London, 1979) 82
Beagle Channel Arbitration
Award of 18 April 1977, HMSO 1977 71
British Guiana *v*. Brazil Boundary Arbitration
11 *RIAA* p. 21 78
British Guiana *v*. Venezuela Boundary Arbitration
92 *BFSP* (1899–1900) p. 160 .... 78, 82
Printed Argument on Behalf of the United States of Venezuela (New York, 1898)
Buttenuth *et al. v.* St Louis Bridge Co.
123 Ill. 535; 17 NE Rep. 439;
Scott's Cases on International Law (Washington, DC, 1922), p. 206 .... 79, 80
Case concerning the Continental Shelf (Tunisia/Libyan Arab Jamahiriya)
ICJ Reports 1982, p. 18 72
Costa Rica *v*. Nicaragua Boundary Arbitration: Decision of 22 March 1888
2 *Moore's International Arbitrations*, p. 1945 73
Costa Rica *v*. Nicaragua (Central American Court of Justice) Decision of 13 September 1916
11 *AJIL* (1917) p. 181 .... 73, 90

Costa Rica v. Panama
11 *RIAA* p. 528 73
Eastern Greenland Case
PCIJ Series, A/B, No. 53 (1933) 70
Francis v. The Queen
(1956) 3 DLR (2d) 641 103
Grisbadarna Arbitration
(1909) 1 *Scott's Hague Court Reports* p. 121 .... 73, 77, 79
Handly's Lessee v. Anthony *et al.*
5 Wheat. 374 .... 79, 82
In re Village of Fort Erie and Buffalo and Fort Erie Public Bridge Co.
 (1927) 61 OLR 502; 4 ILR 121; 8 CILC 433 82
International Military Tribunal (Nuremberg) Judgment and Sentences: 1
 October 1946.
41 *AJIL* (1947) p. 172 110
Iowa v. Illinois
147 US 10 .... 79, 80, 81
Island of Timor case
(1914) 1 *Scott's Hague Court Reports* p. 355 78
Jaworzina Advisory Opinion
PCIJ, Series B. No. 8 (1923) 101
Karnuth v. US
279 US 231 103
Louisiana v. Mississippi
202 US 1 .... 79, 80
Luzern v. Aargau
Schindler, 'The Administration of Justice in the Swiss Federal Court in
 International Disputes', 15 *AJIL* (1921) p. 149 .... 89, 91
Minnesota v. Wisconsin
252 US 273 .... 77, 79
Minquiers and Ecrehos case
ICJ Reports 1953, p. 47
ICJ Pleadings, The Minquiers and Ecrehos case, Vol. 1. 71
Missouri v. Nebraska
196 US 23 80
Nebraska v. Iowa
143 US 359 80
New Jersey v. Delaware
291 US 361 .... 77, 79, 81
North Atlantic Coast Fisheries Arbitration
11 *RIAA* p. 173 102
Proceedings in the North Atlantic Coast Fisheries Arbitration, Washington,
 1912

Table of Cases

Case of the United States: Vol. i; *Appendix to the Case of the United States*, Part I, Vol. ii; *Case of Great Britain*: Vol. iv; *Oral Arguments*, Vol. ix, Part I, and Vol. xi.. 101, 102

North Eastern Boundary Arbitration
1 *Moore's International Arbitrations*, p. 127 78

Rann of Kutch Arbitration
50 ILR 1; 16 *RIAA* p. 1 71

Regina *v.* Mat Erat
(1872) 2 Ky. (Cr.) 86 (Straits Settlements); 8 CILC 379. 82

Society for the Propagation of the Gospel *v.* New Haven and Wheeler
8 Wheaton 464 102

State *v.* Reardon
120 Kansas 614; 245 Pacific Reporter 158 102

State of South Australia *v.* State of Victoria
[1914] AC 283 73

Sutton *v.* Sutton
(1830) 1 R & M 663; 39 English Reports 255; 4 BILC 362 103

Techt *v.* Hughes
229 NY 222; 128 North Eastern Reporter 185 103

Temple of Preah Vihear
ICJ Reports 1962; p. 6
ICJ Pleadings, Temple of Preah Vihear, Vol. ii (1962)................... 70, 73, 83

The Twee Gebroeders
3 C. ROB. 336; 165 English Reports, 485; SC 1 Eng. Pr. Cas. 323 .... 76, 83

Trademark Registration Case: Federal Republic of Germany, 27 September 1967
59 ILR 490 103

Vermont *v.* New Hampshire
289 US 593... 80, 81

Washington *v.* Oregon
211 US 127... 79, 81

Western Sahara Advisory Opinion
ICJ Reports 1975, p. 12 72

Zurich *v.* Schaffhausen: Decision of 9 November 1897
Schindler, 'The Administration of Justice in the Swiss Federal Court in International Disputes', 15 *AJIL* (1921) p. 149 82

Zurich *v.* Schaffhausen: Decision of 28 May 1907
Ibid. p. 168 82

Introduction

The history of the boundary regime between Iran and Iraq in the region of the Shatt-al-Arab river is a long and complex one and, accordingly, there has appeared, over a number of years, a considerable amount of literature on questions relating to the history, politics, and law of this sector of the border. However, this body of work suffers from some difficulties. For one thing, although a number of scholarly studies regarding the Iran–Iraq boundary and the war of 1980 have appeared since the commencement of hostilities between the two States, most of them tend not to be exhaustive legal examinations of the Shatt-al-Arab sector. For another, some of the writings on this topic were written in a period prior to the conclusion of the Baghdad Treaty of 1975 and the developments preceding and succeeding the hostilities. Moreover, some of this work is either inspired by official sources or is not entirely objective in presentation and analysis. Furthermore, in certain cases, writers and commentators have attempted to address themselves to legal questions without adequate knowledge of either the law or the political history of the case, both of which are, as with every boundary case, essential for an objective appreciation of the status of the boundary regime. In view of this situation, and especially the continuing hostilities between Iran and Iraq, a reappraisal of the legal aspects of the boundary regime in the Shatt-al-Arab (hereinafter referred to as the Shatt) region may not necessarily be a superfluous essay. It is recognized that the Shatt boundary is only a very small sector of an extensive 550-mile frontier; but it is this region which has generated problems and uncertainties and consequently the investigation has been confined, in the main, to this sector.

Although the primary objective, as mentioned above, is to provide a legal statement regarding the boundary question, the dispute nevertheless provides an adequate opportunity to reflect upon some of the more important issues relating to the international law of title to territory and, more specifically, boundary matters, with a view to achieving clarity in respect of some of them. Accordingly, within the framework of the Shatt question, an attempt has been made to provide a thoroughgoing statement and analysis of all the relevant issues of the dispute which then leads on to an application of the law to the specific question under consideration. Hence, while each of the questions has been examined in detail, it was inevitable that the *range* of the issues studied, and thus the scope of the work itself, would be limited by those confronting the States party to the dispute. It follows therefore that the book does not pretend to be an exhaustive statement on the law relating to boundaries. At any rate the questions raised by the two States and their predecessors for over a period of almost a century and a half are of fundamental importance to the law and keenly merit close scrutiny.

Furthermore, it is the case that owing to divergent and rather self-favouring interpretations placed upon them by the disputants, several of these issues have become somewhat obscured. This is especially true of the question of the rule of the thalweg and the *medium filum aquae* in navigable rivers, but not only because of the representations made by the parties. The analysis this subject has received by certain writers on international law has been less than satisfactory.

The abrogation of the Baghdad Treaty of 1975 between Iran and Iraq, which delimited the boundary in the Shatt and other sectors of the frontier and which established by way of protocol, *inter alia*, a regime regarding security along the frontier, gives point to the discussion on the law relating to the abrogation of frontier agreements—a matter of cardinal importance to this area of the law and one which constitutes a significant manifestation of the doctrine of continuity and finality of boundary regimes. Inasmuch as the doctrine has been examined by the author in an earlier publication, it does not qualify for more detailed study in the forthcoming pages. Nevertheless, it may be useful to note that the question of abrogation and of revision of the boundary treaties has bedevilled the relationship between Iran and Iraq and the predecessors of the latter.

Similarly it was felt that a more contemporary legal account of the law relative to the effect of war on boundary treaties and regimes was required, an account which attempts to provide modern legal answers to an old problem. The continuing hostilities between the disputing States furnishes an appropriate backcloth, as it were, to a study of the problems the war has succeeded in generating, namely those relative to the questions of unilateral and bilateral modifications to the alignment during and after a war, the roles of aggression and self-defence regarding alterations in the status quo of territory, and the realignment of frontiers after the conclusion of hostilities by way of peace treaty. These questions merit consideration in so far as the conclusions drawn therefrom may serve as guidelines not only for the two belligerents astride the Shatt, but also other disputants in different parts of the world with respect to their mutual rights and obligations and the appropriately limited compass of their powers both before and after the cessation of hostilities.

As in all cases, both international and municipal, a presentation of the facts is an essential preliminary to the legal analysis and accordingly the book has been divided into two main parts. Chapter 1 deals with the historical background to the dispute, while Chapter 2 is concerned with the legal analysis. Chapter 1 is a rather extended survey and is presented in the hope that such a survey will clarify some of the political facts which have over the years been obscured, again, by conflicting claims made by the disputing States. It may lay to rest some of the controversy which surrounds the more important issues of the boundary question, particularly those relating to traditional limits of control and allegiances of the main tribal grouping in the region, the Chaab. A feature which has informed this historical examination is the attempt, at all the appropriate places, to inquire why a specific, particular alignment, both riverain and non-riverain, was proposed, adopted, or rejected. This has resulted in some detailed description of certain sectors of the frontier and accordingly maps have been included to facilitate the following of the lie of the boundary. The approach mentioned above is justified not only because it has resulted in the presentation of a complete and hitherto unpublished record of the evolution of the frontier problem. It highlights the fact that contrary to popular belief, lines on the map were not always drawn by statesmen at their whim and fancy over the negotiating table, but were the results of meticulous research and extensive expeditions in various sectors of the borderlands by trained officials, both civilian and military, of the British government. To say this, of course, is neither to diminish or ignore the role played by the highest echelons of government in eventually arriving at a mutually agreeable frontier; it is only to stress that more often than not the boundaries agreed to by delegates have been those proposed and substantiated by local government officials. With a view, hence, to presenting a balanced picture of the history of the boundary problem, the various diplomatic initiatives made by the parties and superior policy considerations which shaped and affected the lines adopted by them have also been discussed.

In order to succeed in the objectives outlined above, it was necessary to rely almost exclusively on unpublished archival material housed in the India Office Library and Records, a division of the British Library, London.[1] Yet a number of published tracts and monographs on

---

[1] A substantial amount of this material originated in the Foreign Office. The India Office was not only kept informed on all matters which affected British interests in India, the Persian Gulf, and other adjacent areas, but also participated directly by seconding officials for frontier advice, investigations and expeditions, and boundary demarcation. The records referred to belong to the series entitled *Letters, Political and Secret* (L/P&S/), Nos. 10, 11, and 12 (Files and Collections).

the Shatt-al-Arab question have provided valuable information.² It is hoped that an historical record, which succeeds in furnishing essential facts for a legal analysis, will emerge and lend greater perspective to the dispute in consideration.

² Some of the more important published works on this subject in terms of history and analysis are Al-Izzi, *The Shatt-al-Arab River Dispute in Terms of Law* (Baghdad, 1972) and *The Shatt-al-Arab Dispute: A Legal Study* (London, 1981); Ismael, *Iraq and Iran: Roots of Conflict* (Syracuse, 1982); Amin, *International and Legal Problems of the Gulf* (London, 1981) and 'The Iran–Iraq Conflict: Legal Implications', *International and Comparative Law Quarterly*, 31 (1982), p. 167; Tahir-Kheli (ed.), *The Iran–Iraq War: New Weapons, Old Conflicts* (New York, 1983); El-Azhary (ed.), *The Iran–Iraq War* (London, 1984); Dessouki (ed.), *The Iraq–Iran War, Issues of Conflict and Prospects for Settlement* (Princeton, 1981). Some of the older works are: E. Lauterpacht, 'River Boundaries: Legal Aspects of the Shatt-al-Arab Frontier', *ICLQ* 9 (1960), p. 208; Edmonds, 'The Iraqi-Persian Frontier, 1639–1938', *Asian Affairs*, 62 (1975), p. 147 and *Kurds, Turks and Arabs* (Oxford, 1957); Melamid, 'The Shatt-al-Arab Boundary Dispute', *Middle East Journal*, 22 (1968), p. 351; Khadduri and Dixon, 'Passage through International Waterways', in Khadduri (ed.), *Major Middle Eastern Problems in International Law* (Washington, DC, 1972); Akhtar, 'The Iraqi-Iranian Dispute over the Shatt-al-Arab', *Pakistan Horizon*, 22 (1969), p. 213; Ryder, 'The Demarcation of the Turco-Persian Boundary in 1913–1914', *Geographical Journal*, 66 (1925), p. 237. For official governmental publications see *A Review of the Imposed War by the Iraqi Regime upon the Islamic Republic of Iran* (Legal Department, Ministry of Foreign Affairs, Iran, 1983); *Comment on the Iranian Claims concerning the Iraqi-Iranian Frontier Treaty of 1937, and the Legal Status of the Frontier between the Two Countries in the Shatt-al-Arab* (Ministry of Foreign Affairs, Baghdad, 1969): and *Facts Concerning the Iraqi-Iranian Frontier* (Minister of Foreign Affairs, Baghdad, 1960).

I
The History

I GEOGRAPHICAL DESCRIPTION OF THE REGION

The Euphrates and Tigris rivers flow through the Mesopotamian plains in Iraq in a general north-west to south-east direction. The two rivers meet at Kornah (Qornah), and from this point to where they flow into the Persian Gulf, the waters are known as the Shatt-al-Arab river. The areas of land on either side of the Shatt between Kornah and the Gulf are flat and marshy. On the eastern side, the lands are surrounded by the Zagros mountains, which lie wholly in Iran. Informed sources hold the view that the land lying between the Iranian plateau and the Shatt is geographically part of the Mesopotamian plain, the greater part of which is within Iraq today.[1] To the west of the Shatt is an extensive tract of low-lying alluvial desert drained by the Khor Zubair. The latter flows into the Khor Abdulla, a large tidal creek flowing south-east into the Gulf.[2] The belts of land on either side are ringed with date plantations. Low tides uncover vast tracts of marshy land at the mouth of the Shatt.[3] Further to the west, the terrain rises gently to form the great sand-deserts on the northern edges of the Arabian plateau. Downstream from Kornah on the right, or western,[4] bank of the Shatt, lies Basra. Further downstream is Khoramshar or Mohammara as it was once known.[5] It is situate on the left bank and lies astride the Karun river, or the Haffar Canal, which flows into the Shatt from the north-east. The Karun river, which flows in a general south-west direction towards Mohammara joins the Haffar Canal some miles to the east of it. The Bamishere (or Bamanshir) river flows generally parallel to the Shatt on its eastern side,

---

[1] Memorandum on the Frontier between Persia and Turkey, and Persia and Iraq, 1639–1934: Eastern Department, Foreign Office, 8 Jan. 1935: Persia Confidential Print E171/32/34 at PZ462, 1935 in L/P&S/12/2869. (Hereinafter referred to as the Eastern Department Memorandum.)

[2] Naval Intelligence Division, *Iraq and the Persian Gulf* (1944), p. 61.

[3] This phenomenon caused legal problems, see below, n. 267.

[4] In keeping with usage, the terms left and right banks will be employed to refer to east and west of the Shatt. For maps of the region, see Figs. 1, 3, 5, 6, and 7 below.

[5] Although Khoramshar is the current name, Mohammara, for purposes of this study, is deemed to be the more appropriate one inasmuch as the latter name was used throughout the history of the dispute up to 1937. The use of the name Mohammara does not reflect political bias.

and empties its waters in the Gulf. It is believed that at one time the Bamishere constituted the eastern branch of the Shatt; it receives its waters today from the Karun, which it leaves at the point where the latter flows into the Haffar Canal. This configuration has led to the creation of the island of Abadan, or Al Khizr, its earlier name, at the north-western head of which is the port of Abadan. Approximately seventy-five miles to the north of Mohammara is Hawizeh, and south-east of the latter, above thirty miles to the east of Mohammara, is the old town of Fellahiyeh.

II A GENERAL HISTORICAL AND POLITICAL PROVENANCE TO THE BOUNDARY PROBLEM

1. THE LOCATION AND DESCRIPTION OF THE BOUNDARY

The boundary between Iraq and Iran begins in the north near a peak in the Dalamper mountain approximately forty miles north-east of Ruwandiz in Iraq (36° 38' N, 44° 32' E), at north latitude 37° 09' and east longitude 44° 47', the trijunction of Iraqi, Iranian, and Turkish boundaries. It tends generally south-south-east along the high watersheds of the Zagros mountains and then along Baneh, a tributary of the Little Zab or Kalow. The boundary subsequently follows this and a minor affluent thereof in an east-west direction leaving the upper basin of the Qala Chulun tributary of the Little Zab and the upper tributaries of the Diyala to Iraq. Leaving the river and continuing in a south-easterly direction, the river ascends the mountains tending east, south-west, south, and south-east. It crosses the Zimkhan river and runs along a range of mountains which it soon leaves to follow the Sirwan river in a general south-westerly direction. The boundary leaves the river to ascend, and run south-west along, the mountains which leads it to Kasr-i-Shirin and Khanaqin in the Zohab region. These are the so-called 'transferred territories' which were the subject of some controversy in the early part of this century.[6] From this point, the boundary runs south-eastwards along the western edges of the Zagros mountains, or the Pusht-i-Koh, leaving the plains to Iraq in the west and Luristan to Persia in the east. It runs to Al Miqdadiyah, then south-east to Mandali, the river Badra, and to a point approximately thirty-two miles west of Dezful. The alignment then descends southwards into the plains and after following the Doveyrich and Shatt-al-Ama rivers, the boundary tends generally south-west and south through marshy tracts of territory. West of Hawizeh, the boundary line runs in a straight line to 31° parallel at which point it turns east along it up to a point east of the 48° meridian, at Khushk-i-Basri.[7] It

[6] Below, p. 40–8.
[7] For a more detailed description of the line, see below, p. 29–30.

then turns south in a straight line to the Shatt which it strikes about eight miles west of Mohammara.

The boundary south of this point constitutes the main area of controversy and has over the course of more than a century been modified on several occasions. By virtue of the Baghdad Treaty of 1975 and its Protocol on the delimitation of the river frontier, which constitute the latest agreement on the boundary question, the boundary runs along 'the thalweg, i.e. the median line of the main navigable channel at the lowest navigable level, starting from the point at which the land frontier between Iran and Iraq enters the Shatt Al' Arab and [continues] to the sea'.[8]

2. EARLY HISTORY OF THE BOUNDARY QUESTION

The Ottoman Empire began to gain ascendancy in Mesopotamia in the sixteenth century and direct administration began in 1546. After having extended its frontiers, the Ottoman Empire began a series of wars with Persia over questions of territory in Mesopotamia; but the treaties of peace which followed the wars never defined the exact location of the frontier between the Persian and Ottoman Empires. Questions were resolved by vague and general attributions of parcels of territory. Even so, it is believed on authority that 'Since the late middle ages, the frontier between the Persian and Turkish Empires has, speaking generally, followed, in its southern sector the line of division between the Iranian plateau and the Mesopotamian plain and in its northern sector the watershed between Lakes Urumiah (now Rezaiyeh) and Van. The exact line of this frontier has, however, been the cause of incessant quarrels between the two Empires'.[9]

The Treaty of Zohab of 17 May 1639[10] between Sultan Murad IV of Turkey and Shah Safi of Persia is one of the earliest treaties which assigned territories to the two States. While it did not delineate a boundary as such, it appears that the line of delimitation began at a point where the Shatt enters the Gulf and ran along it northwards for about fifty miles till it reached the edge of the Persian plateau. It skirted the plateau, leaving Mandali and Badra to Turkey. After reaching Kurdistan, the boundary ran generally north-westwards along high watersheds. In the far north, the

---

[8] Article 2. Text: *United Nations Treaty Series*, 1017, No. 14903. See also *A Review of the Imposed War*, Annex, p. 163. See Annexes 6 and 7 below.
[9] Eastern Department Memorandum.
[10] For text, see FO Persia Confidential Print 10007, Reg. P1742-3, 6/10 May 1912 in L/P&S/10/266, and *British and Foreign State Papers* (*BFSP*), 105 (1912), pp. 763-6. However, it may be noted that altogether 5 versions of the Treaty were produced at various times at the Conferences at Erzeroum held between 1843 and 1847: see Canning despatch of 18 July 1944 in FO Persia Confidential Print (hereinafter PCP) 12044 of 16 Mar. 1912: Notes on Treaties between Turkey and Persia relative to the Frontier Question: 1639 to 1822, Reg. P1326, 2 Apr. 1912, in L/P&S/10/266.

Suram (Likhi) mountains formed the boundary between Turkey and Persia.[11] On 4 September 1746 the two States signed the Treaty of Kurdan and reaffirmed the territorial divisions of the Treaty of Zohab.[12] These provisions were subsequently confirmed by the Ottoman and Persian rulers in the first Treaty of Erzeroum, signed on 28 July 1823.[13] However, no precise definition or demarcation was attempted. The northern end of the Perso-Russian frontier was determined by the Treaty of Turkmanchai of 1828 between the Persian and Russian Empires: it was defined as lying along the Aras (Araxes) range at Mount Ararat.[14]

The second Treaty of Erzeroum of 31 May 1847[15] also attempted to resolve territorial questions by general attribution of territory, but inasmuch as it did so partly by reference to the Shatt, a degree of delineation and certainty entered the treaty. While a more detailed study of this treaty will be presented subsequently, it may be appropriate to state here that in Article 2 of this agreement, the Ottoman government ceded, or formally recognized, the sovereignty of the Persian government over the city and port of Mohammara, the island of Al Khizr (known today as Abadan Island), the Abadan anchorage, and the territory on the east, or left, bank of the Shatt. Effectively, therefore, a left-bank alignment was created by the parties. Difficulties of interpretation of the text and its meaning will also be presented at a more appropriate place.[16]

3. THE QUESTIONS OF TRIBAL ALLEGIANCE AND TRADITIONAL CONTROL

In the present state of international legal and political orders, it is not unusual for States to raise claims to territory on the bases of tribal and tra-

---

[11] Memorandum on the Persian Frontier, FO Research Department, 31 Jan. 1947, PCP E10136/4029/34, Ext. 1133 in L/P&S/12/1201 (hereinafter referred to as the Research Department Memorandum). See also the Eastern Department Memorandum, 1935, which says that it 'did little more than consecrate the natural geographical division'. Persia pledged not to interfere with the fortresses, burghs, provinces, countries, mountains, or hills lying on the side of Akhaltsik, Kars, Van, Cherizul, Baghdad and, Basra.

[12] Research Department Memorandum; for text see PCP 10007. An annexed article says that 'the frontiers and boundaries of Sultan Murad Khan shall be correctly ascertained and the governors of the frontiers shall refrain from actions which are opposed to friendship': PCP 10007, Reg. P1742. See also Enc. 1 in Lowther to Grey, 23 Apr. 1912, PCP 17845, Reg. P2869–70, 19 July 1912, in L/P&S/10/291.

[13] Research Department Memorandum. For text see PCP 10007.

[14] Ibid.

[15] For text, see *BFSP* 45 (1847–8), p. 874. Parry, *Consolidated Treaty Series*, 101 (1847), p. 86. Both are French language texts. For the English text see Appendix No. 1, in Iraqi letter to Secretary General, Council of the League of Nations, 29 Nov. 1934, *League of Nations Official Journal*, 16 (1935), and Annex No. 1, Al-Izzi, *The Shatt-al-Arab River Dispute*, p. 123. See Annexe 1 below.

[16] See below, subsections 4(a), (b), (c).

The Boundary Problem 9

ditional control. This is true of the history of the frontier problems between the two States under study. Although it is recognized that questions of tribal allegiances and traditional control are not as important as they once were, inasmuch as the rights and obligations of these States are governed, as they have been for over a century, by certain territorial and frontier treaties, they continue to be relevant to the examination of the Perso-Iraq boundary problem. The following account attempts to provide perspective and supply the necessary background for an appreciation of the various claims made by the States on the bases of history, ethnicity, and tradition. For Iraq, these matters are crucial to her traditional claims over not merely half the breadth of, but the entire Shatt.

(a) Tribal allegiance

As regards tribal allegiance, it is to be noted, speaking in broad general terms, that the inhabitants of the region in controversy are Arab, and not Persian, in character. The tribe in question was the Chaab, or Ka'ab, who were originally, according to Major (later Sir Henry) Rawlinson (Political Agent, Turkish Arabia), the inhabitants of the areas surrounding the confluence of the Tigris and Euphrates rivers.[17] They paid *Meer-i-Kalameyah*, or tribute, to the Ottoman governor of Basra.[18] *Circa* 1683, the Chaab are believed to have emigrated to lands on the left bank and the delta of the Shatt.[19] Over a period of years they acquired, 'partly by intimidation and partly by bribe', several tracts of land, including Tamar, El Haffar, Mohammara, El Jadeed, Khomeisah, Shakhura, Nahr Yusuf, Darband, and El Khaiyin, all of which lie on or in the vicinity of the left bank.[20] Some of these tracts came within the jurisdiction of the Chief of Kut-al-Sheikh, who acted as deputy to the Sheikh of Fellahiyeh.[21] It is said that the Chaab paid 300 tons of dates as yearly land rent to the governor of Basra,[22] and

---

[17] Rawlinson Memorandum, which was of considerable importance in shaping the British response to frontier questions, is an enclosure in a letter from the British Minister, Tehran, Col. Sheil, to the Secretary of State for Foreign Affairs, the Earl of Aberdeen, 3 Feb. 1844, PCP 10021, P1916, 1912 in L/P&S/11/16. See also Rawlinson's Observations on a Persian memorandum (undated) Relative to Mohammara: PCP 9997, enclosure in Canning's dispatch of 18 July 1844, Reg. P1230–1, 29 Mar. 1912 in L/P&S/10/266. According to the Turkish delegate at the Conference at Erzeroum, Dervesh Pasha, the Chaab came from Nejd: see enclosure No. 1 in Lowther to Grey, British Foreign Secretary, 19 June 1912, PCP 26634, Reg. P2682, 1912 in L/P&S/10/291; hereinafter referred to as Dervesh Pasha's book (1868).

[18] Rawlinson Memorandum.

[19] Ibid. See also the Memorandum respecting the Frontier between Mohammara and Turkey, 3 Apr. 1912, by A. Parker, PCP 14638, Reg. P1595, 24 Mar. 1912, in L/P&S/10/266, hereinafter referred to as the Parker Memorandum.

[20] Extract from the Rawlinson Memorandum, 16 Jan. 1844, enclosure in Parker to Lt. Col. Sir Percy Cox, Political Resident, Bushire, 18 Mar. 1912, Reg. P1037, 1912, in L/P&S/11/9.

[21] Extract of Rawlinson Memorandum.

[22] Ibid.

that it was paid uninterruptedly up to 1844.[23] A robe of office was allegedly given to the leader of the Chaab tribe.[24] The Chaab also acquired control over Dowasir, situate on the right bank, and over tracts extending northwards to Girdelan on the left; but, by and large, they remained, as regards the Shatt, confined to Tamar.[25]

Chaab expansion further eastwards in Goban, Fellahiyeh, Hindian, and Bend-i-Kir, and towards the north-east in Kut-el-Nawasir, brought them into contact with Persian authorities and it gradually led to the acquisition of a 'permanent footing in a country to which the right of Persia was unquestioned'.[26] It is estimated that four-fifths of the land occupied by this tribe in that period was Persian.[27] The Chaab, accordingly, entered into relations with the relevant authorities and began by offering presents of horses and dairy produce to the Chief of the local Afshar tribe which they had displaced.[28] Subsequently, the annual revenue payable as tribute by the Afshar to the Persian-ruled Vali of Hawizeh was paid by the Chaab.[29] Later, the Chaab became liable in principle (which liability, it is said, was never disputed) to pay 4,000 tomans to the Persian governor of Fars as revenue; in fact only 1,000 tomans were paid.[30] This payment was later made over to the Persian governor of Shiraz.[31] Parker goes on to observe that while the Chaab subsequently began bearing the Persian flag, it cannot be regarded as conclusive evidence of Persian control over the tribe in question.

It seems, that in point of fact, the Chaab were independent of any real control of both the Turkish and Persian authorities. Rawlinson observed that they could be regarded, in respect of lands north of Mohammara, as foreign occupants of Turkish property. He said that after the death of their tribal chief, Sheikh Salman, in 1682, 'the Chaab [became] virtually independent of Busrah, and . . . the notion of the indefeasibility of their allegiance to Turkey is an invention of late years, brought forward as a counterpoise to the claims of Persia upon Mohammara'.[32] As regards the occupation of Fellahiyeh, it appears that the Persian authorities may have

---

[23] Rawlinson Memorandum. Cf. Cox who stated that from 1747 onwards the Chaab paid no tribute, as opposed to land rent, to Turkey, and that by 1769 they had, on account of pressure exerted by the Persian king, become subjects of Persia: Cox to Grey, 20 Mar. 1912 Reg P1037, 1912 in L/P&S/11/9. See also Parker's reply of 12 June 1912: PCP 25042, Reg. P2184, 7 June 1912 in L/P&S/10/266.

[24] Rawlinson Memorandum; Dervesh Pasha's book.

[25] Parker Memorandum.

[26] Ibid.

[27] Rawlinson Memorandum.

[28] Ibid. Also see Dervesh Pasha's book.

[29] Col. Sheil to Earl of Aberdeen, 3 Feb. 1844, op. cit. n. 17 above.

[30] Rawlinson Memorandum. However, in 1818, the Persians demanded and received 13,000 tomans from the Chaab leader on account of accumulated arrears.

[31] Ibid.

[32] Ibid.

considered the Chaab as Turkish colonists who had immigrated to Persia and who had, over the years, become naturalized citizens.[33] Eventually, the distinction between revenue for land and tribute to the Persian Crown may have become blurred.[34] Rawlinson adds that Persia's relations with the Chaab, although in practice closer than Turkey's, 'bore the character of intimidation on the one hand and of concession on the other, rather than of the assertion and fulfilment of the acknowledged rights of a superior Government'.[35]

The growing power of the Chaab brought them into conflict with both the Persian and Turkish administrations. Persia used force twice, once in 1757 and again in 1765, in attempts to bring the tribe firmly under her rule, but failed to reach her objective.[36] Turkey, animated by a desire to test the independence of the Chaab and also to recover Dowasir on the right bank, attacked Mohammara in 1765, but the tribesmen emerged victorious, and it is believed that although there was no formal renunciation of links with, and allegiance to, the Turkish Caliph, the Chaab confirmed their status and were regarded thenceforward as being independent of Ottoman rule.[37] Another attempt was made in 1837 when the Ottoman Pasha of Baghdad razed Mohammara and destroyed its warehouses.[38] Interestingly, whilst the Sheikh of Mohammara, a descendant of the earlier tribal Chaab chiefs, pledged his allegiance to Turkey, Sheikh Jabbir, son of Mirdow, a servant of the Muhaisan tribe entrusted by the Sheikh of Mohammara with the defence of the fort at Mohammara, claimed independence and threatened to secure Persian protection.[39] Persia put forward her claims to Mohammara and demanded indemnity of £1 million from the Ottoman government. In order to avert war, Britain and Russia intervened between the two States.[40] Subsequently in 1843 an armed struggle for supremacy broke out between the Chaab and Muhaisan tribal leaders,[41] and provided the Persian government with an opportunity of bringing the region finally under its control. It occupied Mohammara in the following year and installed a governor therein.[42]

This development, among others, caused further disquiet to the Ottoman government, and once again Britain and Russia mediated to avert a

[33] Parker Memorandum.
[34] Ibid.
[35] Rawlinson Memorandum.
[36] Ibid. See also Eastern Department Memorandum.
[37] Rawlinson Memorandum; Parker Memorandum.
[38] Rawlinson Memorandum; see also Parker Memorandum.
[39] Parker Memorandum.
[40] Ibid.
[41] Rawlinson Memorandum. In 1862, the latter superseded the Chaab, who continued to live at their old capital Fellahiyeh.
[42] Ibid.

war.⁴³ The conferences at Erzeroum, Turkey, which were held from 1843 to 1847 and were attended by the two Mediating Powers, attempted to resolve these difficulties.

The foregoing account sheds some light on the sources of confusion which later led to a long-standing frontier dispute. In sum, it may be said that the Chaab, for one thing, emigrated to a region which was only nominally, and at best partially controlled by Ottoman authorities, and partially by the Persian government. For another, while the Chaab continued to maintain nebulous links with, and to admit tutelage to the Ottoman rulers of Basra, they entered into a burgeoning relationship with the Persians, who eventually succeeded in subjugating them. The Chaab, moreover, never intimated, by declaration or otherwise, to whom, if anyone, they owed their exclusive allegiance; at the same time, the Turkish authorities refused to admit that the connection between themselves and the Chaab tribesmen had been lost. These matters further complicated questions of traditional and territorial control and the limits thereof, an account of which is presented below.

(b) *Traditional limits of control*

The question of historical and traditional limits of Persian and Ottoman control is essential to a correct appreciation of the frontier problem of today. According to Major Rawlinson, who was well acquainted with boundary matters between the two parties:

> The rule of appropriation from the time of authentic history appears then to have been simply this: that the lands deriving water from the Tigris and Euphrates belonged to Irak-i-Arab (Turkey), while the country along the banks of the Karun was within the limits of Khuzistan (Persia). Nothing, perhaps, could be more simple in principle than this distribution, but nothing could be more fluctuating and perplexed than it has proved in practice, owing to the numerous changes in the courses of the rivers.⁴⁴

His study of the Jeyhani maps, produced 400 years after the advent of Islam, showed him that the boundary was a line drawn midway between the mouth of the Bamishere Canal and Khor Musa, the name given to the delta and marshland further east of the canal, and that the line which was prolonged further north-westwards parallel to the Shatt and well away from it did not cross any rivers in this region.⁴⁵ It appears that the boundary shown in these maps was drawn sufficiently away from the river up to

---

⁴³ Other incidents were the Persian occupation of Suleimani (Sulemanyeh) of 1840, and her action in Kasr-i-Shirin in Zohab in 1833: Relations between Persia and Iraq; by C. W. Baxter, 4 June 1928, FO PCP 2936/29/65, Reg. P3641, 1928, in L/P&S/10/1229 (hereinafter referred to as the Baxter Memorandum).
⁴⁴ Rawlinson Memorandum.
⁴⁵ Ibid.

32° of north latitude. In this period, the Bamishere was the left branch of the Tigris and Euphrates. Major Rawlinson speculated that the Karun had deserted its old bed and forced its way into both the Bamishere and the Haffar Canal and, consequently, into the Shatt. Thus, the 'rule of appropriation' was destroyed. The matter was compounded when the Bamishere underwent excessive silting, which prevented navigation of the canal. The inhabitants began to rely heavily on the Shatt which thus became the sole outlet to the Gulf.

In Rawlinson's view, at the time of the commencement of Ottoman rule in Irak-i-Arab in the sixteenth century, the lands on the left bank of the Shatt, from Girdelan, north of Kornah, to the sea, were traditionally dependent upon Basra.[46] Mohammara, it is said, was one of the grants of land made by the Caliph Sultan Salim in 1512 to four holy men. After about two centuries, the Pasha of Baghdad awarded the grant to Salman, leader of the Chaab tribe. At the time of the Treaty of 1639, Goban, which lay on the left bank of the old Karun delta, was ruled by Pashas who were allegedly vassals of the governor of Basra.[47] Rawlinson concluded: 'The right of Turkey, politically and geographically, to all the country which is dependent for its cultivation on the water of the Shatt-al-Arab is, I think, unquestionable.'[48] He recognised, however, that certain changes had occurred in the historic boundary: the Chaab tribe had come under Persian influence and had effectively broken away from Ottoman rule. Rawlinson then drew a line which, according to the map, depicted the 'actual boundary'. It began at a point south of Shoaib, at approximately north latitude 31° 29' and 47° 51' east longitude west of Hawizeh, and ran southwards about six to seven miles away from and parallel to the Shatt on the left bank to Abou Jazee, a small town. It then ran south by west to the Shatt and lay along it till it reached the mouth of the Haffar. The boundary then ran across the mouth of the Haffar and regained land at Al Khizr or Abadan island. It then ran along the left bank of the Shatt to the sea. His proposed boundary, however, attributed approximately half of Abadan to Turkey and the other half to Persia. Mohammara was assigned to the former and the line between Abou Jazee and Shoaib was not altered.[49]

This view of the traditional and prevailing boundary finds confirmation in other accounts. Mr Alwyn Parker of the Foreign Office pointed out that

---

[46] Ibid. Rawlinson added that he did not know on what grounds Persia claimed the left bank as the boundary: the only connection she had to it was that the lands were at one time occupied by the Chaab which she regarded as her subjects. These observations are particularly worthy of note inasmuch as the British government wished to gain an accurate description of the status quo.

[47] Ibid.

[48] Ibid.

[49] Map accompanying Rawlinson's Memorandum, enc. in Canning, British Ambassador to Turkey, to FO: No. 70, 27 Apr. 1844; copy in Parker Memorandum.

most of the maps submitted at the Erzeroum Conferences between 1843 and 1845, including the one prepared by MacDonald Kinneir, showed the Shatt as the boundary.[50] Colonel Sheil, the British Minister at Tehran, communicated a Persian Memorandum to the Foreign Office on 16 April 1844.[51] 'The right', declared the memorandum, 'of Turkey to the ports which are situated on the western bank of the river is not contested, but those to the east of the Shatt al Arab which forms the boundary of Fars, depend upon that province.'[52] In this connection Persia's claim-line at the Erzeroum Conferences may also be mentioned.[53] This line ran along the left bank of the Shoaib river which flows into the Shatt a few miles south of Kornah; it then lay along the left bank of the Shatt up to the point where it meets the Haffar.

Similarly, the British Minister of Constantinople between 1877 and 1880, Sir Henry Layard, who was concerned with the problem of the location of the Turco-Persian boundary, wrote that, traditionally speaking, the Persian frontier had never quite reached the delta for it was the Ottoman government which controlled both the Bamishere and the delta.[54] 'The Porte', he wrote, 'contended, not without reason, that as the Euphrates was a Turkish river, running through the dominions of the Sultan from its source, it was unjust and against universally recognised principles to give to Persia the control of its outlet into the sea, merely because a Persian stream had changed its course . . . .'[55]

Another early source is that of General Monteith, who, in a despatch to the Foreign Office in February 1843, suggested that the line ran from Kermanshah to Banilla on the [Hawizeh] river which flows north-east to south-west into the Karun river. He added that this led the Persians to claim the entire tract of land occupied by the Chaab up to eight miles from Basra, including Mohammara.[56] Russia, it is to be noted, claimed on behalf of Persia all the territory situate on the left bank between Haffar–Mohammara and the sea.[57] Dervesh Pasha, the Turkish delegate of the Turco-Persian Delimitation Commission, wrote in his book that the

[50] Parker Memorandum.

[51] PCP 9997, Reg. P1230–1, 29 Mar. 1912, in L/P&S/10/266; see also Appendix E, Parker Memorandum.

[52] Ibid. In a report submitted to the Turkish Grand Vizier, the Persian Frontier Commission wrote that the boundary south of Hawizeh (or Ahwaz) lies along the eastern side of the Goban: see enc. in Lorimer to Lowther, 15 June 1912, Reg. P3317, 1912, in L/P&S/10/266.

[53] See the map accompanying Parker Memorandum. See Fig. 1.

[54] Extract from *Early Adventures in Persia, Susiana and Babylonia* . . . (London, 1887): Appendix C, Parker Memorandum.

[55] Ibid.

[56] Notes made by General Monteith in Feb. 1843 for the Foreign Office: Appendix D, Parker Memorandum.

[57] Parker Memorandum. See below.

boundary, beginning at a point on the Persian Gulf, ran northwards leaving Mohammara, north and south Goban, Haffar, and [Moaviyeh] to Turkey; it then passed on to Kut-el-Abd, situate about five and six hours east of Mohammara on the right bank of the Karun.[58] From the latter point, the boundary, according to Dervesh Pasha, ran northwards between Kasr-i-Basra and Kasr-i-Hawizeh, dividing the old *Sanjaks* of Shoaib and Nervesh, dependencies of Basra, from the lands depending upon Hawizeh. It then ran to Sheira, situate on the left bank of the Shoaib river, which flows into the Shatt at a point half a mile distance from Kornah.[59] This description is clearly not conclusive of the matter and has only been cited here in order to indicate Turkey's general position regarding the location of the frontier. At any rate, it was not only incompatible with, but also far in excess of what the British government were willing to let Turkey acquire under the prevailing circumstances.[60]

The Eastern Department Memorandum, which was prepared by the Foreign Office in the period preceding the conclusion of the Treaty of 1937,[61] and which constituted guidance for its officials, observed that it was probable that in 1639 neither Turkey nor Persia exercised effective control over the territories in question; but that the acknowledged dependencies of Basra, with which the treaty forbade the Shah of Persia to interfere, included the country on both banks of the Shatt.[62] At a later period the Pashas of Basra had extended up to Bandar Shahpur on Khor Musa. It went on to point out that the Turkish view that Persia had never possessed any recognized legal right to the Shatt nor to any territory adjoining the left bank prior to 1847, 'finds support in the fact that even prior to 1847 [the date of the conclusion of the Second Treaty of Erzeroum] Persian vessels using the river did in fact have to pay dues to the Ottoman authorities'.[63]

Finally, reference may be made to the line proposed by the British and Russian Mediating Commissioners to the Ottoman and Persian Boundary Commissioners in 1850. It ran in a straight line south from Hawizeh to a point near the junction of the Karun with the Shatt. It then followed the left bank of the Shatt southwards to the sea. It is true that the line was a compromise between the extreme claims of the Turkish and Persian representatives;[64] nevertheless, as Parker observed in his memorandum:

The line proposed by the Mediating Commissioners is important, inasmuch as it

---

[58] See Dervesh Pasha's book.
[59] Also see map accompanying Parker Memorandum; and also the one accompanying Lowther to Grey, 17 June 1912, PCP 26630, Reg. P2586, 27 June 1912, in L/P&S/10/291. See Fig. 1.
[60] See below, subsection 4(*a*) and (*b*).
[61] See below, subsection 4 (*f*).
[62] PZ462 1935 in L/P&S/12/2869.
[63] Ibid. See also Parker Memorandum.
[64] See subsection 4(*b*) below and Fig. 1.

represents, *except insofar as proof may be adduced to the contrary*, what was the conclusion of the Mediating Commissioners on the important question of where, in the year 1850, Persian territory ended and Turkish territory began . . . [I]t was the impartial interpretation, and practical application of the terms of the Treaty of Erzeroum and of the 'Explanatory Note' by the Mediating Commissioners on the spot.'[65]

From the foregoing it appears that there is support for the view that, traditionally speaking, Iraq and her predecessors had extended to an appreciable degree to the country on the left bank of the Shatt, but that, over a considerable period of time, she had lost control of and title to these tracts of land, owing to political and historical circumstances over which she had little or no control. In such a situation, it was perhaps natural that the adjacent State assumed ascendancy over the tracts in question. Iraq, however, managed, by maintaining full and effective control over the Shatt, to limit Persian administration to the land territory to the east of the river.[66] In time to come, however, Iraq's predecessors were to abandon control over large parts of the river. This latter development will be presented at a more appropriate place (in subsections 4(*d*), (*f*), and (*g*) below).

4. THE DEVELOPMENT OF THE FRONTIER QUESTION AFTER 1843

(*a*) *The Conferences and Treaty of Erzeroum, 31 May 1847*

At the Conferences of Erzeroum, both Persia and Turkey advanced claims to Mohammara and the lands to the north and east of it, including Tamar and Haffar, and submitted evidence in respect thereof.[67] The Ottoman delegate produced deeds of sale, of foundation in mortmain, court rolls, witnesses, and maps. The tribal chief of the Chaab, Sheikh Thamir, stated, in the capacity of witness, that the Chaab were actually and had always been under the dominion of the Sultan.[68]

The British Commissioners, Colonel Williams and Mr Robert Curzon, concluded that on the balance of probabilities Turkey had valid rights to Mohammara.[69] On 27 April 1844 Sir Stratford Canning (later Lord), the British Ambassador at Constantinople, proposed adopting the Rawlinson line. He added that if this could not be agreed owing to difficulties in navigation of the Bamishere, it would be advisable to place Mohammara under the control of the Chaab and to grant a common right of access to the town by both parties. However, the Russian Vice-Chancellor, Count Nessel-

---

[65] Parker Memorandum (emphasis original).
[66] It is interesting to note that throughout the course of the Tigris, and for about three-quarters of the (upper) Shatt, the boundary runs well away to the east of the river.
[67] Parker Memorandum.
[68] Ibid.
[69] Ibid.

The Boundary Problem

rode, recommended that Mohammara and the left bank be ceded to Persia and that she be assured the freedom of navigation in the Shatt. He drew attention to the fact that the Shatt was southern Persia's sole outlet. Count Nesselrode argued that the principle of *uti possidetis* should apply.[70] Canning agreed with the application of this principle but advised that care be taken not to give Persia any extension of territory unwarranted by fact. He said that the line of actual control was the edge of the Shatt, and in its instructions to him the British government emphasized that the principle of compromise should be that of 'undisturbed possession of long standing'. In March 1845 the British and Russian envoys jointly recommended the cession by Turkey of Mohammara and of all the places dependent upon Persia, and that the latter be granted full rights of navigation in the Shatt.[71]

Turkey agreed in principle to cede Mohammara, but she made it clear that she would have 'rights of property to the river, the course of which was still to belong wholly and exclusively to the Porte, which only granted freedom of passage to Persia . . . '.[72] A draft treaty was drawn up in which Article 2 stipulated that Turkey agreed to cede to Persia the city, port, and anchorage of Mohammara and the island of Al Khizr. The left bank was referred to as the boundary, but there was no indication regarding its northern extent. The Porte, however, refused to put even a preliminary signature to a treaty in the absence of assurances regarding the meaning of some articles and insisted that Persia agree with these interpretations.[73] At this stage, the latter took no part in the proceedings. Britain and Russia agreed and their representatives at Erzeroum gave written assurances that in ceding the city, port, and anchorage of Mohammara and the island of Khizr, the Sublime Porte did not cede any other territory or any other ports which may be in the region. They also stated that the districts on the left bank which belonged to Turkey were to continue to belong to her, notwithstanding the fact that these districts may have been occupied by Persian tribes.[74] It was agreed that the Persian plenipotentiary would be

---

[70] Ibid. It appears that the term *uti possidetis* was employed to mean the line of actual control, and that it had little to do with the doctrine of *uti possidetis* claimed by the Latin American States.

[71] Ibid.

[72] Lord Palmerston to Lord Bloomfield, 12 July 1850, Appendix H, Parker Memorandum.

[73] Ibid., and Parker Memorandum. Some detail of this aspect of the negotiations has been included in this study inasmuch as both States have, over the years, regularly challenged and defended the validity of the so-called 'explanatory note' appended to the treaty. It is of little legal significance today.

[74] Palmerston to Bloomfield, op. cit. n. 72 above. For the published text of the written assurances, see Appendix No. 1 to Iraq letter to Secretary General, Council of the League of Nations, 29 Nov. 1934, and Annexe No. 2, Al-Izzi, *The Shatt-al-Arab River Dispute*, pp. 126–8. Other assurances included statements to the effect that Persia would not be entitled to put forward claims in regard to regions on the right bank, and that both parties would abstain from fortifying the banks of the Shatt. For Ottoman reply, see Appendix No. 1 to Iraqi letter of 29 Nov. 1934. For Persian delegate's reply, see Appendix 6 to Persian letter to Security Council, 8 Jan. 1935, *League of Nations Official Journal*, 16 (1935) p. 216.

18   *The History*

informed of these assurances *after* the treaty had been signed, but *before* proceeding to ratification.[75] The Mediating Powers hoped to induce Mirza Mohammed Ali Khan, the Persian Plenipotentiary, to accept the assurances before the treaty was ratified, and thereby provide him with an opportunity of considering the matter before ratification.[76] Turkey warned the Mediating Powers that if Persia failed to adopt the assurances the treaty would be considered *nul et non avenu*.[77] The two contracting States signed the treaty, but when the question of ratification came before the Persian representative, he refused to adopt the explanatory notes and to ratify the treaty, pleading want of authority.[78] Pressure was brought to bear upon him by the Mediating Powers and eventually he 'acceded . . . to the demands of the Porte in the form of an official note addressed to the Mediating Representatives'.[79] Turkey then requested a formal statement of the assurances from Britain and Russia. The 'explanatory note' was communicated to Turkey by Britain on 26 February 1848 and in the following month she ratified the treaty.[80]

Article 2 of the Treaty of Erzeroum stipulated that the 'Ottoman Government formally recognizes the unrestricted sovereignty of the Persian Government over the city and port of [Mohammara], the island of Khizr, the [Abadan] anchorage, and the land on the eastern bank—that is to say, the left bank—of the Shatt-al-Arab, which are in the possession of tribes recognized as belonging to Persia. Further, Persian vessels shall have the right to navigate freely without let or hindrance on the Shatt-al-Arab from the mouth of the same to the point of contact of the frontiers of the two Parties.' The Persian government abandoned all her claims to the city and province of Suleimani. Article 2 also recorded an undertaking given by the Persian government 'to cede to the Ottoman Government all the lowlands—that is to say, the land in the western part of the province of Zohab . . . '. The Ottoman government undertook to cede the eastern or mountainous part of the said province. Article 3 of the treaty provided for the appointment of commissioners 'for the purpose of determining the frontiers between the two States in conformity with the preceding article'.

(b) Demarcation attempts: 1850–1852

Two Boundary Commissioners from Persia and Ottoman Turkey and two Mediating Commissioners from Britain and Russia assembled at Moham-

[75] Parker Memorandum.
[76] Ibid.
[77] Ibid.
[78] Ibid. Cf. Lowther to Grey, 5 Apr. 1912, No. 81 M, Reg. P1326, 1912, in L/P&S/10/266.
[79] Parker Memorandum.
[80] Ibid. See also Shipley Report: *The Turco-Persian Frontier Commission*, 1912: PCP 12714: 19 Mar. 1913, Reg. P1353, 4 Apr. 1913 in L/P&S/10/267. See Annexe 1 below.

The Boundary Problem

mara in 1850 and at Zohab in 1851 and 1852.[81] Turkey and Persia failed to adopt a mutually acceptable interpretation of Article 2 of the treaty. While the Ottoman Commissioner agreed to cede the town and port of Mohammara, he refused to transfer even 'an inch of the surrounding territory'.[82] The Ottoman claim-line was drawn due south of Hawizeh in a straight line to a point where it reached a set of pillars (or ruins) just south of the 31st degree of north latitude. The line then tended sharply south-east cutting across the Karun and the Serahi Canal, and terminated at the coast, running parallel in a straight line to the Bamishere.[83] The arguments advanced were generally to the effect that the cession of Mohammara and Abadan did not imply that the boundaries between them lay in that direction: Abadan was an island and Mohammara an enclave. All that was required of the Commissioners was the determination of the frontier between Turkey's left-bank possessions and Persia's Khuzistan dominions. Support for this was based upon the provisions of the explanatory note,[84] namely that only Mohammara and Khizr [Abadan] had been ceded and that all the lands on the eastern side of the river belonging to Turkey were to continue under her administration. Essentially, of course, Turkey relied upon the facts of traditional control in order to support her claims to the line proposed by her Boundary Commissioner during the demarcation proceedings. The British Commissioner, Colonel Williams, could not agree to this interpretation of the treaty and the explanatory note and in a letter dated 4 February 1850 to Sir Stratford Canning advised that the Turkish line had not been contemplated at Erzeroum.[85] Canning warned that the Turkish line would establish not one but three frontiers running parallel to each other,[86] and Lord Palmerston, the Foreign Secretary, noted the conspicuous silence maintained by the Ottoman government regarding Al Khizr's eastern edge and the Bamishere canal.[87] He recalled that in the period preceding the exchange of ratifications, Colonel Williams had wished to avoid giving the impression to the Turkish plenipotentiary that the explanatory note was susceptible of being interpreted in a manner which would allow Turkey to put forward extensive claims to tracts lying to the east of the river; and that he had stated this in a note dated 26 April 1847, which note was eventually withdrawn: the Turkish Minister for Foreign Affairs gave a verbal assur-

---

[81] Parker Memorandum; Eastern Department Memorandum.
[82] Parker Memorandum.
[83] See Col. Williams's map in Parker Memorandum, but see the line claimed as depicted in the map accompanying the despatch from Lowther to Grey, 17 June 1912. See Fig. 1.
[84] Lord Palmerston to Lord Bloomfield, Appendix H, Parker Memorandum.
[85] Parker Memorandum. He suggested that the purpose of Turkey advancing such extensive claims was to calm her suspicions against Persian claims to Kornah.
[86] Sir Stratford Canning to Lord Palmerston, Constantinople, 30 May 1850, Appendix G, Parker Memorandum.
[87] Palmerston to Bloomfield.

ance that his government would not aspire to areas the Commissioners declared were Persian territories.[88] Nevertheless, the Eastern Department Memorandum observed that the assignment to Persia of Mohammara and other territories on the left bank was regarded by Turkey as a Persian intrusion into Turkish territory, and was acceptable only if viewed as an offset to the abandonment by Persia of her territorial claims further north. 'This point', it said in 1935, 'is of importance in any consideration of the ownership of the Shatt-al-Arab, since the Turkish view was that previous to 1847, Persia had never possessed any recognised legal right to any territory adjoining the left bank of the river, and had consequently never had even a pretence to sovereignty over the river itself.'[89]

The Persian claim-line, it will be recalled, ran south-west from Hawizeh along the left bank of the Shoaib (or Jaab) river to its confluence with the Shatt to the south of Kornah. It then ran south-east along the middle of the Shatt to the sea.[90] On 4 February 1850, Colonel Williams proposed a line which, he said, would keep Turkey away from territories east of Mohammara and Al Khizr, and Persia away from the islands in the Shatt: an alignment which would 'demonstrate the justice of our award'. It ran from the mouth of the Shatt along its left bank and lay across the Haffar canal; it then ran 'up the Shatt al Arab to the mouth of the Abu Djudei [or Jidiyeh] canal, a distance of a geographical league from the Haffar; and thence in as straight a line as circumstances will admit of to the town and district of Hawiza [Hawizeh], passing through the towers named by Dervish Pasha'.[91] Just opposite the mouth of the Abu Jidiyeh canal, which flows into the Shatt north of Mohammara, stood Falliyeh,[92] a place of some importance to the Sheikh of Mohammara.[93]

The British and Russian governments pronounced themselves in favour of Colonel Williams's proposal and at first the Persian government maintained that the line would be acceptable if the point at which it left the river were

---

[88] Palmerston to Bloomfield; but see letter from Col. Sheil to the Grand Vizier of Persia of 20 Mar. 1850, namely that the explanatory note attempts only to aid mutual interpretation and says only that which is self-evident: enclosure in Grey to Lowther, 14 May 1912, PZ1826, 1912, in L/P&S/11/16. At the Erzeroum Conference the British delegate emphasized that the explanatory note was 'a mere repetition of what the treaty contains': Parker Memorandum.

[89] Eastern Department Memorandum.

[90] See Col. Williams's map in Parker Memorandum (Fig. 1, p. 21). It is to be noted, however, that the map shows a left-bank boundary from Kornah to the Haffar Canal; and that in a marginal note, Parker adds that according to the journal of the 2nd Conference at Mohammara the line should have been drawn in the middle of the Shatt: see map opposite p. 25 of the Memorandum.

[91] Col. Williams as quoted in Parker Memorandum. The distance, however, was really two and a half miles, ibid. The towers mentioned may be the ruins depicted on Col. Williams's map.

[92] Not to be confused with Fellahiyeh, the Chaab capital east of Bamishere.

[93] Below, p. 26. See Wilson to Cox, 12 Mar. 1910, enc. 2 in Cox to Grey, 8 May 1910, PCP 18938 in Reg. P1356, 12 Apr. 1912, in L/P&S/10/266.

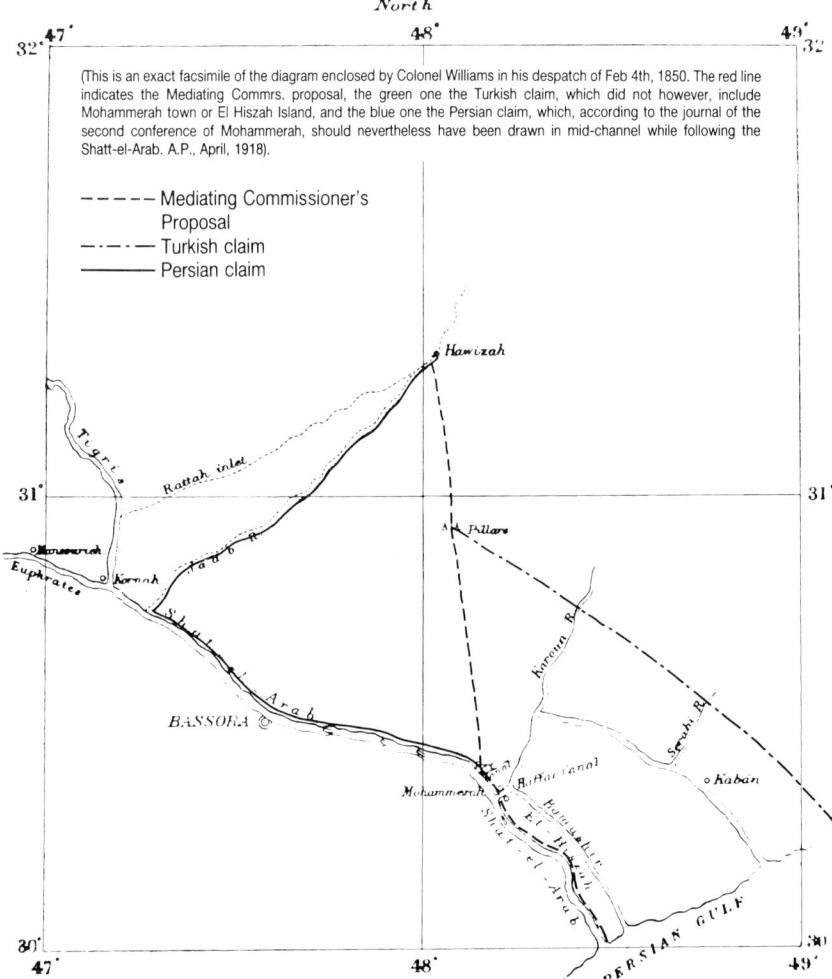

FIG. 1. Turkish, Persian, and Mediating Commissioners' claim lines in 1850

drawn four to six miles further west along the bank near Tamar, 'the argument being that a portion of the Cha'ab resided on, and was in actual possession of, the land up to the above spot, if not beyond it'.[94] The Eastern Department Memorandum of 1935 noted that the Persian government did not make any reservations about the Shatt at that time. However, Persia's recommendations were not acceptable to the British government. The

---

[94] Parker Memorandum. See also letter of Persian Prime Minister to British and Russian Ministers, 25 May 1850, Eastern Department Memorandum.

mouth of the Abu Jidiyeh Canal recommended itself as the point at which the boundary ought to leave the river in view of the fact the Britain did not wish traders bound for Basra to be exposed to Persian musketry as they would have been had Tamar been selected as the relevant point. 'Thus', Col. Williams said, 'we offer to Persia free entrance to, and security in, her port of Mohammara, at the same time ensuring to Turkey the navigation of the Shatt-al-Arab by the destruction of the fort (at Feylieh [Falliyeh]) built by Sheikh Jabir during the Conferences of Erzeroum.'[95]

On British insistence, however, Persia agreed on 25 May 1850 to accept the British proposals, provided the Chaab tribesmen cut off at Falliyeh were transferred to Persia.[96] The Turkish government rejected the proposed line, 'and it was agreed, but as a purely provisional arrangement, and expressly pending a final adjustment, to accept the status quo . . . but a long wrangle took place as to what was the status quo, and nothing precise was generally accepted'.[97] It is clear therefore that the demarcation proceedings failed to establish a mutually acceptable definitive frontier line. Nevertheless, the boundary in principle, if not in fact, continued to be governed by the provisions of the treaty of 1847.

(c) The Identic Map and the Agreement of 1869: further attempts at demarcation

In 1869, the British and Russian ambassadors in Constantinople presented the Turkish Foreign Minister with what subsequently came to be referred to as the 'Identic Map'.[98] It was prepared on a scale of 1:73500 and covered the entire length of the Turco-Persian borderlands between latitude 30° in the south on the Gulf, to latitude 40° in the north in the Caucasus mountains.[99] The areas covered lay within a 'frontier zone' ranging from twenty to fifty miles, but no line was delineated upon it. The ambassadors urged the Ottoman government to agree a boundary with Persia by delineating a line within the stipulated zone, and suggested that if there were any difficulties in this respect it could refer to the British and Russian govern-

---

[95] As quoted in Parker Memorandum. At first, Col. Williams had drawn the line $5\frac{1}{2}$ miles away from the Haffar Canal. Traders had no alternative but to navigate on the eastern side of the Shatt: the western half was not suitable. See also Cox's Note IV, enc. in Cox to MacMahon, Secretary to Government of India, Foreign Department, 21 May 1912; copy enclosure in Cox to Parker (DO at IO), 21 May 1912, PCP 25042, Reg. P2184, 7 June 1912 in L/P&S/10/266, in reference to comments on Parker's Memorandum; and Grey to Buchanan, 11 Apr. 1912, Reg. P1356, 12 April 1912 in L/P&S/10/266.

[96] Parker Memorandum and Eastern Department Memorandum. The British and Russian governments could not and did not agree to forced expatriation of tribes cut off by the border.

[97] Parker Memorandum.

[98] Eastern Department Memorandum. A copy of this map, prepared by the Southampton Survey is in the possession of the India Office Library. See Fig. 2, p. 24–5.

[99] Ibid. See also Research Department Memorandum and Wilson to Cox, 26 May 1909, enc. 2 in Barclay to Grey, 9 Sept. 1909, PCP 35732, Reg. P1356, 1912, in L/P&S/10/266.

ments.[100] On 3 August 1869, Turkey and Persia concluded an agreement for the preservation of the status quo regarding the frontier 'such as was defined by the Commissioners of the four Powers'.[101] In 1870, the British and Russian representatives in Tehran communicated a copy of the Identic Map and their proposals to the Persian government.[102] Four years later the agreement, or Protocol as it was also called, was renewed[103] and Persian and Turkish Boundary Commissioners met in 1874 in Constantinople to proceed with the demarcation of the frontier on the basis of the detailed Identic Map.[104] They were joined by British and Russian representatives in 1875 and 1876, whose efforts none the less failed to induce the Turkish and Persian Commissioners to delineate, either by delimitation or demarcation, a mutually acceptable frontier.[105]

(d) The Tehran Protocol of 1911 and the Boundary Protocol of 1913

The unsettled state of affairs at the frontier continued to engender political difficulties between the two States. It appears that Turkey began attempting to assert her influence in Mohammara in 1892–93 when she claimed the right to collect duty on goods emanating from or bound for Mohammara on the ground that the latter constituted Turkish and not foreign territory.[106] In 1899, the authorities at Basra organized the construction of an embankment at Diaji which would have extended across the local lines of control. The Sheikh of Mohammara protested and the authorities ceased construction.[107] In 1905, Turkish troops advanced into Urmia, which lay well on the Persian side of the frontier zone,[108] and in 1908, the Porte stepped up its attempts to acquire greater influence at Mohammara, a development which the British government viewed with alarm.[109] In addition to these problems, one of the prime objectives of British policy was the establishment of a Commission for the superintendence of the Shatt with powers of levying dues on shipping. This inadvertently raised the issue of rights in the Shatt. The Political Resident, Bushire, Major (later Sir) Percy Cox believed that while Persia had no right to be considered for

---

[100] Eastern Department Memorandum.
[101] Ibid. For text, see Parry, *The Consolidated Treaty Series*, Vol. 139 (1869), pp. 425–6 (French language translation). See Articles 2, 4, and 7.
[102] Eastern Department Memorandum. See also Wilson to Cox, 26 May 1909 (n. 99 above).
[103] Wilson to Cox, 26 May 1909, op. cit. n. 99 above.
[104] Eastern Department Memorandum.
[105] Ibid.
[106] Consul McDouall to Cox, 12 June 1909, enc. 4 in Barclay to Grey, 9 Sept. 1909, op. cit. n. 99 above.
[107] Ibid.
[108] Baxter Memorandum.
[109] Generally, see Grey to Sir N. O'Conor, British Ambassador to Turkey, 25 Feb. 1908, PCP 5428, Reg. P2914, 6 Mar. 1908, in L/P&S/10/132.

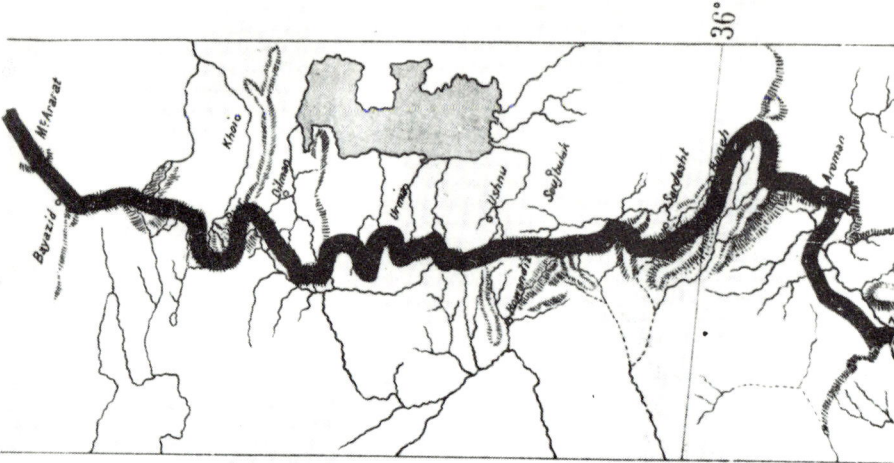

participation at the bar of the Shatt, she had rights on the levying of dues inasmuch as most of the shipping was bound for either Mohammara or Abadan.[110] It was clear that the British government had in mind the exclusion of Persia from these operations and he advised against it because the Sheikh of Mohammara, who had received guarantees of protection from the Persian government, had always, in conjunction with the latter, been considered as having the responsibility of maintaining safety of commerce in the river.[111] Furthermore the India Office considered the strategic importance of the Persian Gulf to India to be axiomatic.[112] Supremacy, it was said, depended not only on naval power but also on 'a network of political relations', and those existing at the head of the Gulf were regarded as being 'the most valuable'.[113] The traditional friendship of, *inter alia*, the Sheikh of Mohammara fell in this category. 'There is a consensus of opinion', wrote Alwyn Parker, 'as to the importance of securing the most favourable settlement possible for the Sheikh'.[114] Sir Edward Grey, Secretary of State for Foreign Affairs, urged the British Ambassador at Constantinople, Sir Nicholas O'Conor, to make clear to the Porte that 'His Majesty's Government are not prepared to recognise any other frontier

[110] Cox to MacMahon, 9 Mar. 1912, Reg. P1356, 12 Apr. 1912, in L/P&S/10/266.
[111] Ibid. See also Viceroy's telegram to IO, 4 Apr. 1912, Reg. P1317, 1912, in L/P&S/10/266.
[112] *The Mesopotamian Expedition*, 1916: Statement by the Political Secretary, IO: B236 in L/P&S/18.
[113] Ibid.
[114] Parker's remarks to Cox, letter of 23 May 1912: see enc. in FO to IO, 31 May 1912, PCP 22191, Reg. P1950-1, 1912, in L/P&S/10/266.

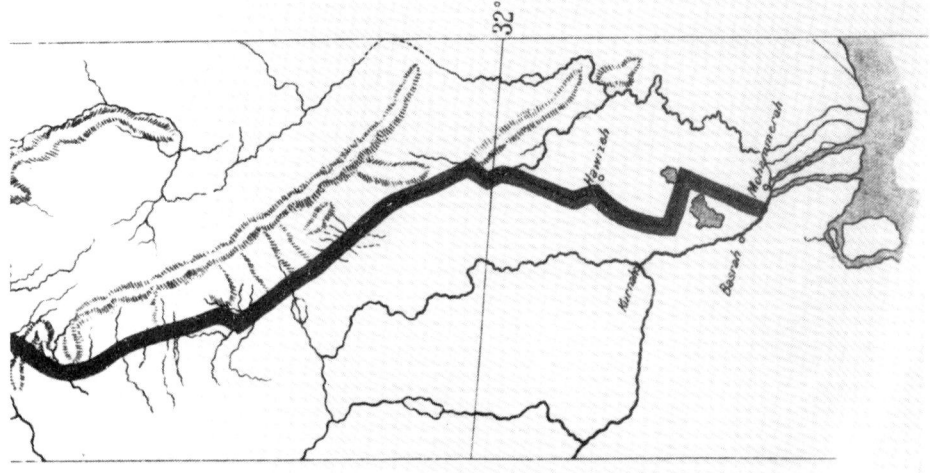

FIG. 2. Sketch showing approximate Turco-Persian frontier

than that laid down by the Mediating Commissioners in 1850.'[115] In order to facilitate a resolution of the frontier questions, fresh negotiations between the two disputing governments and the Mediating Powers were initiated. Russian interests in securing a frontier settlement covered an area ranging from Mount Ararat, the trijunction of Russian, Ottoman, and Persian boundaries, to the 36th degree of north latitude, and British interests dominated the sector between the 32nd degree of north latitude up to the Gulf. The former sector was generally referred to as the Russian sector and the latter as the British sector. Inasmuch as this work is generally confined to the examination of the 'British sector' of the frontier it will be necessary to restrict its scope to the role played by British interests in the development of the frontier question. However, in the areas lying between the 32nd and 36th degrees of north latitude there was an overlap of British and Russian interests. This sector, moreover, generated a considerable degree of controversy between the two contracting States before agreement was reached in the Protocol of 1913. Accordingly, a study of this sector is relevant to the main work.

In order to determine the situation at the borderlands, investigations were carried out by officials of the Foreign Office and government of India. In a letter to Major Cox dated 12 March 1910, Lt. Wilson reported that the boundary in the Shatt region as observed locally was different from the one

---

[115] Grey to O'Conor, 25 Feb. 1908, op. cit. n. 109 above. He said that any 'disturbance of the *status quo* of Mohammara would affect British interests, and might . . . lead to the active intervention of His Majesty's Government who have given the Sheikh [of Mohammara] certain assurances in regard to his territory'.

laid down in 1850.[116] He said that while the latter alignment ran along the left bank and left it at the eastern bank of the Abu Jidiyeh Canal west of Falliyeh and ran northwards to Hawizeh, the locally observed line ran midstream along the main channel of the river from its mouth in the Gulf to a point about one and a half miles above Falliyeh, and then along a narrow [Khaiyin] Canal formed by the presence of three long islands close to the left bank. Near Diaji, he wrote, the boundary ascends 'a well-defined mud-wall' and runs northwards some ten miles west of Hawizeh.[117] There was evidence to show that Turkish authorities had never challenged the local boundary, but on the contrary, had actually buried some coal in a pit as a permanent boundary mark;[118] and that the periodic cleaning of the Khaiyin Canal was undertaken by the Sheikh, while the cleaning of the Diaji Canal was carried out by Turkish *mudirs*.[119] Apart from that, the Sheikh's palace and offices were situate in the tracts of land lying between Falliyeh and Diaji, a fact inconsistent with the 1850 line.[120] He urged the British government to abandon the 1850 line in favour of the locally observed frontier, and Major Cox wrote as much to the Government of India and the Foreign Office.

The India Office was quick to acknowledge the importance of the change, and in a letter to the Foreign Office, the Secretary of State for India, the Earl of Crewe, recognized that Turkey had a right to control the Shatt from bank to bank, subject to Persia's freedom of navigation.[121] Even so, he added, the Turkish government 'have allowed a situation to grow for sixty years in which mid-channel has, without challenge, been accepted by local usage as the boundary, and that is consequently the *status quo* on the observance of which His Majesty's Government must insist.'[122] At the Foreign Office, Mr Alwyn Parker urged the British government not to recommend a mid-line boundary in the Shatt, but agreed that the line be extended further eastwards along the left bank for about six and a half miles to the west of Falliyeh in order to assign the palace and offices of the Sheikh to Persia.[123] Major Cox wrote convincingly in favour of the latter

---

[116] Letter of 12 Mar. 1910, enc. No. 2 in Cox to Grey, 8 May 1910, PCP 18938, Reg. P1356, 12 Apr. 1912. See also Wilson to Cox, 5 May 1912, enc. in Cox to Hirtzel, 5 May 1912, No. M11, Reg. P2016, 1912, in L/P&S/10/266. See Fig. 3, p. 27.

[117] Letter of 12 Mar. 1910.

[118] Wilson to Cox, 5 May 1912.

[119] Ibid.

[120] Ibid. Also see Wilson to Cox, 12 Mar. 1910; Parker Memorandum; Grey to Buchanan, 8 Apr. 1912, Reg. P1326, 2 Apr. 1912; and Grey to Buchanan, 11 Apr. 1912, Reg. P1356, 12 Apr. 1912, in L/P&S/10/266.

[121] IO to FO, 3 June 1911, Reg. P974/1038: 15 Mar. 1912, in L/P&S/10/266. See also Viceroy to Secretary of State of India, 7 June 1912, Reg. P2184, 1912; and cf. minute note to File Reg. P1950-1, 23 May 1912, in L/P&S/10/266.

[122] IO to FO, 3 June 1911.

[123] Parker Memorandum. He urged that the 1850 line be adopted as a basis for negotiations.

The Boundary Problem

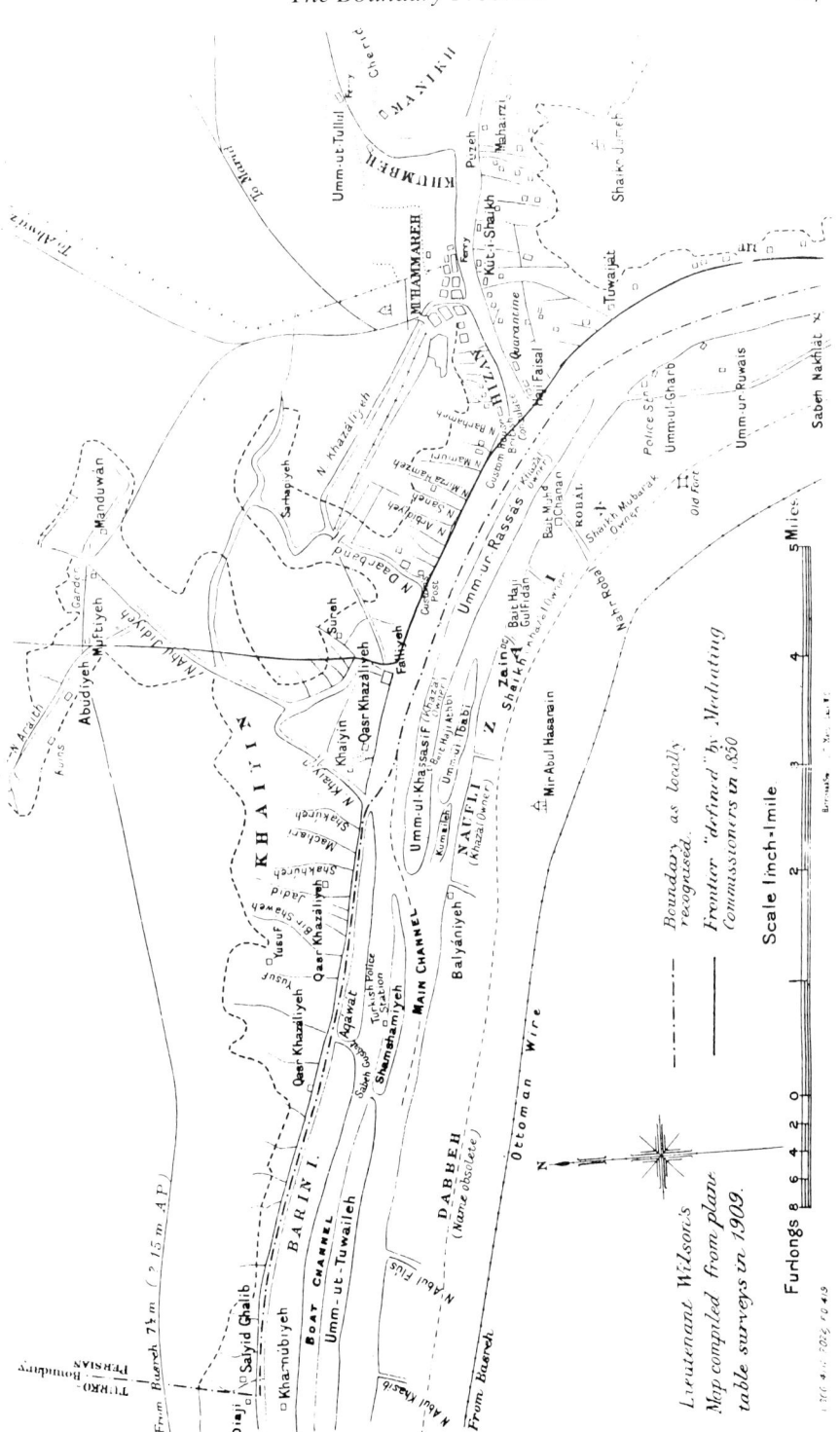

Fig 3. Lt. Wilson's map compiled from Plane Table Surveys in 1909

proposition. 'Local Turkish authorities', he wrote, 'have accorded unequivocal and repeated recognition of the present boundary by erection of marks and maintenance for many years of [a] permanent frontier customs posts at Diaiji [Diaji] such action should make it impossible for them after a lapse of sixty years to claim another frontier to which their pretensions are at least doubtful.'[124] He also observed that the Sheikh regarded the nature of his tenure in the territory between Falliyeh and the locally recognized boundary at Diaji to be identical with his status at Mohammara and elsewhere.[125] This, he said, was supported by the fact that he recognized the difference between the nature of his territorial possessions in certain islands in the Shatt and his proprietary interests on the right bank which were indisputably under Turkish sovereignty.[126] Major Cox relied also upon legal arguments in favour of the mid-line boundary,[127] and although the Foreign Office was not entirely convinced that a *medium filum aquae* could be urged in view of the provisions of the Treaty of Erzeroum,[128] it decided nevertheless to urge the Turkish government to recognize Persia's prescriptive title of sixty years to the mid-line.[129] At the same time, the British government realized that it could not abandon the left bank boundary in its entirety. In a letter to Sir George Buchanan, the British Ambassador at St Petersburg, Sir Edward Grey observed that having regard to the Treaty of Erzeroum, nothing more could be claimed in principle for Persia apart from her freedom of navigation, Turkey having taken great pains to assert her ownership over the entire waters of the Shatt.[130] He recognized that although the argument of *uti possidetis*, (that is, the line of actual control) could not be entirely ignored, it was doubtful whether, on a strictly legal interpretation, the argument would prevail owing to the reservations contained in the Turco-Persian Protocol of 1869.[131] Notwithstanding the

---

[124] Cox to FO, 23 May 1912, Reg. P1950-1, 23 May 1912. See also telegram to IO and FO, 23 May 1912, Reg. P1950-1; Cox to MacMahon, 21 May 1912, enc. in Cox to Hirtzel, 21 May 1912, Reg. P2184, 7 June 1912, in L/P&S/10/226; to IO, 6 May 1912, Reg. P1700, 6 May 1912, in L/P&S/10/266 and Memorandum, 4 July 1909, enc. No. 7 in Barclay to Grey, 9 Sept. 1909, Reg. P1356.

[125] Cox to government of India, 5 May 1912, enc. No. 2 in IO to FO, 30 May 1912, PCP 23058, Reg. P2016, 25 May 1912, in L/P&S/10/291. Cf. Parker, who said that Persian claims to sovereignty between Falliyeh and Diaji were not of 'uniform validity': Parker comments to Cox letter, PCP 25042, Reg. P2184.

[126] Cox to Government of India, 5 May 1912.

[127] Annexe Note VI, Cox to MacMahon, 21 May 1912. See also Cox telegram to FO and IO, 23 May 1912, Reg. P1950-1, 23 May 1912. In the telegram, he relied upon Wheaton's treatise on international law, and on the legal notions of prior occupation and long undisturbed possession.

[128] FO to IO, 31 May 1912, Reg. P2072, 1912, in L/P&S/10/266. See below, regarding FO Legal Advisers' opinion, p. 83.

[129] FO to IO, 31 May 1912, PCP 22191, Reg. P1950-1, 1912 in L/P&S/10/266.

[130] Grey to Buchanan, 11 Apr. 1912, Reg. P1356, 12 Apr. 1912; see also minute note to Reg. P2184, 7 June 1912, in L/P&S/10/266.

[131] Grey to Buchanan, 11 Apr. 1912.

above, Sir Edward Grey observed that the line in 1850 had been drawn at Abu Jidiyeh to assure the safety of navigation for Basra, but the experience of sixty years had showed that this fear had been groundless. He therefore requested the Ambassador to inform the Russian government that the British government effectively intended claiming the territories up to Diaji. Clearly, hence, the Foreign Office was disposed in favour of adopting a balanced course of action in which the 1850 line was to continue in principle, while the locally observed boundary was to be urged only for specific areas in order to accommodate important Persian grievances. Thus, the Falliyeh–Diaji extension would allow the Sheikh to continue to enjoy his rights in those areas, while a mid-line boundary opposite Mohammara would enable Persia to continue to control the anchorage and other parts of the river in that direction. Quite apart from the boundary issue, Major Cox made clear that the Sheikh of Mohammara claimed on behalf of the Persian government certain islands in the Shatt, namely Mohalla and Bahriyeh, the four islands between Shutait and Moaviyeh, and the two islands opposite Mankoli (Manquli). He said that they were in possession of Persia and had never been under Turkish control. Major Cox claimed that they formed part of Abadan and that all islands subsequently forming on the Persian side of the mid-channel line should be *ipso facto* Persian.[132]

As regards the frontier in the sector between the Shatt and Hawizeh, the reports and recommendations made by Major Cox and Lt. Wilson, who both visited the region in 1912, were to carry decisive weight. The area in question was regarded as a recognized district of the Persian province of Khuzistan, whose tribes, the Beni Salih, Beni Sukain, and Beni Turuf, were the sole inhabitants paying tribute to the Vali of Hawizeh.[133] Bisaitin, which stood about eighteen miles north-north-west of Hawizeh, was regarded as the limit thereof in this direction.[134] While these tribes drew a distinction between their tribal limits and the frontier of Persia, the 'universal view', as expressed to Cox by the tribes in 1912, was that the boundary of Hawizeh was coexistent with the Turco-Persian frontier.[135] In July 1912, Lt. Wilson reported that the tribes claimed that the frontier lay along the Dawairij river: it began at a point where the river leaves the Pusht-i-Koh in the far north and ran past the Turkish frontier-post on the

[132] Telegram from Cox to IO, 10 July 1912, Reg. P2701, 1912, in L/P&S/10/266.
[133] See Wilson Report regarding the Position of Hawizeh and of the Turco-Persian Frontier as locally observed west and north-west of Hawizeh, Wilson to Cox, 5 July 1912, enc. in Cox to MacMahon, 19 July 1912, Reg. P3317, 1912, in L/P&S/10/266; and Cox to Government of India, 6 May 1912, enc. No. 5, in IO to FO, 30 May 1912, PCP 23058, Reg. P2016, 25 May 1912, in L/P&S/10/291; Cox to IO, 4 July 1912, Reg. P2617/3154, 1912, in L/P&S/10/291; Cox to Government of India, 21 May 1912, PCP 25042, Reg. P2184, 1912, in L/P&S/10/266. See Fig. 4, pp. 32–3.
[134] Wilson Report, loc. cit.
[135] Ibid., and see Cox to Government of India, 6 May 1912, Enc. No. 5, IO to FO, 30 May 1912.

Amarah [Amara]–Dezful track along the western boundary. It thereafter struck the locality called Khaiyit-as-Sultan. It then lay along the old main (dry) channel called Shatt-al-Alma, or the Ghor-i-Muhaisin, as it was called on the map prepared by the Mediating Commissioners. The frontier then tended towards Azam, a small sheet of open water in the middle of the marsh to the west of Shoaib, and it then followed the Shoaib marsh stream southwards until the boundary turned towards the Khushk-i-Basri (30° 57′ N and 48° 02′ E).[136] However, on arriving at the frontier, Lt. Wilson discovered that the tribes were unable to take him to Ghor-i-Muhaisin lest they should bring 'all sorts of calamities' upon themselves, and accordingly stopped at Ghor-i-Douvil, or Umm-Chir, a river (now dry) which flowed north and south and east and west into the Ghor-i-Muhaisin, about eight miles north-west of Bisaitin.[137] He concluded that while the boundary recognized by Turkey and claimed by Persia lay along the Ghor-i-Muhaisin, the line observed locally by the tribes was the Ghor-i-Douvil where it ran north to south about seven miles east of the Ghor-i-Muhaisin.[138] He recommended, however, a line which lay along the Dawairij and Ghor-i-Muihaisin in view of the fact that it was a natural frontier which passed through uninhabited areas and was not prone to disturbance by silt.[139] There would, he added, be no clashes with tribes. The line would then follow the traditional boundary south to Azam and run along the edge or middle of the marsh to Shoaib.[140] At a point just south of the 31st degree of north latitude the line was drawn straight east to Khushk-i-Basri. Cox then drew the line south in a straight line to Diaji on the Shatt. He explained that the formation of a sharp angle was necessary because the southernmost limits of the Hawizeh tribes were determined by the extent of their water supply from a winter lake in Yafair, and that this 'limit is considered to be reached at Khushk-i-Basri, where the ruins of an extensive building of great age form a convenient land mark.'[141]

Meanwhile, on the diplomatic level, the Ottoman and Persian governments had concluded a protocol at Tehran on 21 December 1911 in respect of the establishment of a basis of negotiations and the procedure to be fol-

---

[136] Wilson Report; Cox to IO, 4 July 1912.
[137] Wilson Report. Apparently, this stream carried the bulk of the waters of the Dawairij river.
[138] Ibid. See also Cox to IO, 4 July 1912.
[139] Wilson Report, and Cox to Government of India, Enc. No. 5, IO to FO, 30 May 1912, and Cox to IO, 4 July 1912.
[140] Ibid.
[141] Cox to Government of India, Enc. No. 5. See also Memorandum on Mohammara Frontier communicated to Turkish Ambassador, 17 July 1912, in Grey to Buchanan, 17 July 1912, PCP 30379, Reg. P2981–2, 25/29 July 1912, in L/P&S/10/291, and map accompanying letter: above, n. 83.

lowed for the delimitation of the boundary.[142] A Commission of an equal number of delegates of either party was to meet a Constantinople with a view to the settlement of the frontier question. It was agreed that the work of the Joint Commission would be based on the provisions of the Treaty of Erzeroum. Negotiations opened at Constantinople in March 1912 and ran into difficulties on the question of the validity of the explanatory note.[143] The Turkish government insisted that the Persian delegate accept the note as valid, while the latter argued that his government had had no knowledge of the existence and contents of the note and it could not, therefore, constitute an integral part of the Treaty of Erzeroum.[144] It was also contended that the note constituted a modification of the relevant provisions of the treaty, and that the Persian plenipotentiary had not possessed full powers either to conclude or modify a binding treaty.[145] Eventually, however, pressure was brought to bear upon the Persian delegate and his government agreed to accept the explanatory note. At the sitting of 15 August 1912, the Persian delegate announced that the government in Tehran had decided, while reserving its position in principle, to accept the explanatory note unconditionally.[146]

On 18 July 1912, the Secretary of State for Foreign Affairs communicated a memorandum regarding the location of the Turco-Persian frontier to the Turkish Ambassador, Hakki Pasha, in London.[147] In this letter, Sir Edward Grey maintained that the view of the British government regarding the alignment between Hawizeh and the sea was based upon historical evidence, extensive research in archives, and investigations carried out in the areas concerned. The line proposed by him followed the recommendations made by Major Cox and Lt. Wilson. The Hawizeh–Shatt sector described above was urged on the basis of history and tradition, and references were also made to natural frontiers formed by the edges of the marshland. As regards the sector between Shatt and the sea, Sir Edward Grey maintained that the locally observed frontier was a line which entered the Khaiyin Canal at a point between Nahr Diaiji [Diaji] and Nahr Abul Arabid and followed it mid-stream to the point where the Nahr Nazaliyeh,

[142] Text: Parry, *Consolidated Treaty Series*, 215 (1911–12), p. 138: French language. For English language texts, see Appendix 7, Persian reply to Secretary General, League of Nations, 8 Jan. 1935, Annexe No. 3, Al-Izzi, *The Shatt-al-Arab River Dispute*, p. 129. See Annexe 2 below.
[143] See Lowther to Grey, 5 Apr. 1912, Reg. P1326, in L/P&S/10/266; Eastern Department Memorandum.
[144] Shipley Report, op. cit., n. 80 above.
[145] Ibid.
[146] Ibid. See also his draft letter of acceptance, PCP 35866, Reg. P3624, 11 Sept. 1912, in L/P&S/10/267.
[147] See Enc. No. 1: Memorandum on Mohammara Frontier Communicated to Turkish Ambassador, in Grey to Buchanan, 17 July 1912, PCP 30379, Reg. P2981–2, 25 July 1912, in L/P&S/10/291. See Figs. 5, 6, and 7, pp. 36–9.

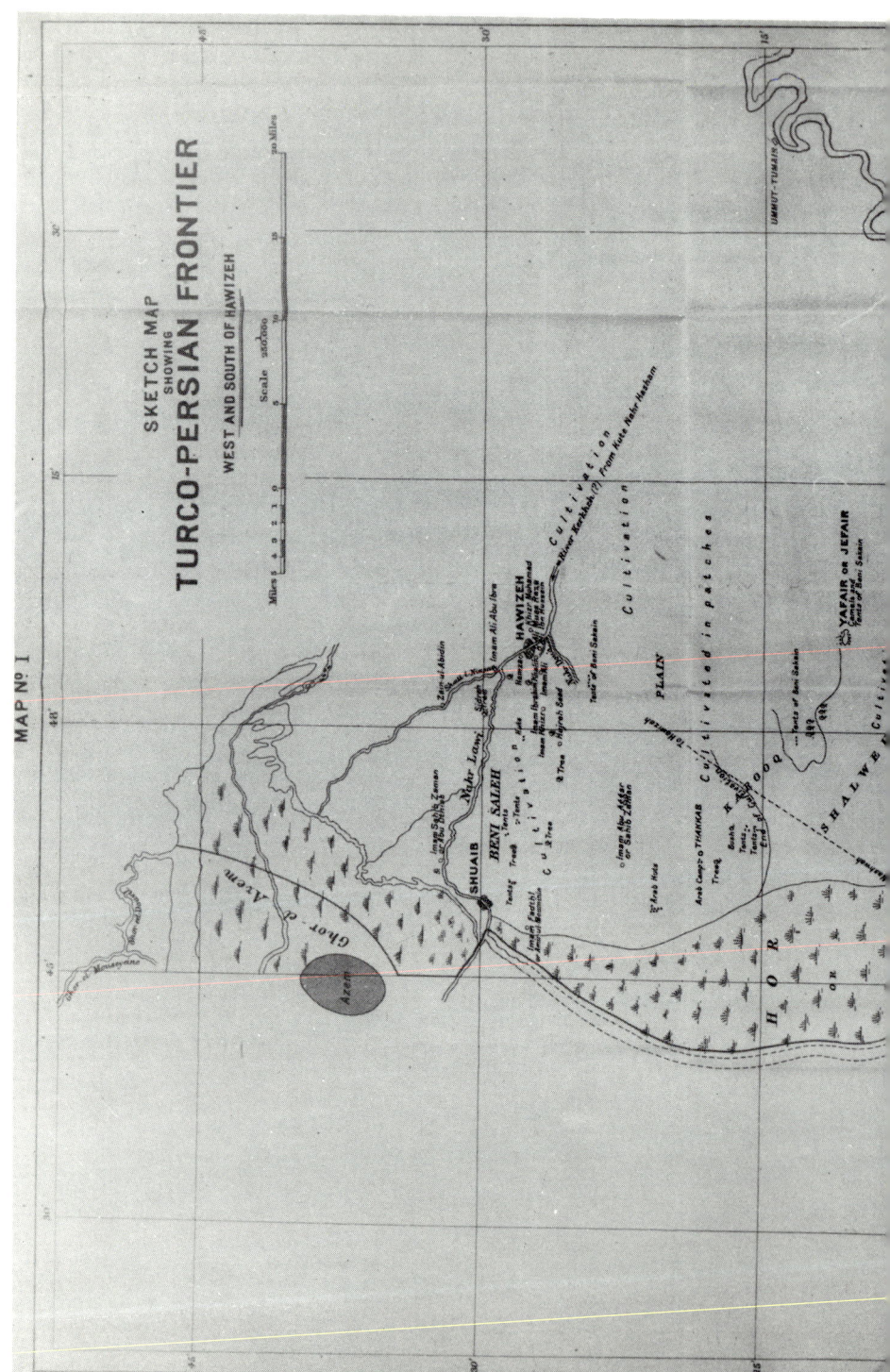

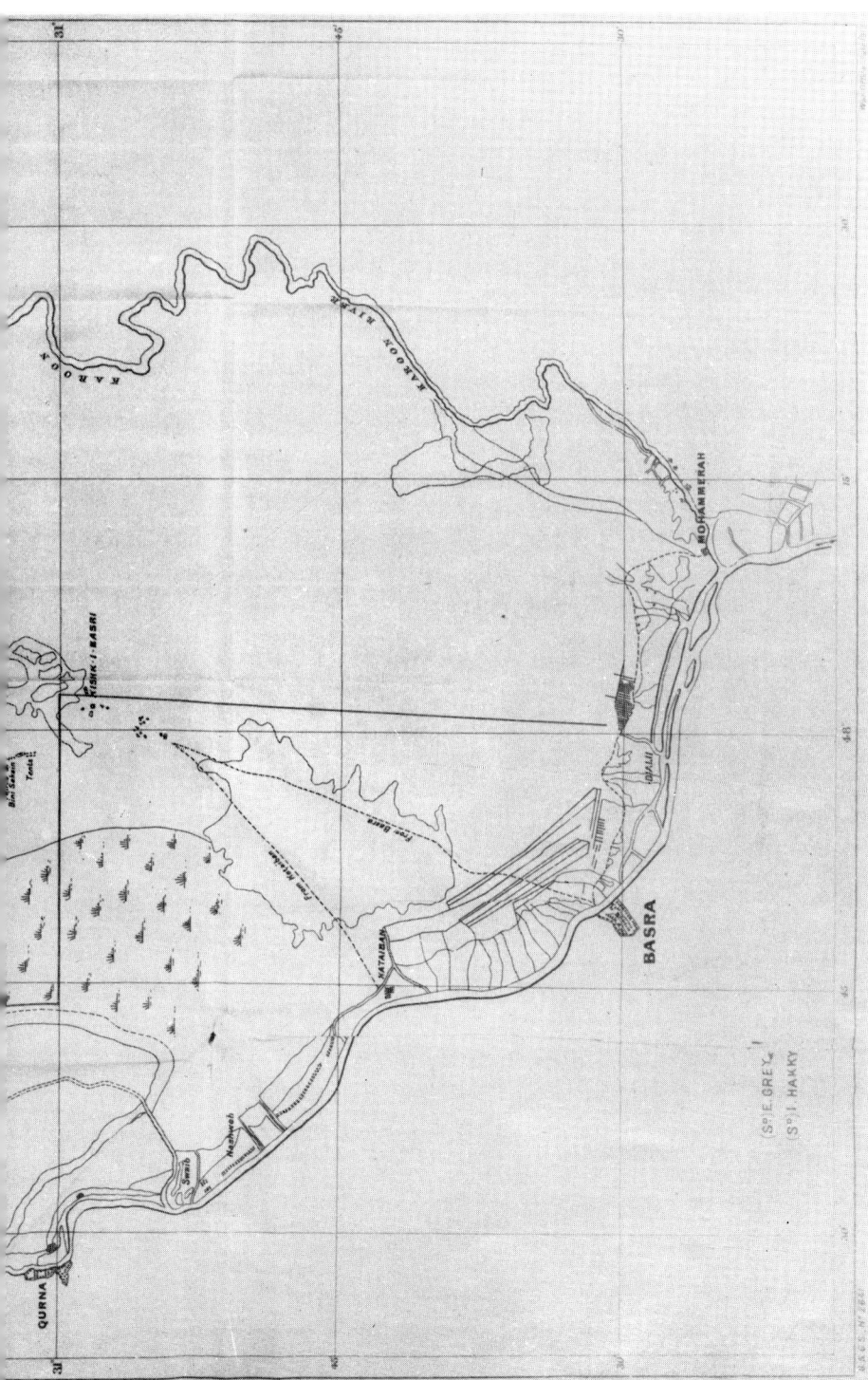

Fig 4. Sketch showing Turco-Persian frontier west and south of Hawizeh; delimited in 1913

(which flows into the Shatt from the north-east and is shown as the Khaiyin Canal in Fig. 3) and the Khaiyin Canal meet the main channel of the Shatt. It then followed the main channel of the Shatt in mid-stream until it reached the Persian Gulf. He reiterated some of the facts cited by the local officials in support of this boundary and noted that such a boundary was also in accordance with the general presumption that where a navigable river forms the boundary between coterminous States the middle of the channel or thalweg is the actual line of separation. 'Such a presumption may, however,' he wrote, 'be swept away, either by proof of prior occupancy and long undisturbed possession on the part of one of the two States, or by express treaty stipulation.'[148] He added that although his government could 'press for' the adoption of this line, he proposed that Turkey accept the line between Hawizeh and the point where the Khaiyin and Nazaliyeh entered the Shatt. With regard to the sector beyond the latter point, he offered to influence Persia and the Sheikh of Mohammara to accept Turkish claims to the whole of the Shatt, provided Turkey would agree to the view, *inter alia*,[149] that the modern port and anchorage of Mohammara, which lay in the main stream of the Shatt above and below its junction with the Karun, was situated within the limits of Persian jurisdiction. Effectively, therefore, the line, according to the accompanying map, ran along the *medium filum aquae* from a point where the land frontier joined the narrow Khaiyin Canal at Diaji to Tuwaijat, a point south of the Mohammara anchorage in the Shatt. He also pressed Turkey to agree [by way of *quid pro quo*] that the islands of Mohalla and Baliriyeh, their four smaller islands, and any other island now or in the future which may be connected with Abadan at low water or with the Persian bank below the Nahr Nazaliyeh, to be within Persian territorial limits.

It was clear, however, that if the Turkish Government were to be induced into accepting these proposals along with those submitted by Russia in respect of the sector between latitude 32° and Mount Ararat, some concessions would have to be made to Turkey in order to make the outcome appear as a compromise and not 'Turkish surrender'.[150] Hakki Pasha informed Mr Parker that while Turkey wished to satisfy Britain in the south and Russia in the north, she wished to obtain concessions in the

---

[148] He also claimed that the Treaty of Erzeroum contained no express provisions regarding the ownership of the river. Cf. Cox, who told the Sheikh of Mohammara on 20 Aug. 1912 in respect of the memorandum, that the treaty and the explanatory note assigned the whole river to Turkey: enc. in Cox to MacMahon, 25 Aug. 1912, Reg. P3572, 25 Aug. 1912, in L/P&S/10/266. The latter view was the more prevalent one at the Foreign and India Offices.

[149] Other conditions included an assurance that Persia's existing fishing rights would not be interfered with and that Turkish jurisdiction would not extend to land on the Persian bank which may be covered temporarily with water. See Article 1 of the Protocol of 1913, paragraphs (c) and (d). See also text to n. 150 below.

[150] Grey to Lowther, 6 Mar. 1913, Reg. P1048, 13 Mar. 1913, in L/P&S/10/267.

middle of the boundary, that is in the Zohab province, which is situate between the 32nd and 36th degrees of north latitude, and which was occupied by Persian troops when the Ottoman Empire was at war with Greece.[151] On 7 March 1913, Hakki Pasha reported that he was disposed to accept the line proposed by the British and Russian governments. This acceptance, however, was bound up with the question of the location of the boundary in the Zohab sector, the discussion of which is presented in some detail in a different part of this work. It will, accordingly, be sufficient to state here that it was this sector, and not the question of the location of the line in the Shatt, that constituted the chief source of difficulties in the negotiations leading up to the Protocol of 1913.[152]

On 29 July 1913, Sir Edward Grey and Hakki Pasha signed in London a 'declaration' with regard to the 'British sector' of the Turco-Persian frontier.[153] The frontier adopted in this declaration was based on the proposals communicated by Sir Edward Grey to the Turkish Ambassador on 18 July 1912. The lines have been described in sufficient detail above and need not be repeated here. It may be appropriate, hence, to elicit only the salient features of and changes made in the 'declaration'. The text of the draft declaration communicated to the Turkish Ambassador in Britain on 18 July 1912 had not stipulated for a mid-stream boundary in the Khaiyin Canal, whereas the accompanying map had shown it running along the *medium filum aquae*. This discrepancy was resolved in the definitive declaration by the provision of an express stipulation to the effect that the boundary in the Khaiyin Canal ran along the midpoints thereof.[154] The accompanying map depicted the boundary regaining the left bank at Tuwaijat.

Important changes were made in the Shatt–Hawizeh sector. In April 1913, Turkey had proposed the adoption of a line which began at a point where the Shatt-i-Niasan ran into the Ghori-i-Azam, a point situated a few miles west of Hawizeh between Nesheva and Hawizeh.[155] The Ottoman line was then drawn along the eastern edge of the Ghori-i-Azam in a south-westerly direction leaving effectively the entire *Ghor* or marsh north and north-west of Shoaib to Turkey. The Cox–Wilson alignment had assigned it to Persia. The new boundary proposed by Turkey regained the Cox–Wilson alignment at the point where Nahr Lawi ran into the *Ghor* just west

---

[151] Parker Minute, 4 Mar. 1913, PCP 10716, Reg. P1048, 1912; of 7 Mar. 1913, PCP 11389, Reg. P1142, 1913, in L/P&S/10/267.
[152] Persia, it may be noted, played a marginal role in these negotiations. See below, pp. 40 *et seq*.
[153] PCP 35336, 29 July 1913, Reg. P3371, 15 August 1913, in L/P&S/10/430. See Figs. 4, 5, 6 and 7, p. 32–3, 36–9.
[154] Louis Mallet (at the FO) to Hakki Pashi, 8 July 1913, Asiatic Turkey and Arabia Confidential Print 30014, Reg. P2935, 25 July 1913, in L/P&S/10/267.
[155] Grey to Townley, 9 Apr. 1913, Reg. P1395, 25 July 1913 in L/P&S/10/267. See Fig. 4, p. 32–3.

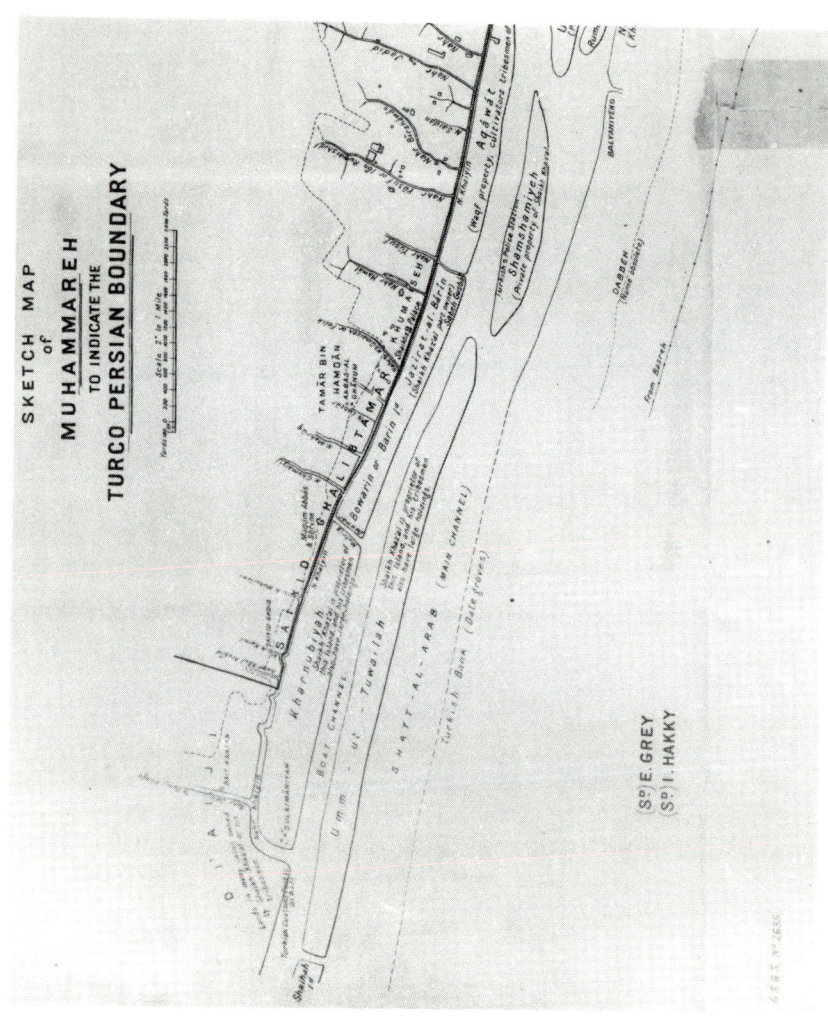

Fig 5. Sketch of Mohammarah to indicate the Turco-Persian boundary; delimited in 1913

The Boundary Problem

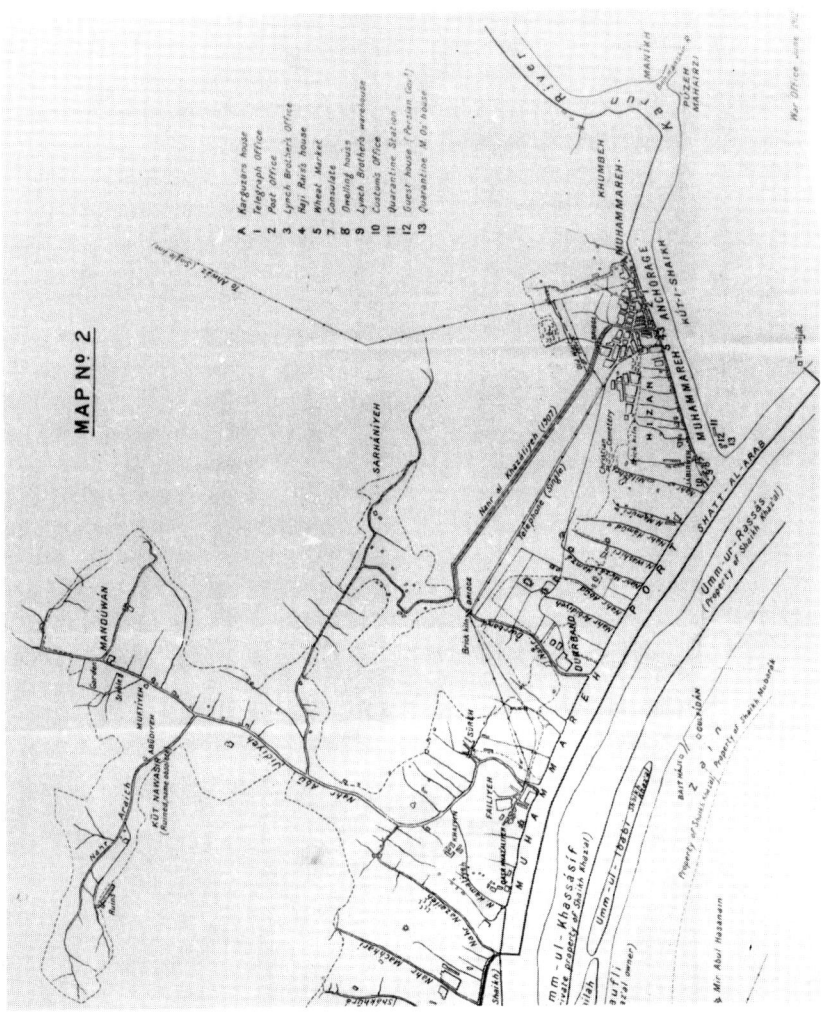

Figs 6 and 8. appear as foldout-maps between pp. 40 and 41

Fig 6. The Shatt-al-Arab and Bamishere; delimited in 1913
Fig 8. Sketch of the province of Zohab

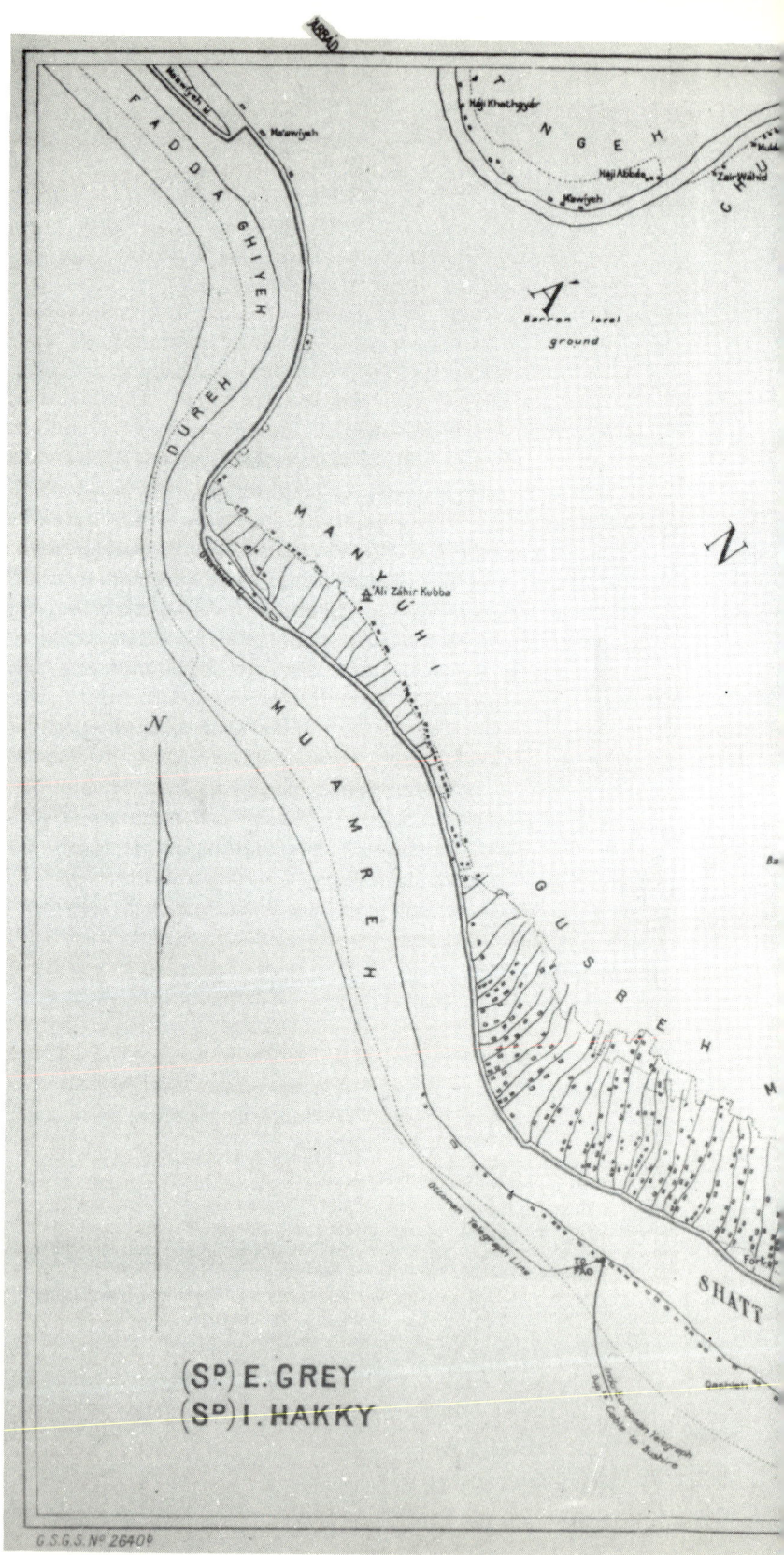

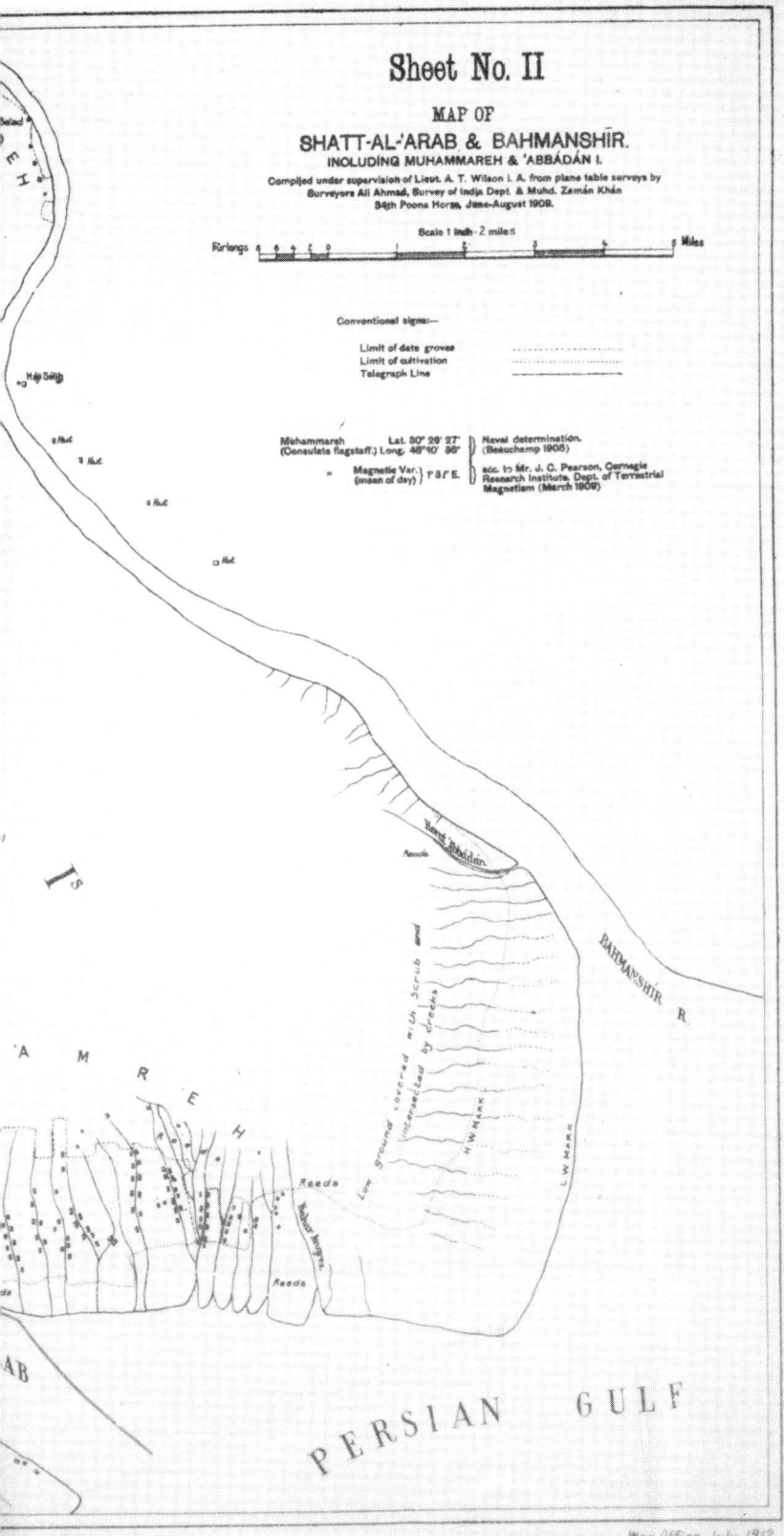

FIG 7. The Shatt-al-Arab and Bamishere up to the sea

of Shoaib, leaving to Persia all of the *Ghor* south of the latter town. At about north latitude 31° 08', that is a point which is approximately level with Khushk-i-Basri, the new Turkish line left the Cox–Wilson alignment and ran south-eastwards in the direction and to the north of some encampments of the Beni Sukain leaving them to Turkey. It then passed south of Khushk-i-Hawizeh and north of Khushk-i-Basri leaving the former to Persia and the latter to Turkey. The Cox–Wilson alignment ran straight eastwards to Khushk-i-Basri. After crossing east longitude 48° 15', the new Turkish line was drawn generally south-west and struck the Shatt at a point opposite the island of Umm-el-Hassaissif, leaving Falliyeh to Persia.[156] Sir Edward Grey was antipathetic to the prospect of allowing Turkey a line close to Mohammara much as he was against assigning the Beni Sukain tribes dependent upon Hawizeh to Turkey.[157] Major Cox, whose opinion was sought, advised that the reason why he had recommended the delimitation north of Shoaib was in order not to grant Turkey a footing on *terra firma* to the edge of the marsh as it lay within the influence of the Beni Turuf.[158] The exit of the boundary at the Shatt-i-Niasan was regarded as being inconvenient because it was not accurately fixed.[159] He recommended that the boundary begin at a point nine miles east of the terminus proposed earlier, that is the point at which the Ghor-i-Douvil left the Ghor-i-Azam: the Umm-Chir reported by Lt. Wilson in July 1912.[160] From that point, Cox proposed that the line be drawn south-west to rejoin the Cox–Wilson alignment at the southern extremity of Azam, an open sheet of water. He observed further that as regards the rest of this sector of the boundary, he saw no 'serious objection to the angle of our line at Khushk-i-Basri being shifted northwards just sufficiently to bring that point into the corner of Turkish territory, but at any rate not higher than the 31st degree of latitude', provided that the earlier Cox–Wilson alignment between Khushk-i-Basri and the Shatt was accepted without further modification. These recommendations were adopted by the British government and communicated to Hakki Pasha,[161] whose government issued a declaration on 6 May 1913 accepting the British government's modifications to its latest proposals.[162] The line adopted in the declaration ran in the manner described above.

The Zohab sector boundary was an area of mutual concern for Britain

---

[156] Ibid. This island lies opposite the Khaiyin Canal and Nahr Nazaliyeh junction and extends up to the Shatt–Haffar Canal junction and beyond. See Fig. 3, p. 27. The Nahr Nazaliyeh is shown as the Khaiyin, and the island is shown as Umm-ul-Khassassif.
[157] Ibid.
[158] Cox to Grey, 11 Apr. 1913, Reg. P1455, 1913, in L/P&S/10/267.
[159] Ibid.
[160] Ibid.
[161] Letter of 15 Apr. 1913, PCP 16898, Reg. P2087, 1913, in L/P&S/10/267.
[162] Declaration by Ottoman Turkey, 6 May 1913, Reg. P271B, 8 May 1913, in L/P&S/10/267.

and Russia and they accordingly collaborated with each other in the determination of a line which would be acceptable to all parties. It is bounded in the north by the Shemiran plains, and in the south by the town of Mandali, and is drained by the rivers Sirwan, Kuretu, and Elvand. While the Shia Senjabis inhabit the Kermanshah areas in Persia, their traditional winter home and pastureland was the region lying to the south of the Kuretu up to Mandali. Approximately thirteen miles to the north of Kasr-i-Shirin were situate the oil wells of Chia Surkh operated by the Anglo-Persian Oil Company. The area was investigated by Messrs Soane, Vice Consul, Kasri-i-Shirin, and Orlof, Russian Consul-General at Baghdad in 1912–13, in order to determine the location of the prevailing local boundaries and to make recommendations in respect thereof.[163] The frontier observed locally was described as being the southern limits of Shemiran, which followed the Sirwan river south-westwards to Bughaz, and then south-east along the Qashaan range towards Markaz and Khalifa Murad. It then ran due south along a road flanked by Turkish towers and forts to Kani Biz on the Elvand. This boundary then tended south-west towards the road running between Khanaqin and Qala Naft which it then ascended and ran along up to Qala Naft, leaving the Baghcha mountains and Qatar to Persia. It then lay south-south-east to Qala Naft on the Aab-i-Naft and thence ascended the Kumezang range south-east to Kali Shaun on the Gangir river, west of Mandali. Soane and Orlof recommended three lines. The first, or Proposition No. 1, was drawn solely on the consideration of leaving the oil wells at Chia Surkh to Persia.[164] It began at the confluence of the Zimkhan with the Sirwan and ascended the Baizal range to the south and then ran along the Tavghuz belonging to the Babajani Kurds. It then tended south along the Cham-i-Zirishk to a point nearly opposite the source of the Dar-i-Zengena stream which marked roughly the separation between the Sharafbaini and Babajani Kurds to the north and Guran to the south. The line was then drawn south-westwards along this river up to its confluence with the Ikhtiarabad stream. It then ascended the Darband-i-Ur range, and then lay westwards along the Abbasin river to Mamishan. It ran west across the north of the Serkala plains to the Tilaku ruins, and then, continuing in the same direction, the line ascended the summit of Dar-i-Divan; thence west to a point on the Sirwan, a few miles north of Bughaz, leaving Serkala to Persia. The boundary then ran along the locally observed line up

---

[163] Report by Soane, 9 Nov. 1912, Enc. No. 2 in Lowther to Grey, 12 Dec. 1912, PCP 53486, Reg. P106, 1913, in L/P&S/10/430; and Note accompanying Map of Frontier between Shemiran and Mandali, 13 Jan. 1913, Enc. No. 2 in Lowther to Grey, 25 Feb. 1913, PCP 9829, Reg. P1048, 1913, in L/P&S/10/267; hereinafter referred to as the Soane Report and Soane Note respectively. See Fig. 8, p. 39.

[164] Ibid. See Fig. 9, p. 44.

to Mandali.¹⁶⁵ It assigned the Senjabi winterlands to Persia,¹⁶⁶ but was considered wanting owing to the absence of marked physical features.¹⁶⁷

The second line, or Proposition No. 2, began near the Sirwan–Zimkhan confluence at Pusht-i-Shemiran and lay along the Zimkhan to a point opposite the northern end of the Khushik mountain range which it then ascended.¹⁶⁸ It ran south to Darband-i-Ur, the Salman ridge, Taktak mountain, and Bagh-e-Kuna just east of Mount Zengler. It was then drawn south-east along the Karamiz mountains to the Kuretu river and Tangi Hamam further south. The boundary followed the river westwards to Kuretu town after which point it lay straight westwards across the Akdagh [Aghdagh] mountains to a point north-east of Markaz, and thence it was co-existent with the locally observed frontier up to Mandali. Proposition No. 2 also assigned Senjabi lands to Persia, but left Chia Surkh to Turkey. Although he regarded this alignment as being the most advisable, inasmuch as it followed marked physical features, Soane qualified his proposals by suggesting that he would recommend following either the Kattar hills (to the west of Kuretu) to the Elvand, and then the Baghcha and Qatar mountains, thus attributing their western slopes to Turkey;¹⁶⁹ or following Proposition No. 1 up to Darband-i-Ur and from there, Proposition No. 2 to Mandali.¹⁷⁰ The advantage in the latter alignment lay in that the Babajani and Sarafbaini Kurds would be attributed undivided to Turkey. He pointed out that while Pusht-i-Shemiran was regarded locally as being under Persian control, Pusht-i-Kula was considered to be Ottoman in character.¹⁷¹ Proposition No. 3 was based on the desirability of following the roughly defined boundary between the Kalhur and Senjabi, leaving the former to Persia and the latter's winterlands to Turkey.¹⁷² It followed Proposition No. 2 to the Kuretu river; it then lay south to the Baz-i-Devaz range and then south-west to the Aab-i-Gilan and the Charmiah range. It continued in this direction till it struck the Shah Kuh knot of mountains and then joined the Aab-i-Naft along which it lay westward to Qala Naft. It then ascended the Kumezang mountains and ended at Kali Shaun. Soane drew attention to the fact that this alignment left the Senjabi lands to Turkey, cutting them off from their summer homes in Kermanshah, Persia.¹⁷³ Sir Edward Grey was disposed to adopt Proposition No. 1 as far as Darband-i-Ur and Proposition No. 2 between the latter and the Samaur plains near

---

¹⁶⁵ Soane Note.
¹⁶⁶ Soane Report.
¹⁶⁷ Soane Note.
¹⁶⁸ Soane Note and Report.
¹⁶⁹ Soane Report.
¹⁷⁰ Soane Note.
¹⁷¹ Ibid.
¹⁷² Ibid.
¹⁷³ Soane Note.

Kali Shaun.[174] He proposed the inclusion, if such a line were finally adopted, of a saving clause to protect the interests of the Anglo-Persian Oil Company at Chia Surkh.[175]

On 22 August 1912, the Russian Ambassador at Constantinople, M. de Giers, asserted in a letter to the Ottoman Minister for Foreign Affairs that, as regards Zohab, the whole of the territorial question was exhausted by virtue of Article 2 of the Treaty of Erzeroum which stipulated that the Persian government should undertake to cede to the Ottoman government all the lowlands, namely the western part of Zohab, while the latter was required to transfer all the mountainous regions thereof to Persia.[176] He also made proposals in respect of the 'Russian sector' of the boundary. The attitude of the Ottoman government was generally favourable, and on 7 March 1913 (mentioned earlier in respect of the Hawizeh sector) the Turkish Ambassador in London agreed to urge the Ottoman Grand Vizier to accept the lines proposed by the British and Russian governments in their notes of July and August 1912. As for the regions lying between the 32nd and 36th degrees of north latitude, he agreed to accept the prevailing status quo in return for compensation in the regions lying north and south of the town of Zohab, the district occupied by Sunni tribes, and the Mandali region. Other areas, he suggested, would be determined subsequently. Hakki Pasha agreed that the towns of Zohab and Kasr-i-Shirin would continue to remain in the possession of Persia.[177] The Ottoman reply of 31 March 1913 contained, *inter alia*, proposals regarding the boundary.[178] The line proposed therein was identical to the Soane–Orlof Proposition No. 1 up to Darband-i-Ur. It then tended south along the Salman, Taktak, Bagh-i-Koh, and Zengler mountain ranges attributing Dasht-i-Khyzl in equal parts to Turkey and Persia. After crossing the Kuretu river, the line ran westwards at a short distance away from the river, till it reached the Akdagh chain of mountains, which it then ascended and continued south to the Elvand river. It crossed the Elvand at Kani Biz and then followed its general direction at varying distances away from it on its left bank, tending north-east until it arrived first at Sar Pul and then Rijab. The proposed line then lay along the crest of the Kuh-i-Noa, Aarak, and Zelezerd mountains to the south and ended at Zorbatieh, about forty-five miles south of

---

[174] Grey to Lowther, 6 Mar. 1913, PCP 9829, Reg. P1048, 13 Mar. 1913, L/P&S/10/267. The Russian Ambassador in Constantinople was generally favourable: see Lowther to Grey, 18 Apr. 1913, Reg. P1048, 1913, in L/P&S/10/267.

[175] Grey to Lowther, 6 Mar. 1913.

[176] Enc. No. 2 in Buchanan to Grey, 24 Aug. 1912, PCP 36335, Reg. P3519, 1912; and Marling to Grey, 24 Aug. 1912, Reg. P3343, 1912, in L/P&S/10/291.

[177] Minute by Parker, 7 Mar. 1913, PCP 11389, 7 Mar. 1913, Reg. P1142, 1913 in L/P&S/10/267; and Grey to Buchanan, 9 Mar. 1913, Reg. P939, 10 Mar. 1913, in L/P&S/10/430.

[178] Prince Said to Russian Ambassador to Turkey, enc. in Lowther to Grey, 5 Apr. 1913, PCP 16221, Reg. P1713, 24 Apr. 1913, in L/P&S/10/430.

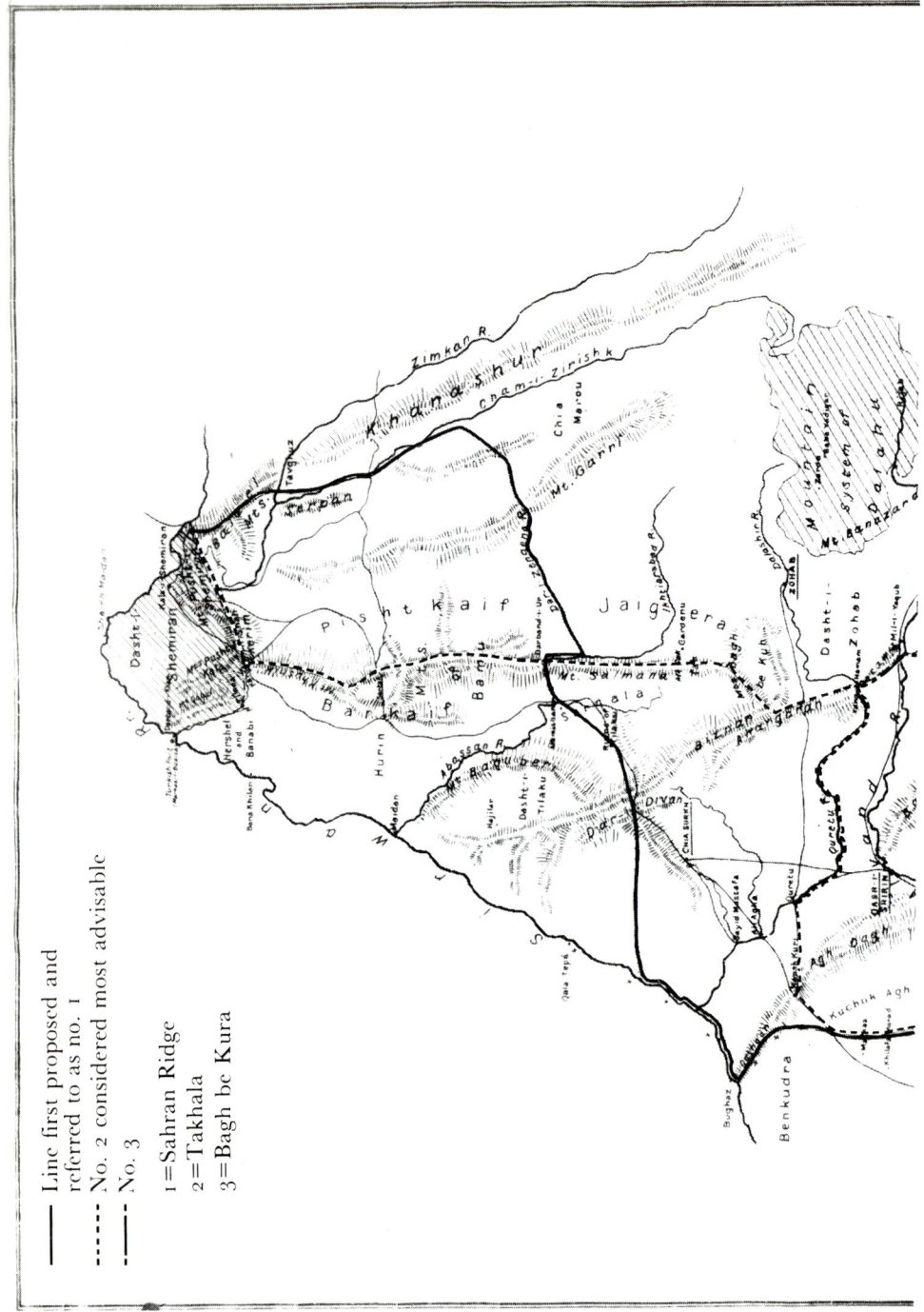

Fig 9. Sketch of the province of Zohab showing the Soane–Orlof proposals

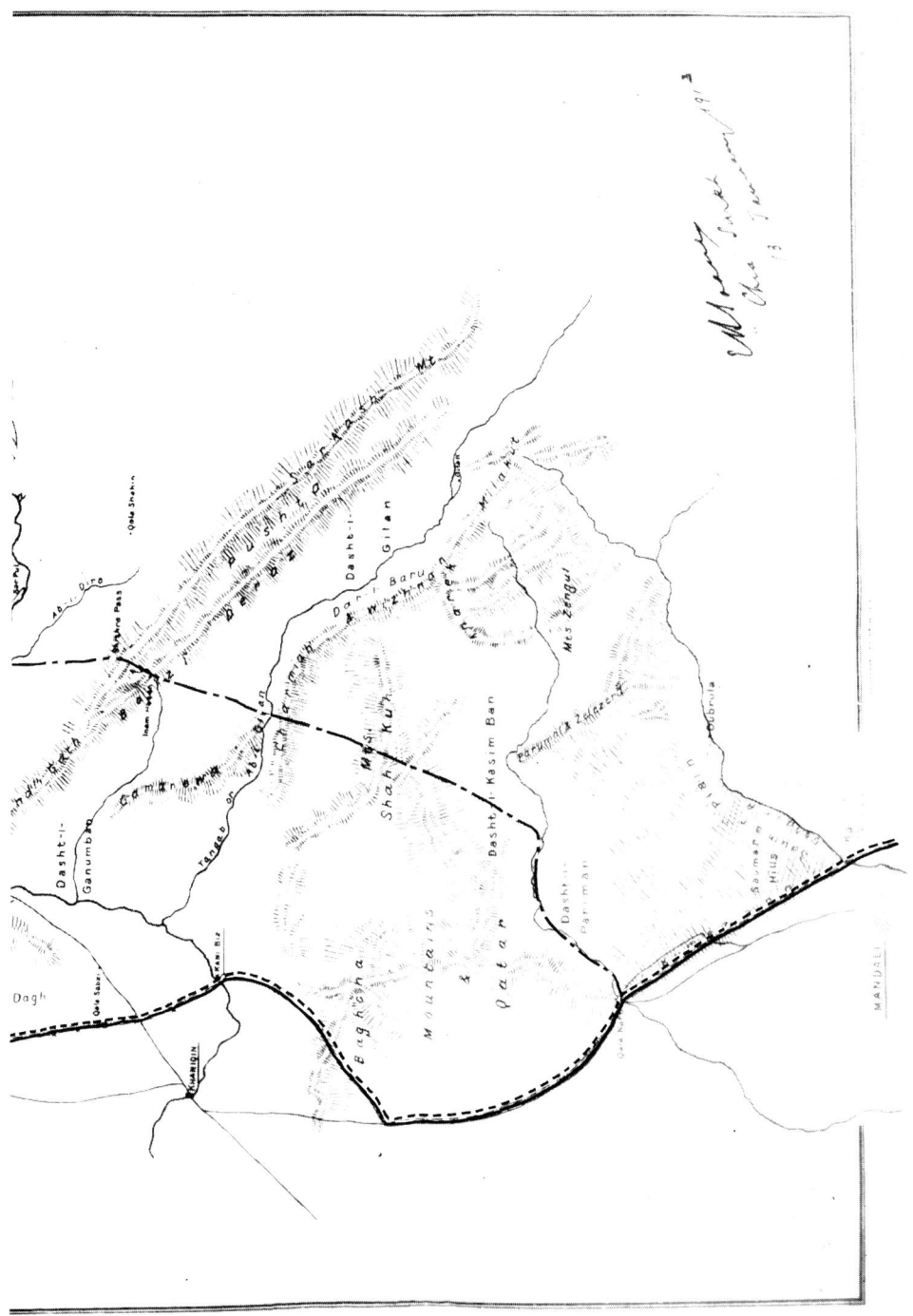

Mandali.[179] The Turkish line was not regarded as altogether acceptable in so far as it assigned the oil wells at Chia Surkh and excessive Shia Senjabi winterlands to Turkey[180] and encroached upon the Pusht-i-Koh.[181] The Russian Ambassador at Constantinople urged his government to accept in general terms the Turkish proposals subject to the proviso that all Sunni tribes were to be assigned to Turkey, while the pasturelands of Shia tribes would be allocated to Persia.[182] At the same time, he advised the British Ambassador to agree to a concession, that is to exchange the south-western districts of Shemiran (Chia Surkh), if need be, with the Porte.[183] He feared that there would be no chance of the Turkish government acceding to the proposals of the Mediating Powers which left the Senjabi and Kalhur (both Shia) countries south of the Elvand and oilfields to Persia; and that such proposals would endanger the whole course of the negotiations.[184] Sir Edward Grey concurred with the views of the Russian Ambassador, but advised Sir Gerald Lowther, the British Ambassador at Constantinople, 'to make it plain that the Anglo-Persian Oil Company would retain exactly [the same] position which they now hold at [Chia Surkh] and are not liable to the Porte for royalties . . . .'.[185]

On 26 April 1913 Sir Gerald Lowther proposed adopting a new line based none the less on the Soane–Orlof Proposition No. 2 up to Kuretu on the Kuretu river.[186] It provided for the cession of Chia Surkh to Turkey but it differed in that it assigned the district south of Shemiran to the east of Bamu mountains and the Serkala valley to Persia.[187] In his letter to Sir Edward Grey, he explained this by saying that the retention of Shemiran was essentially a bargaining position and that the Russian Ambassador was unwilling to cede Serkala to Turkey in view of its strategic value, that is the facility it offered for attack on the town of Zohab.[188] Beyond Kuretu, it was recommended that the line be drawn south between the paths of the Kuretu group of villages and Kouch-Khouyek up to and along the Akdagh range of mountains. The boundary would then be drawn further south, following the line of Turkish posts up to Kani Biz on the Elvand. The recom-

---

[179] See Lowther to Grey, 28 Mar. 1913, Reg. P1255, 1913 in L/P&S/10/267; and ibid. letter of 5 Apr. 1913, PCP 16221, Reg. P1713, 1913 in L/P&S/10/430.
[180] See letters cited n. 179 above; and Grey to Lowther, 11 Apr. 1913, Reg. P1455, 1913 in L/P&S/10/267.
[181] Lowther to Grey, 28 Mar. 1913.
[182] Lowther to Grey, 11 Apr. 1913, Reg. P1455, 1913; and id. letter of 28 Mar. 1913, in L/P&S/10/267.
[183] Lowther to Grey, 16 Apr. 1913, Reg. P1495, 1913, in L/P&S/10/267.
[184] Ibid.
[185] Grey to Lowther, 18 Apr. 1913, Reg. P1588, 1913; and Grey to Russian Ambassador to Britain Count Benckendorff, 24 Apr. 1913, PCP 18556, Reg. P2087, 1913, in L/P&S/10/267.
[186] Lowther to Grey, 26 Apr. 1913, PCP 19795, P2087, 1913, in L/P&S/10/267.
[187] Ibid.
[188] Lowther to Grey, 26 Apr. 1913, PCP 19795.

mended frontier then ran parallel to the Sirwan river and upon arriving at its left branch, that is the Kand-i-Bor, the boundary ran along the latter up to a point closest to the summit of the Kutchuk-Baghcha range. Having ascended this range the boundary would proceed along it southwards up to Jebel Louti-Baghcha chain in the Jebel Hamrine complex of mountains. Arriving at Aab-i-Naft, the recommended boundary ran along the summits of Varbulend, Kohnerig, and Kali Shaun which constitute an extension of the Jebel Hamrine, and ended at Mandali.[189] Effectively, therefore, the British and Russian governments decided to leave only the areas to the west of the Baghcha mountains, namely a relatively small section of the winter pasturelands of the Senjabi, to Turkey.

Identical notes incorporating these proposals were communicated by the British and Russian Ambassadors at Constantinople to the Turkish Minister for Foreign Affairs on 3 May 1913. The Grand Vizier advised them that although these proposals were not in principle entirely acceptable, he was inclined to agree with the northern section of the line and proposed the adoption of a modified line in the southern sector.[190] He suggested that he would not be able to defend any other boundary before Parliament. Both Hakki Pasha and the Grand Vizier insisted that the new Turkish line represented the actual status quo.[191] This line was formally proposed in the Turkish response of 12 July.[192] The Sublime Porte agreed to accept the Anglo-Russian line between the Shemiran river, the north terminus, and the Akdagh range. The new line differed in that it ran past Kani Biz to a point near the Gilan confluence with the Elvand. It then joined the Naft-i-Sou by curving around Ab-i-Bachan and ran on to Naft-i-Hane, situate west to the point at which the longitude 46° 40′ north cut the Aab-i-Naft. It then followed the latter south-westwards up to a point where the road from Kasr-i-Shirin joined the river. The sector of the line which lay along the Varbulend, Kohnerig, and Kali Shaun was accepted and the line was drawn in the direction of the 'local boundary' formed by the ranges of Jebel Guerbi, Goulan, Tizavouk, Bendi Kouli, and Burzuk until it reached and stopped at Guenjiadjim.[193] The major effect of this line was that inasmuch as it lay to the east of the Baghcha mountains and for some distance along the Aab-i-Naft it attributed relatively more areas of the Senjabi to Turkey.

[189] Ibid. See draft memorandum submitted by Russian Ambassador, annexed to his letter to the Sublime Porte: Enc. 2 in Lowther to Grey, 26 Apr. 1913. See also Lowther to Grey, 29 Apr. 1913, PCP 20331, Reg. P2087, 1913.

[190] Lowther to Grey, 27 May 1913, Reg. P2140, 1913, in L/P&S/10/267.

[191] Lowther to Grey, 19 June 1913, PCP 28576, Reg. P2715, 1913; and Grey to Lowther, 29 May 1913, Reg. P2140, 1913, in L/P&S/10/267. Hakki Pasha said that if the Anglo-Russian line were adopted, Turkey would lose revenue derived from naphtha products: Grey to Lowther, ibid.

[192] Enc. No. 1 in Marling to Grey, 11 July 1913, Asiatic Turkey and Arabia Confidential Print 32900, Reg. P3137, 1913, in L/P&S/10/267.

[193] Ibid.

It was for this reason that Sir Gerald Lowther had regarded the line as generally unacceptable.[194] In his letter to the British Foreign Secretary he suggested, nevertheless, that if Turkey's desires were met in the south he would be able to abate her demands in the north.[195] The Foreign Secretary agreed to adopt the Turkish line between Kuretu and Mandali subject to the concurrence of the Russian government in this regard.[196] In August 1913, Orlof confirmed that the local boundary between the Kuretu river and the Elvand was identical with the line proposed by the Ottoman government in July 1913. However, the Turkish line between the Elvand and Mandali did not correspond with the 'present boundary' barring small tongues of land south of Kani Biz, that is Dasht-i-Dourvue, Nazar Ali Beg, and Naft Maidan, which were unquestionably Turkish.[197] Thus in further identical notes communicated to the Ottoman Minister for Foreign Affairs on 5 August 1913, the British and Russian Ambassadors agreed to adopt the line proposed by them in May and the Ottoman government in July 1913.[198] The boundary proposed on 5 August followed the Soane–Orlof recommendations referred to as Proposition No. 2 as far as Kuretu, and for the sector between Kuretu and Mandali, the Mediating Powers agreed to accept the boundary proposed by the Ottoman government. Thus effectively the Mediating Powers agreed to the cession of the south-western parts of Shia land to Turkey. The Sublime Porte accepted these proposals on 23 September 1913.[199] Thereafter there were no major difficulties in settling the location of the line in this sector.[200] As regards the sector between Mandali and Shoaib it was agreed on all sides that there was little knowledge in respect of the status quo in this area, and the parties were inclined to leave the provisions relating thereto 'necessarily vague' so that a definitive alignment could be established at the time of demarcation on the basis of tribal and geographical considerations.[201]

The government of Persia took no part in the negotiations which were

---

[194] Lowther to Grey, 27 May 1913.
[195] Ibid.
[196] Grey to Lowther, 29 May 1913, Reg. P2140.
[197] Marling to Grey, 14 Aug. 1913, PCP 38476, Reg. P3619, 1913, in L/P&S/10/267.
[198] Enc. 1 and 2 in Marling to Grey, 21 Aug. 1913, PCP 39480, Reg. P3735, 1913 in L/P&S/10/430. See also Marling to Grey, 14 Aug. 1913, PCP 3847, Reg. P3619, 1913 in L/P&S/10/267.
[199] Said Halim Pasha to Marling, 23 Sept. 1919 enc. in Marling to Grey, 25 Sept. 1913, PCP 44174, Reg. P4234, 1913, in L/P&S/10/430.
[200] There were some difficulties regarding the exact location of the Aab-i-Naft, and Turkey was anxious not to grant any future rights in oil to the APOC, apart from the prevailing rights in Chia Surkh: Pasha to Marling, 23 Sept. 1913, PCP 44672, Reg. P4234, 1913 in L/P&S/10/430. These matters were quickly resolved. See Article 7 of the 1913 Protocol; and APOC to FO, 12 Nov. 1913, PCP 51583, Reg. P4806, 1913 in L/P&S/10/430.
[201] Marling to Grey, 14 Aug. 1913, PCP 38476 in Reg. P3619, 1913, also see telegram from Grey to O'Beirne, 7 Sept. 1913, Reg. P3735, 1913, in L/P&S/10/430; and Marling to Grey 13 Aug. 1913, Reg. P3301, 1913, in L/P&S/10/267.

being conducted between the two Mediating Powers and the Ottoman government at Constantinople. However, at the meetings of the Turco-Persian Frontier Commission, which were also being held at Constantinople, Persia did participate and submitted claims in respect, *inter alia*, of the Zohab boundary.[202] Extensive debates were held between, and evidence was submitted by, the Turkish and Persian delegates; but these were ineffectual inasmuch as the more meaningful discussions were being held between the British and Russian Ambassadors and the Ottoman government, discussions from which Persia had been excluded. It appears, however, that the British Ambassador in Tehran had, from time to time, consulted and conveyed information to the Persian government regarding these discussions.[203] 'It is', wrote Sir Walter Townley, the British Ambassador at Tehran, 'by no means unlikely that the Persian government may resent not having been consulted about the last details of the Turco-Persian frontier, and that we may experience some difficulty in securing their concurrence.'[204] He added that at any rate Persia feared Turkish aggression and was anxious to settle. The justification, it seems, for assuming full control over these negotiations was perhaps articulated most appropriately by Charles Marling (later Sir), Councillor of the British Embassy in Constantinople, who, in a letter to Sir Edward Grey wrote:

Indeed the view of the two Governments has been that if by their [sc. British and Russian] efforts they have succeeded in bringing about in Persia's interest a final settlement of this long-standing question, a settlement, moreover, which is far more favourable to Persia than she could ever had hoped to have reached without their intervention, it is but reasonable that Persia should consent to some sacrifice of territory.[205]

Nevertheless, these negotiations resulted in agreement in principle alone and were understood as requiring formal Persian concurrence, albeit of a nominal kind. Thus, Sir Edward Grey was able to telegraph the British Councillor at St Petersburg, Mr H. J. O'Beirne, that no further communication on the question of the frontier was to be made to the Persian government until Turkey had definitively accepted the line on the map. 'We can', he advised 'then telegraph a full description of it to Tehran, and place before the Persian government a line for the whole frontier, urging its immediate acceptance.'[206] A joint note was addressed to the Persian Prime

---

[202] See Shipley Report, op. cit. no. 80 above. See also Marling to Grey, 31 July 1912, PCP 32938, Reg. P3245, 1912 in L/P&S/10/291.
[203] Townley to Grey, 18 Aug. 1913, Reg. P3372, 1913, and Grey to O'Beirne, 30 May 1913, P2196, 1913, in L/P&S/10/267. Also Marling to Grey, 21 Aug. 1913.
[204] Letter of 18 Aug. 1913, Reg. P3372, 1913, in L/P&S/10/267. He wrote: 'I don't know how much Persian Ambassador at Constantinople has been kept informed, but hear complete ignorance of what is taking place is affected.'
[205] Marling to Grey, 21 Aug. 1913.
[206] Grey to O'Beirne, 30 May 1913.

Minister on 27 October 1913 in which the Russian and British Ambassadors exhorted Persia to accept the boundary decided upon by the representatives of the three States and advised the Persian government to be ready to make concessions (or 'sacrifices') in territory.[207] It urged her to send a delegate in the capacity of demarcation officer *'sans retard'* to Mohammara with authority to effect a final settlement regarding the districts under dispute.[208] The Persian Prime Minister is reported as having said 'it was true that Persia acquired a large portion of the disputed territory in some parts of the frontier, but . . . in other parts she [had] lost large tracts of territory [which] had been considered her undoubted possession for centuries.'[209] A Conference, attended by all four States, was convened in November at Constantinople. The Persian Foreign Minister pointed out to the British Ambassador that the Persian representative at Constantinople had been instructed to sign the frontier protocol with the reservation that Persian sovereign rights over the river were to be maintained, especially in view of the fact that the new line followed the left bank instead of the middle line.[210] The British Foreign Secretary advised Sir Walter Townley to emphasize that formerly the alignment ran along the left bank and not otherwise.[211] However, while several questions relating to different points along the frontier were raised by Persia at the Conference, no issue regarding the boundary in the Shatt was brought up.[212] The [Boundary] Protocol was signed on 17 November 1913[213] without any reservations submitted by Persia or Turkey. However, the Persian Prime Minister alleged that this was so because instructions regarding the boundary in the Shatt had failed to reach the Persian representative in accurate form by telegram.[214] The boundary between Hawizeh and the sea, the sector with which this study is primarily concerned, was that which had been settled between Sir Edward Grey and Hakki Pasha on 29 July 1913.[215] The island of Mohalla, its two

[207] Enc. No. 1 in Townley to Grey, 27 Oct. 1913, PCP 52062, Reg. P4900, 1913; and ibid., 28 Oct. 1913, PCP 49098 Reg. P4721, 1913, in L/P&S/10/430. See also *Memorandum*: Enc. No. 2 in Townley to Grey, 27 Oct. 1913.
[208] See Enc. No. 1 in Townley to Grey, 27 Oct. 1913, and *Memorandum*: Enc. No. 2, ibid.
[209] Townley to Grey, 27 Oct. 1913.
[210] Townley to Grey, 16 Nov. 1913, Reg. P4743, 1913 in L/P&S/10/430; Eastern Department Memorandum.
[211] Grey to Townley, 18 Nov. 1913, Reg. P4743, 1913, in L/P&S/10/430. See also Eastern Department Memorandum. Persia continued to raise vague demands of 'riverain rights', which were noted as containing the 'germs of continual future disagreement', but Grey made clear that 'there can be no question of Persian sovereign rights over the Shatt, whole of which is Turkish': Grey to Townley, 25 Jan. 1914, Reg. P357, 1914, in L/P&S/10/272.
[212] Meetings of 4, 5, 6, 8, and 9 Nov. 1913: Wratislaw's Notes of Meetings of Frontier Delegates at Constantinople, 10 Nov. 1913: Enc. No. 1 in Mallet to Grey, 10 Nov. 1913, PCP 51683, Reg. P4986, 1913, 5 Dec. 1913 in L/P&S/10/430.
[213] For text see Appendix II of the Iraqi letter to the Secretary-General, Council of the League of Nations, 29 Nov. 1934, and Al-Izzi, Annexe IV, The *Shatt-al-Arab River Dispute*, pp. 131–41. See Annexe 3, below.
[214] Eastern Department Memorandum.
[215] Above, p. 31.

The Boundary Problem

smaller islands, the four islands between Shutait and Moaviyeh, and the islands opposite Mankoli were transferred to Persia. However, her freedom of navigation was not reconfirmed in the Protocol. Article 5 provided that as 'soon as part of the frontier has been delimited, such part shall be regarded as finally fixed and shall not be liable to subsequent examination or revision.' While the protocol was concluded and the boundary demarcated on the mutual understanding that the alignment in question was a result of the interpretation of the general terms of the Treaty of Erzeroum, no specific provision to this effect was included in the said Protocol. However, references to the treaty do exist. Thus, in Article 1 it is provided that the 'parts of the frontier not detailed in the above-mentioned frontier line shall be established on the basis of the principle of the *status quo* in conformity with the stipulations of Article 3 of the Treaty of Erzeroum'.

(e) Boundary demarcation proceedings, 1914

Demarcation proceedings were initiated in January 1914, and the sector between the mouth of the Shatt and the Khaiyin Canal–Nazaliyeh junction was demarcated at the second and third meetings on 12 and 16 January 1914.[216] In his report, Colonel Ryder wrote, 'The frontier along the Shatt al Arab was the left or Persian bank, and the Commission only had to make a trip in steamer down to the mouth of the river to make "*une acte de presence*" and mark the frontier line on the map . . . '[217] The islands transferred to Persia were recorded, and the southernmost point, or terminus, of the boundary was fixed at two miles south of Sheikh Khazal's (the Sheikh of Mohammara) fort whose azimuth with the north was fixed at 87°.[218] On 19 January the Commission proceeded to determine the boundary to the north of the 'fixed point' from where the frontier line was to leave the Shatt to turn towards Khushk-i-Basri.[219] This point (boundary pillar No. 2) was about 400 feet west of the junction of the Nahr Abul Arabid with the Khaiyin (30° 20' 00" north latitude and 48° 03' 00" east longitude). Six boundary pillars were placed at the extreme edge of the lands drained by the Khaiyin, and the *medium filum aquae* at Tuwaijat extending northwards was determined accurately and recorded. The distance between Tuwaijat and the Khaiyin-Nahr-Nazaliyeh junction is about four

---

[216] Ryder Report, undated, Reg. 1577, 1 Apr. 1915; and Wratislaw Notes of Turco-Persian Frontier from Mohammara to Vazneh, enc. in Wratislaw to Grey, 21 Dec. 1914, Persia and Central Asia Print 88900, Reg. P2202/5094, 4 June 1915 in L/P&S/10/522. See also Proceedings of the Boundary Commission (translation) in Reg. 7173, 1920 in L/P&S/10/932.

[217] Ryder Report.

[218] Proceedings of the Boundary Commission, op. cit. n. 216 above. See also description in tabular form: Enc. in Chief Political Officer, Basra to Officer-in-Charge, Arab Bureau, Director Military Intelligence (DMI) Cairo, 28 May 1917, Reg. P2852, 1917, (part of Reg. P5094, 1917) in L/P&S/10/522.

[219] Proceedings of the Boundary Commission, op. cit.

and three-quarter miles. By 27 February 1914, the boundary up to Ghor-i-Douvil, which was the northernmost point of the British sector, had been demarcated,[220] albeit on the map alone inasmuch as the land was marshy and featureless;[221] and by 28 October 1914 the entire boundary, barring a small section in Kotur, had been marked out on the ground up to Mount Ararat.[222] Inasmuch as the latter sector now lies in Turkey, it follows that the entire frontier between Iraq and Iran stood demarcated on the basis of the Protocol of 1913. The Boundary Commission recorded its work in eighty-seven subsidiary protocols and a *tableau descriptif* of the frontier.[223] The demarcated line was drawn on ten sets of the Identic Map, and upon ten sets of twenty-five sheets of a supplementary map; each sheet was signed.[224] However, the proceedings were never ratified, a fact which was to raise some difficulties at a later period of time.

(f) *The Treaty of* 1937

At the end of the Great War, Turkey concluded the Murdos Armistice and thereby handed over control of Mesopotamia to British forces. Subsequently, the territory was placed under a British mandate. Questions of rectification of the frontier were first raised in 1919 by Persia, who, at the time of the conclusion of the Anglo-Persian Agreement of August 1919,[225] made certain proposals relative thereto.[226] Sir Percy Cox, now acting British Minister in Tehran, gave assurances to the Persian government that he would attempt to realize its claims regarding rectification of the frontier in the Mandali region.[227] Although the India Office admitted that some difficulties did exist in certain sectors of the boundary,[228] it advised the government that it would not be appropriate for Britain, as Mandatory Power, to seek revision of the boundary laid down in 1913–14.[229] The Foreign Office relied upon Article 5 of the Protocol and dismissed the argument that the proceedings were without binding effect because they

---

[220] Ibid.
[221] Wratislaw Notes, op. cit. n. 216 above.
[222] Ryder Report. See also Minute Note by Major Marrs, 6 Feb. 1921, Reg. P7173, 1920 in L/P&S/10/932.
[223] For text, see Appendix IIB of Iraqi letter to Secretary-General, Council of the League of Nations, 29 Nov. 1934, *League of Nations Official Journal*, op. cit. n. 74 above; see letter of 28 May 1917 cited in n. 218 above.
[224] Eastern Department Memorandum.
[225] 9 Aug. 1919, Cmd. 300, Persia No. 1 (1919); *BFSP*, 112 (1919), pp. 763–4.
[226] Marrs Minute Note to Reg. P7173, 1920 in L/P&S/10/932; Eastern Department Memorandum.
[227] Eastern Department Memorandum. Curzon repeated the assurance.
[228] Minute Note to Reg. PZ6702, 1934, in L/P&S/12/2869.
[229] Minute Note by Major Marrs, Reg. P7173, 1930.

The Boundary Problem

had not been ratified.[230] Earl Curzon of Kedleston, the British Foreign Secretary, advised that the delimitation had resulted from the Protocol of 1913, which Protocol had been ratified by the parties, and therefore no further ratification was required.[231] On 11 February 1920 the Persian Minister of Foreign Affairs wrote to Sir Percy Cox saying that he had ordered the Vali of Hawizeh to respect the boundary in view of the hard labours of the Commission;[232] and in June 1920, officials of the Persian and Iraqi governments inspected the frontier between the two States.[233]

The British Mandate over Mesopotamia lapsed and Iraq emerged as an independent State on 3 October 1932. In 1921 Raza Shah ascended the Persian throne and brought with him a vigorous nationalist foreign policy.[234] For a variety of reasons,[235] general and specific questions continued to be raised in respect of territories and frontiers. First, Iran raised questions regarding the validity of the Protocol of 1913, which agreement, by ceding Chia Surkh and other prospective oil-bearing regions to Iraq, had deprived Iran of revenues which would have otherwise accrued to her.[236] Secondly, she had failed to reconcile herself to the fact that apart from the cession at Mohammara, Iran had no lawful rights to the Shatt. To be sure, Iran's grievance in this matter was not entirely groundless. For one thing, ships anchored at Abadan, now a major port with its British oil refinery, were, in contrast to the situation at Mohammara, in Iraqi national waters.[237] For another, the Port Authority at Basra was exclusively responsible for the lighting, buoying, and dredging of the bar and safe navigation in the river. It was the sole authority which could and did impose on all shipping in Shatt. Inasmuch as she did not participate in any of these activities, the existing state of affairs had become unacceptable to Iran, more so in view of the fact that an estimated 80 per cent of the shipping, which generated one-third of the revenues for Basra Port Authority, was bound

---

[230] See FO to Baghdad High Commissioner, 30 July 1934, PCP E3859/197/34 in PZ5610, 1934, in L/P&S/12/2869.

[231] FO to IO, 19 Feb. 1921, Reg. P1020, 1921, in L/P&S/10/932. See also Dobbs, High Commissioner, Iraq, to Clive, British Minister, Tehran, 31 Mar. 1927, P2008, 1929 in L/P&S/12/2870; and Baxter Memorandum.

[232] Clive to Dobbs, 14 May 1927, in P2008, 1929.

[233] Ibid; and Dobbs to Clive, 31 Mar. 1927, P2008, 1929.

[234] Although it is perhaps more appropriate to refer to Persia as Iran in this and subsequent periods, and although the latter name has been adopted in the following pages, a strict adherence to this change is unhelpful in view of inevitable references to pre-transition days, concurrent usage, and citation of official documentation.

[235] Some of the sources of hostility between the Parties were related to Shia–Sunni animosity, to the fact that certain holy cities of Persia were in Iraq, and to the general political disappointment of the Arabs. See Baxter Memorandum.

[236] Baxter Memorandum. See also letter from British Embassy at Baghdad to FO, 29 Mar. 1933, Reg. PZ2502, 1933 in L/P&S/12/2869: Iran wanted the creation of a zone for joint exploitation of all minerals which lay between the 1913 and 1847 lines.

[237] Clive to FO, 4 Mar. 1929 in Reg. P1993, 1929, in L/P&S/10/1098.

for either Abadan or Mohammara.[238] It was clear therefore that the existence of Basra as a first-class port depended on the Abadan trade.[239]

Support for the claim that the 1913-14 settlement was invalid was secured by reference, *inter alia*, to the fact that the Turkish government had renounced the Protocol of 1913 in so far as it applied to the Iraqi-Turkish frontier.[240] 'Furthermore', added Sir Robert Clive, the British Minister at Tehran, 'Persia feels that times have changed sufficiently since [the] Treaty of Erzeroum to justify her in wishing for equal rights in the river with Iraq whom we have made the inheritor of ancient Turkish privileges and who, without our aid, could not maintain them'.[241] The general Iranian claim was that the boundary in the Shatt region ran in the middle and not along the left bank of the river.[242]

The British government, who continued to exercise a significant measure of influence in the foreign affairs of Iraq, recognized the fact that the 1913-14 settlement was valid and binding upon the parties; and therefore a claim to a mid-line boundary could not, in principle, be upheld in law or urged in diplomacy. Hence, it refused to 'push' for a revision of the entire boundary along the left bank.[243] Apart from that, it was observed that it was 'physically impossible' to divide equally the waters of the Shatt 'for the thalweg does not follow the line of midstream but crosses from one side of the river to the other; and an alteration of the frontier to the centre of the thalweg is impracticable owing to the shifting nature of the banks forming the bars and shallower parts of the river'.[244] Nevertheless, the British government appreciated the significance of Iran's grievances, especially in the matter of the anchorage at Abadan,[245] and believed that if the Iranian

---

[238] Baxter Memorandum. Also see Iran Minister at Baghdad to Iraqi Foreign Minister, 18 Aug. 1936, enc. in British Embassy, Baghdad to FO, 22 Aug. 1936, Reg. PZ6431, 1936, in L/P&S/12/3803. By 1935, 90 per cent of the dredging dues came from ships calling at Abadan only: see Appendix A, Report of Narrative of Events, 28 Nov. 1935, PCP E69949/32/34, Reg. PZ170, 1936 in L/P&S/12/2870. All shipping at Abadan was British.

[239] See Appendix A, Report of Narrative of Events, op. cit. Also see Clive to FO, 9 Jan. 1929, Reg. P364, 1929 in L/P&S/10/1098.

[240] Clive to Chamberlain, 12 Jan. 1928, PCP (E587/55/34). Reg. P774, 1928 in L/P&S/10/1229.

[241] Clive to FO, 4 Mar. 1929.

[242] See generally, Iranian letter to Clive, 1 Apr. 1928, cited in Baxter Memorandum. See generally Reg. P364, 1929 and Reg. P2171, 1929 in L/P&S/10/1098; Reg. P774, 1928 in L/P&S/10/1229; Reg. PZ2502, 1933, in L/P&S/12/2869. See also *Correspondence Regarding the Perso-Iraq Frontier*: Reg. P2008, 1929 in L/P&S/12/2870.

[243] FO to Clive, 14 Feb. 1928, Reg. P774, 1928. See also, generally, Reg. P364, 1929 in L/P&S/10/1098; and FO to Tehran, 22 Nov. 1928, No. 561, E5367/55/34, Reg. P6284, 1928 in L/P&S/10/1229; Reg. PZ7287, 1933, PCP E5741/91/34 in L/P&S/12/3802; Reg. P2171, 1929 in L/P&S/10/1098. The FO pointed out to the CO (25 May 1927) that the Iranian Majlis had tacitly accepted the boundary for more than twelve years: see Baxter Memorandum. See also the Memorandum on the 1913 Frontier Report on the Shatt, 1934: Committee of Imperial Defence, 13 Sept. 1934, E5719/197/34, Reg. PZ6165, 1934 in L/P&S/12/2869.

[244] FO to Clive, 8 Feb. 1929, next to Reg. P1174, 1929, in L/P&S/10/1098.

[245] Baxter Memorandum, op. cit. Also see *Perso-Iraq Frontier: Proposals for a New Policy*, 30 Dec. 1936, E7925/10/34, next to Reg. PZ500, 1937 in L/P&S/12/3803.

government were to abandon Abadan and select either Khor Musa or Bandar Abbas as alternative ports away from the Shatt, it would seriously affect the viability of the Basra Port Authority.[246] In addition to that, there was the problem of the Karun which flowed uncontrolled into the Shatt, and brought with it large quantities of mud making the channel below Mohammara unnavigable.[247] It was also believed to be cutting into the south bank of the Shatt at the big bend above Abadan.[248] Participation, therefore, of Raza Shah's government in conservancy measures was considered to be essential. Accordingly, on 11 March 1929 the British Ambassador in Tehran gave a formal assurance to the Persian Foreign Minister in terms to the effect that if the Iranian government were to recognize Iraq, the British government, having been apprised of the practical difficulties prevailing at the frontier, would lend assistance as regards her reasonable demands for further rectification.[249]

The Iranian government recognized Iraq on 20 April 1929 and, in a letter dated 20 September 1931, its legation in Baghdad informed Iraq that the agreement of 1913–14 had not been officially recognized.[250] It pressed the British Minister in Tehran and the Iraqi government to accept the Persian claims.[251] The government of Iraq reiterated its claims to the whole of the Shatt and denied that there was any frontier question apart from genuine Iranian grievances respecting conservancy and navigation.[252] This period, thus, was marked with frontier incidents in the Shatt[253] as well as in the areas to the north, including Amarah Liwa, Kut[Liwa] and Diala Liwa.[254] The Iraqi government protested against Iranian police and customs patrolling in the Shatt and objected to Iranian men of war ignoring the

---

[246] Memorandum by Committee on Imperial Defence, op. cit. n. 243 above; Clive to FO, 9 Jan. 1929, Reg. P364, 1929; FO to Clive, 8 Feb. 1929, Reg. P1174, 1929; Clive to FO, 4 Mar. 1929, Reg. P1993, 1929, in L/P&S/10/1098.

[247] Memorandum on 1913 Frontier: Committee of Imperial Defence.

[248] Ibid.

[249] Eastern Department Memorandum. See also Minute Note to Reg. P2171, 1929. Cf. Britain's earlier position on the matter: namely that it could give no commitment in this regard inasmuch as it was a matter entirely for the Iraqi government to settle: see Clive to FO, 6 Dec. 1928, Reg. P6572, 1928 in L/P&S/10/1229.

[250] Reg. PZ6689, 1931 in L/P&S/12/43.

[251] Mallet to Sir John Simon, British Foreign Secretary, 7 Sept. 1933, PCP E5741/91/34, Reg. PZ7287, 1933; see also Humphrys to Simon, 24 Nov. 1932, PCP E6410/20/34 Reg. PZ7861, 1932. in L/P&S/12/3802.

[252] Conversation between Iraqi Foreign Minister and Persian Minister in Baghdad, 12 Mar. 1933, as reported in enc. in Baghdad Embassy to FO, 6 Apr. 1933, Reg. PZ2502, 1933, in L/P&S/12/2869.

[253] See generally Regs. PZ6028, 1933; PZ7798, 1934; PZ5610, 1934; and Minute Note to Reg. PZ6702, 1934, in L/P&S/12/2869.

[254] Iraqi Minister for Foreign Affairs to Persian Minister, Baghdad, (?)14 Aug. 1934, Reg. PZ5847, 1934; and Iraqi Minister for Foreign Affairs to Secretary-General, League of Nations, Nov. 1934, enc. in Humphrys to Simon 22 Nov. 1934, PCP E7220/197/34, Reg. PZ7798, 1934, in L/P&S/12/2869.

instructions and regulations established by the Director, Basra Port Authority.[255] 'We have', said the Iraqi Foreign Minister, 'on numerous occasions invited the Persian government's attention to the contraventions committed by their vessels in the Shatt-al-Arab . . . '[256] The Eastern Department Memorandum observed that since 1926 Iranian jurisdiction in the Shatt arose partly as a result of an unofficial arrangement between local Iranian and Iraqi authorities, and partly in open defiance of the Iraqi Government.[257] The combination, however, of boundary matters with conservancy questions complicated the negotiations and prevented progress, especially in view of the fact that Iran's main source of grievance was related to the matter of the mid-line boundary and not conservancy measures. On 29 November 1934, Iraq requested the Council of the League of Nations to intervene on the question of the boundary and the 1913–14 settlement.[258] Both parties submitted comprehensive statements on their positions and interpretation of the legal and political facts of the problem.[259] These statements will be referred to in greater detail at a more appropriate place and it will hence be sufficient to state here that the Italian Ambassador Baron Aloisi, who was appointed Rapporteur, submitted a report to the Council on 25 May 1935 regarding consultations he had had with the disputing parties.[260] From a perusal of the records it appears that he proposed that the boundary in the Shatt be drawn along the thalweg between Khaiyin Canal–Shatt junction and Tuwaijat and from the latter point to Buwarda. Between the point where the 1913–14 line began, that is two miles below the Sheikh's fort, and the open seas, the boundary lay along the left bank. At Abadan the Rapporteur envisaged a limited degree of rectification of the line in order to leave part of its waters to Iran.[261] He also

---

[255] Iraqi Minister for Foreign Affairs to Secretariat of the Council of Ministers, Baghdad, 18 Apr. 1934, enc. in Ogilvie-Forbes to Simon, 30 May 1934, Eastern (Iraq) Confidential Print, E3859/197/34, PZ5610, 1934, in L/P&S/12/2869. See also FO to Sir Eric Drummond, British Ambassador, Rome, 21 Feb. 1935, E1101/32/34, Reg. PZ2004, 1935; Clive to Persian Acting Foreign Minister, 20 Apr. 1928, Reg. PZ2008, 1929, in L/P&S/12/2870; Iraqi Minister for Foreign Affairs to Persian Minister, Baghdad, 11 July 1936, enc. in Bateman to Eden, 15 July 1936, E4626/10/34, Reg. PZ5889, 1936 in L/P&S/12/3803.
[256] See letter from Iraqi Foreign Minister to Secretariat of Council of Ministers, 18 Apr. 1934. See also FO to Drummond, 21 Feb. 1935.
[257] Eastern Department Memorandum.
[258] See her letter to Secretary-General, Council of the League of Nations, 29 Nov. 1934 in *League of Nations Official Journal*, 16 (1935), p. 196. For Persian reply, 8 Jan. 1935, ibid., p. 216.
[259] See Minutes of the 84th Session of the Council, Feb. 1935, ibid., p. 113 *et seq.*, in reference to addresses of Nuri Pasha (Iraq) and Kazemi (Iran).
[260] *Report on the Work of the League of Nations since the Fifteenth Session*, 1935, Part 1, p. 32–1. (A.6.1935). See also above vol. of *Official Journal* pp. 651–2.
[261] See Appendix E and F to Memorandum on the Iraqi-Iranian Boundary Dispute by C.J. Edmonds, Second Adviser, Iraqi Ministry of Interior, 11 June 1935, PCP 14641, Reg. PZ4787, 1935 in L/P&S/12/2870, and FO to Seal, 13 July 1935, PCP E3958/32/34, Reg.

recommended the establishment of a Conservancy Board to regulate navigation in the Shatt.[262] However, in view of the progress made in the negotiations between the States, the petition pending at the League of Nations was 'adjourned' in May 1935. A brief account of these proceedings follows below.

In January 1936, the government of Iraq made new proposals to break the deadlock in the negotiations. It recommended first the postponement of negotiations in respect of a conservancy and navigation treaty and, second, the adoption of a boundary agreement. To this effect, it proposed ceding the anchorage, as opposed to half the width of the river, opposite Abadan to Iran. The line between the southern terminus and the sea was left indeterminate. As *quid pro quo*, Iran was to acknowledge the alignment of 1914.[263] Although the response was generally favourable, the Iranian government had misgivings about references to a '1914' alignment[264] and urged that the line be described from north to south.[265] It proposed that the line opposite Abadan be about twelve miles long and lie in the middle of the Shatt.[266] The Iranian government also recommended a median line between the southern terminus of the boundary and the point where the river actually met the sea.[267] In a series of proposals submitted

---

PZ4859, 1935 in L/P&S/12/2870. Baron Aloisi's proposals were not published in the *League of Nations Official Journal*.

[262] Appendix E and F, op. cit. See also Report of the Rapporteur, Appendix I in Edmonds Memorandum, ibid.

[263] Knatchbull-Hugessen (Tehran) to FO, 6 Jan. 1936, Reg. PZ213, 1936; 15 Jan. 1936, Reg. PZ399, 1936, in L/P&S/12/3803. It also recommended a treaty of friendship.

[264] Knatchbull-Hugessen to FO, 12 Jan. 1936, Reg. PZ399, 1936 in L/P&S/12/3803.

[265] Clark Kerr (Baghdad) to FO, 11 Feb. 1936, Reg. PZ1086, 1936, in L/P&S/12/3803. Although the Protocol of 1913 had described the boundary from north to south, the boundary demarcation had been carried out from south to north and the latter constituted the more authoritative of the two delimitations. It was felt that a description of the boundary from north to south would have confused matters and was unacceptable to both Iraq and Britain. The south to north description was repeated in the Baghdad Treaty of 1975.

[266] Ibid.

[267] Ibid. Although the southern terminus was regarded as the point at which the river met the sea, difficulties arose when large bodies of marshy land were exposed at low tides south of the terminus on both sides of the mouth. The tracts on the left bank were known as Abadan Marakat and the one on the right as Abdallah Marakat. The Rooka Channel, which lay partly closer to the left bank and partly in the middle of the river in the waters between the two Marakats, lent significance to the two drying tracts. The question was whether the tracts could legitimately be considered land territory. If the Marakats were to be regarded as land territory, the frontier would continue to run along the left bank and would leave the Rooka Channel within Iraqi national waters; but if they were not part of land territory, the Iranian Government would be free to determine its territorial waters from a point south of the southern terminus, with the result that the channel, or part of it, would be assigned to Iran. It was, hence, in Iraq's and Britain's interest to deem the Marakats as land territory and it was this position which British officials maintained in their confidential correspondence. However, the question of the status of the Marakats or the Rooka Channel never occupied great prominence, although Britain urged Iraq to fortify her position by treaty arrangement in the negotiations leading up to the 1937 treaty.

to the Iranian Authorities in April 1936, the Iraqi government recommended a line which continued along the low water mark on the left bank up to the mouth of the Shatt. It agreed to give a quarter of the width of the Shatt opposite Abadan to Iran. The limit of Iraqi national waters, beyond which lay her territorial seas, was a line which joined the outer edges of the Marakats.[268] There were, however, indications that Iraq was prepared to cede more than the anchorage, and that the line acceptable to her was the thalweg in the vicinity of Abadan.[269] These facts were viewed with considerable caution by the Foreign Office and Admiralty inasmuch as it was considered essential that ships be able to proceed to Basra without passing through Iranian waters.[270] The Admiralty, moreover, were initially in favour of a lease as opposed to a cession, of Abadan anchorage;[271] or a cession limited to one hundred yards in width opposite the anchorage.[272]

In a letter communicated to the government of Iraq on 18 August 1936, the Iranian Minister in Baghdad suggested that the proposed treaty declare the Shatt to be open to passage of merchant ships of all nations equally and without discrimination.[273] She also urged for the joint determination of all matters relating to the regulation of navigation, dredging, and conservancy in the Shatt and the collection of dues. It was claimed that both parties had equal rights of fishing, industrial exploitation, and agriculture.[274] Iraq replied by stressing that Iran must recognize the 'original boundary' in the proposed treaty and reiterated her proposals to cede the Abadan anchorage, subject to the provision of certain safeguards regarding the freedom of navigation by Iraq through the anchorage in peace and in war and the retention of the right to dredge the ceded part of the river.[275] In a letter of 20 January 1937 submitted as a response to the Iraqi proposals, Iran agreed to recognize the Protocol of 1913 and the procès-verbaux of the demarcation of the frontier of 1914 subject to the cession of the anchorage at Abadan which would be effected by the drawing of a line four miles in length along either the middle or the thalweg of the river between Jetty No. 1 and the upper or northern end of Shutait island.[276] She repeated her earlier proposals to the effect that the Shatt be regarded open for passage

---

[268] Proposals of 1 Apr. 1936 submitted to Iranian delegation: Enc. No. 1 in Clark Kerr to FO, 15 April 1936, Reg. PZ2963, 1936 in L/P&S/12/3803.
[269] Clark Kerr to FO, 15 Apr. 1936.
[270] FO to Clark Kerr, 16 Dec. 1936, Reg. PZ9016, 1936, in L/P&S/12/3803.
[271] Admiralty to FO, 24 July 1935: MO472/10/35, Reg. PZ5078, 1935 in L/P&S/12/2870.
[272] FO to Clark Kerr, 16 Dec. 1936. See Fig. 10, p. 60–1.
[273] Enc. in British Chargé d'Affaires, Baghdad to FO, 22 Aug. 1936, Reg. PZ 6431, 1936, in L/P&S/12/3803; Bateman (Tehran) to FO, 21 Aug. 1936, Reg. PZ6125, 1936, in L/P&S/12/3803.
[274] See letters cited in n. 273 above.
[275] Reply of 28 Nov. 1936, enc. in Clark Kerr to FO, 26 Dec. 1936, Reg. PZ8816, 1936; and Clark Kerr to FO, 1 Dec. 1936, Reg. PZ8816, 1936, in L/P&S/12/3803.
[276] Clark Kerr to FO, 23 Jan. 1937, Reg. PZ667, 1937, in L/P&S/12/3803.

The Boundary Problem

of merchant ships of all States on equal terms; that the Shatt be open to warships of Iraq and Iran; and that both sides agree to conclude an agreement concerning the organization, maintenance of the channel, and matters subsidiary to these.

Iraq found herself in agreement on the essential features of this draft treaty.[277] Her Foreign Minister submitted to Iran a draft agreement in which the former agreed to the extent of the cessation of the Abadan anchorage proposed by Iran and drew the line along the thalweg.[278] He also effectively accepted Iran's proposal that the Shatt would be open to navigation for ships of all nations and the warships belonging to the contracting parties. The Iraqi draft included a provision which would have enabled her, in the absence of agreement between the parties, to dredge and carry out other works necessary for the maintenance of the navigable channel in conditions suitable for navigation on both sides of the thalweg boundary.[279] The view of the Foreign Office was that any express reference in the draft treaty to the freedom of navigation of Iraqi warships in the Shatt was superfluous: Iraq already possessed this right, a concomitant of the fact that she had always exercised sovereignty in the river. It added, however, that it would have been a different matter if the inclusion of the provision in question was to ensure the right of Iraqi warships to navigate freely in the *ceded* part of the Shatt.[280]

The question, thus, of the recognition and location of the boundary as such had been settled in principle by February 1937. The delay, however, in the conclusion of the treaty was caused by difficulties regarding the nature of the rights which Iran was effectively to exercise in the Shatt and the precise drafting of the provisions therein. To the extent that these matters bear upon the question of the status of the boundary, it may be of some use to refer briefly to the progress of the negotiations leading to the conclusion of the treaty. In this context, it may be noted that one of Iran's long-standing claims is that the government of Iraq owes her a certain sum of money which constitutes her share of the dues collected from shipping in the Shatt.

---

[277] Clark Kerr to FO, 29 Jan. 1937, Reg. PZ771, 1937 in L/P&S/12/3803. See also Iraqi Foreign Minister to Iranian Minister, Baghdad, 26 Jan. 1937, enc. in Clark Kerr to FO, 29 Jan. 1937, REg. PZ957, 1937 in L/P&S/12/3803.

[278] Proposals of 3 Feb. 1937: Clark Kerr to FO, 3 Feb. 1936, Reg. PZ1008, 1937 in L/P&S/12/3803. See also provisional draft in Clark Kerr to FO, 29 Jan. 1937. Col. Ward had assured the Iraqi Foreign Minister that the extent of the waters on the Iraqi side of the thalweg was sufficient to allow shipping without impinging upon Iranian waters: see Clark Kerr to FO, 4 Feb. 1937, Reg. PZ1008, 1937, and telegram of 12 Apr. 1937, Reg. PZ2549, 1937 in L/P&S/12/3804.

[279] Proposals of 3 Feb. 1937. This meant dredging etc. in Iranian national waters.

[280] FO to Clark Kerr, 15 Feb. 1937, Reg. PZ1158, 1937 in L/P&S/12/3803. The FO was inclined to think that the Iraqi Minister for Foreign Affairs was 'allowing his anxiety for settlement to obscure his judgment upon vital issues': FO to Clark Kerr, 20 Mar. 1937, next to Reg. PZ2261, 1937, FO No. E1547/73/34, in L/P&S/12/3803.

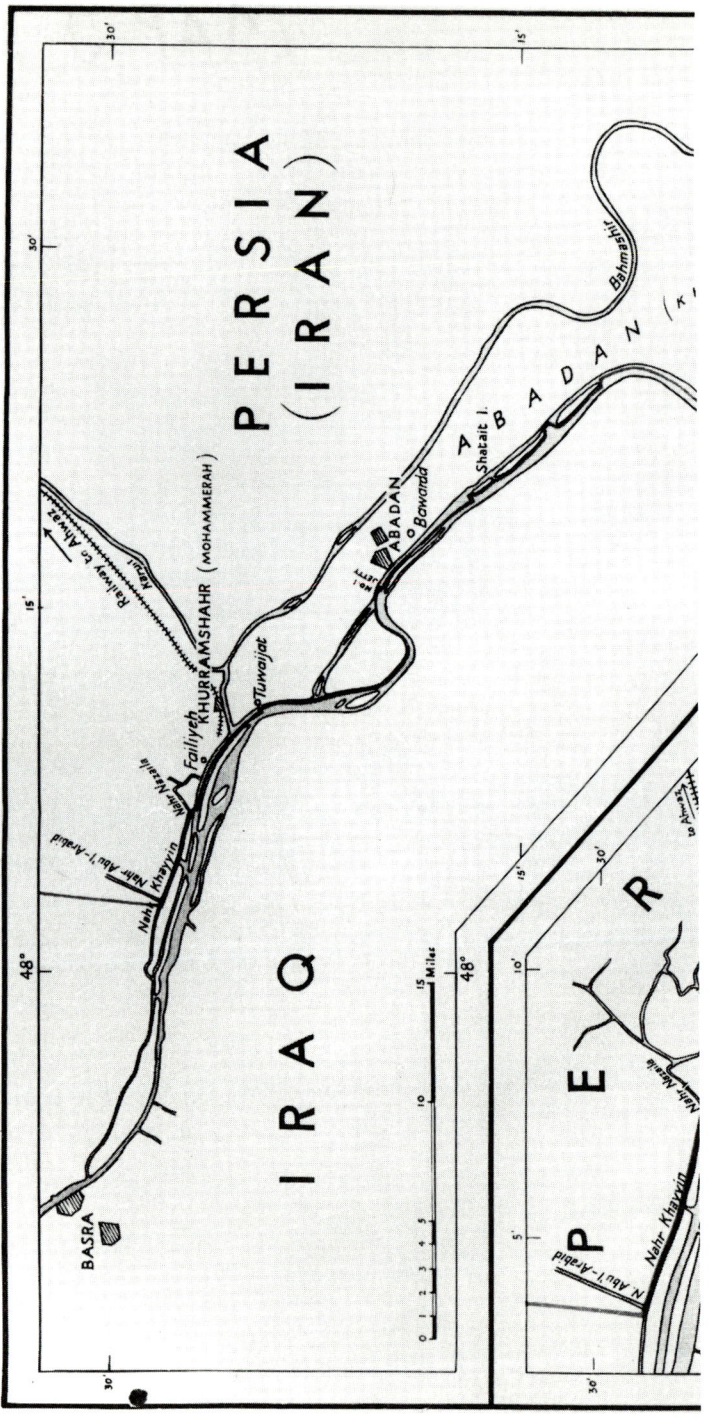

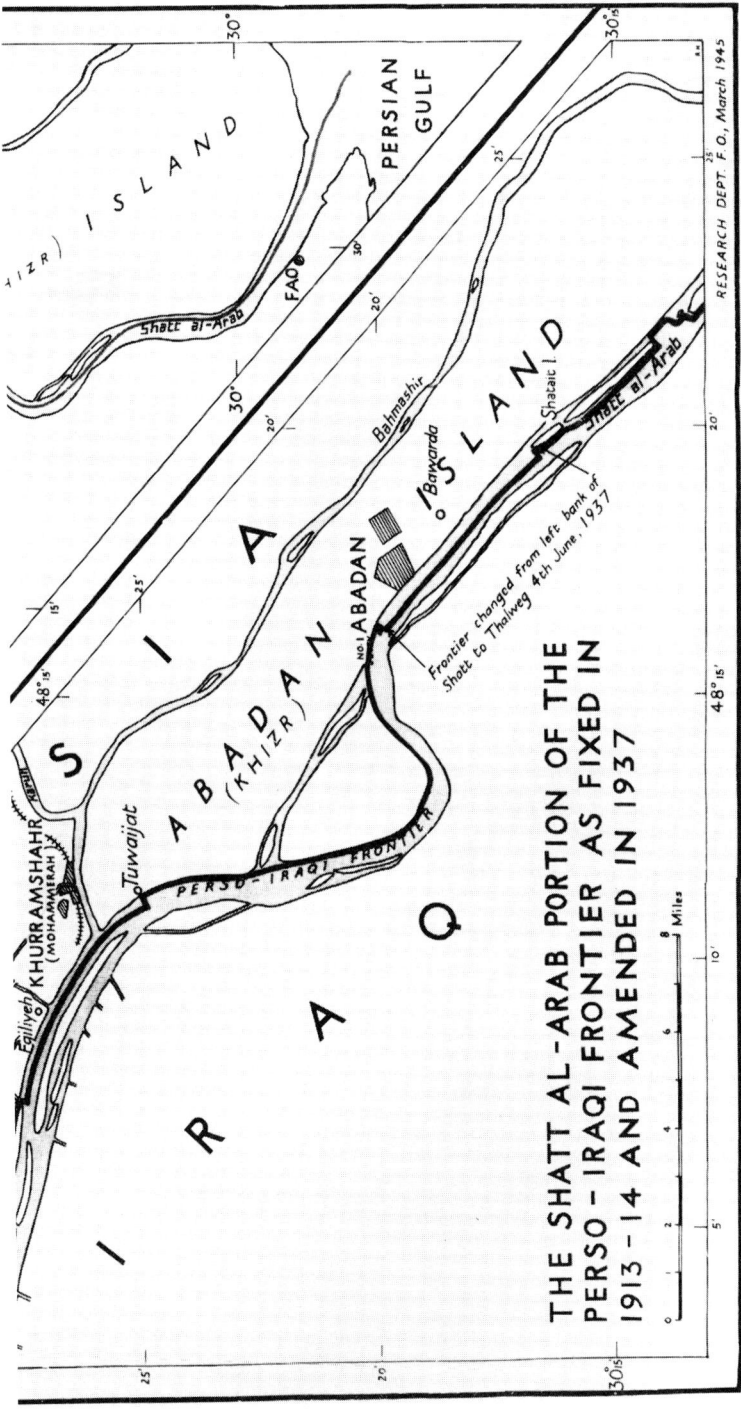

Fig 10. The Shatt-al-Arab portion of the Perso-Iraqi frontier as fixed in 1913–14 and amended in 1937

Iran resisted Iraq's right to dredge and carry out necessary works on the Iranian side of the navigable channel in the absence of an agreement to this effect, and insisted that she give a commitment regarding the conclusion of an agreement which dealt with the joint control of dredging, maintenance of the navigable channel, and other questions concerning navigation and prevention of smuggling.[281] She also asserted an equality of interest in the question of navigation of the Shatt. In her counter-draft of April 1937, Iraq, heeding the advice of the British Foreign Office, excluded reference to the right of navigation of the Shatt by Iraqi warships and proposed instead that it be agreed that the Shatt shall remain open to passage by ships of war and other vessels used for non-commercial purposes belonging to the Iranian government.[282] The draft now provided for the continuation of Iraq's *droit d'usage* in the ceded part of the river and reiterated her 'right and duty' to maintain both sides of the thalweg where it constituted the boundary in the absence of an agreement between the two States. Importantly, while Iraq agreed to conclude an agreement relative to the maintenance, improvement, and dredging of the navigable channel and all other questions relating to navigation in the Shatt, she denied any reference to an 'equality of interests' of the parties, in matters of navigation and maintenance of the Shatt and insisted that till such time as the treaty was concluded the Basra Port Authority would continue to exercise all its present functions.[283] However, Iran was to continue to insist on references to equality of interests in the Shatt and to rights of Iraqi warships in the river.[284] She went on to claim *droit d'usage* for herself as well as Iraq in the Shatt, and added that she was prepared to give a verbal commitment to the effect that the Basra Port Authority would continue to exercise its present functions. The Iranian draft broadened the areas of joint control in the Shatt.

In his reply of 16 June 1937, the Iraqi Minister for Foreign Affairs agreed to the mention of rights of navigation of warships and of the *droit d'usage* of both contracting States in the Shatt.[285] He also agreed to delete references to Iraq's right to maintain and dredge the navigable channel on both sides of the thalweg boundary near Abadan in the absence of an especial agreement. However, in order to avoid conceding a general Iranian equality of interest in the Shatt, he proposed admitting such a right specifically in the context of the freedom of passage of trading ships of all nations

---

[281] Reply of 1 Mar. 1937, enc. in Clark Kerr to FO, 5 Mar. 1937, Reg. PZ2261, 1937 in L/P&S/12/3803.

[282] Iraqi counter-draft of 11 Apr. 1937, enc. in Clark Kerr to FO, 10 Apr. 1937, Reg. PZ2549, 1937; and Clark Kerr to FO, 12 Apr. 1937, Reg. PZ2549, 1937 in L/P&S/12/3804.

[283] Ibid.

[284] Persian Memorandum, *c*. June 1937, on Iraqi proposals of Apr. 1937, enc. in Clark Kerr to FO, 4 June 1937, Reg. PZ3956, 1937; and Clark Kerr to FO, 3 June 1937, Reg. PZ3772, 1937, in L/P&S/12/3804.

[285] Enc. in Clark Kerr to FO, 19 June 1937, Reg. PZ4274, 1937, in L/P&S/12/3804.

The Boundary Problem

and warships and *droit d'usage* of the contracting parties. Soon afterwards, the aforementioned minister proceeded to Tehran where brief but conclusive discussions were held. As a compromise, it was agreed that Iraq would continue to carry out conservancy measures for a period of one year and for any further period extended by common accord.[286] 'This arrangement', the British Minister in Tehran wrote, 'is obviously not fully satisfactory but the Iraqi Minister for Foreign Affairs says that he only obtained it with difficulty . . . '.[287] It is particularly interesting to note that in these negotiations Iraq, being the weaker of the two States, worked under the close supervision of Britain, whereas in the negotiations preceding the Protocol of 1913 the latter had supported Persia in her claims against the more powerful Ottoman Empire. However, there is no evidence in the records to show that Iran insisted upon the adoption of a median line in the Shatt. The evidence is quite to the contrary, namely that Iran was content with the acquisition of four miles of the thalweg boundary and the cession of the Abadan anchorage. A treaty was signed at Tehran on 4 July 1937[288] incorporating the terms of the agreement mentioned in the preceding pages. Iraq subsequently raised questions, albeit on a confidential level, with Britain as to whether it would be advisable to withhold ratification of the treaty, and the Foreign Office advised against adopting such a course of action.[289] Ratifications were exchanged by the parties at the Central Bureau, Ministry for Foreign Affairs, in Baghdad on 20 June 1938.[290] On 8 December 1938 the two States concluded a treaty which provided for the constitution of a boundary commission with powers to reinstall frontier pillars in accordance with Article 3 of the Treaty of 1937.[291] The Commission met in the same month and (in addition to the existing sixty pillars[292]) installed sixty-eight new boundary pillars, the first of which was located at

---

[286] Seymour (Tehran) to FO, 4 July 1937, Reg. PZ4480, 1937 in L/P&S/12/3804. See FO to Seymour, 3 July 1937, Reg. PZ4415, 1937, in L/P&S/12/3804.

[287] Seymour to FO, 4 July 1937. See also Seymour to FO, 14 July 1937, PCP E4510/73/34. Reg. PZ5584, 1937 in L/P&S/12/3804: 'This agreement obviously contains the seeds of future dispute . . . '.

[288] For text see *League of Nations Treaty Series*, 90 (1938), No. 4423, p. 241; *BFSP* 141 (1937), p. 1081. See Annexe 4 below.

[289] It reasoned that non-ratification would leave all matters undecided: Memorandum on Perso-Iraq Frontier, Baggallay, E566/127/34, 27 Jan. 1938, Reg. PZ916, 1938, in L/P&S/12/3804. See also McDougall, Legal Adviser, Iraqi Ministry for Foreign Affairs, Baghdad: Memorandum of 13 Apr. 1938, enc. in Baghdad despatch, 22 Apr. 1938, Reg. PZ4026, 1938, in L/P&S/12/3804. Other questions raised related to Iraq's rights in the ceded waters in the absence of an agreement regarding the conservancy question.

[290] Peterson (Baghdad) to Halifax (FO), 28 June 1938, PCP E4194/127/38, Reg. PZ5924, 1938 in L/P&S/12/3804; Consul-General for Iraq at Bombay to Government of India, External Affairs Department, 7 July 1938, Reg. PZ5281, 1938, in L/P&S/12/3804.

[291] Peterson to Halifax, 22 Dec. 1938, PCP E75/75/34, Reg. PZ1001, 1939, in L/P&S/12/3804. Text: enc. in ibid.

[292] Al-Izzi, *The Shatt-al-Arab River Dispute*, p. 39, quoting Al Rawi, *International Borders* (Cairo 1970), p. 501. (Arabic language).

64   *The History*

the confluence of the Shatt with the Khaiyin, and the last, at Khushk-i-Basri.²⁹³ It appears that Iran unilaterally withdrew from the demarcation proceedings in May 1940.²⁹⁴ Negotiations between Iraq, Iran, and Britain regarding the conclusion of a convention in respect of the conservancy and control of the Shatt were undertaken, but no favourable progress was made, and the negotiations were abandoned at the outbreak of the war of 1939–45.²⁹⁵

(g) The Algiers Protocol and Baghdad Treaty of 1975

Notwithstanding the Treaty of 1937, the Shah of Iran, Raza Shah, and his son, who ascended the throne in 1941, continued to raise questions regarding the boundary in the Shatt and refused to accept the left bank as the dividing line.²⁹⁶ In April 1969, matters came to a head and Iraq threatened not to allow any Iranian ship to navigate in the Shatt.²⁹⁷ On 27 April 1969, the Ministry of Foreign Affairs, Iran, announced that the Treaty of 1937 had been abrogated.²⁹⁸ Of course, this announcement did not necessarily constitute a legally effective act. Support, at any rate, for this measure was based on arguments to the effect that the treaty perpetuated a fundamental inequality of the contracting parties; that Iraq had not carried out her obligations accruing under the treaty and it was therefore she who had effectively abrogated the treaty; that the treaty was invalid on grounds of a fundamental change of circumstances; and that the treaty had failed to apply the thalweg or median line principle.²⁹⁹ The validity of these arguments will be analysed elsewhere.³⁰⁰

Relations between the two States continued to decline and a military clash occurred in April 1971 in the Khanaqin region. Thereafter intermittent border incidents continued to occur between the two States in the period 1971–4.³⁰¹ 'The Kurdish rebellion', wrote Professor Ismael, 'was a

---

²⁹³ Facts concerning the Iraqi-Iranian Frontier, Ministry of Foreign Affairs, [Baghdad] 1960.
²⁹⁴ Ibid.
²⁹⁵ *Aide-Mémoire*, Baghdad Embassy, Apr. 1945, Reg. PZ1930, 1945 in L/P&S/12/3804.
²⁹⁶ Ismael, *Iraq and Iran: Roots of Conflict* (Syracuse, 1982), pp. 18–20; Amin, *International and Legal Problems of the Gulf* (London, 1981), pp. 74–5.
²⁹⁷ See generally, *Yearbook of the United Nations*, 23 (1969), pp. 245–6: Letters exchanged between Iran, Iraq, and President, Security Council, between April and July 1969. Also see Amin, 'The Iran–Iraq Conflict: Legal Implications', *ICLQ* 31 (1982) p. 167 at p. 173; Ismael, *Iraq and Iran*, pp. 18–20.
²⁹⁸ See references cited immediately above.
²⁹⁹ See generally, Iranian letters to President, Security Council, 1 and 9 May 1969: S/9190 and S/9200, and of 2 Sept. 1969: S/9425; *Yearbook of the UN* 23 (1969) p. 246. See also addresses of Iranian Minister for Foreign Affairs to UN General Assembly, Oct. 1969 (24th Session), *UN Monthly Chronicle*, 6 (1969), Nov., pp. 120–1; and of Iranian Permanent Representative, Mr Vakil, Oct. 1971, *UN Monthly Chronicle*, 8 (1971), Oct. p. 164.
³⁰⁰ Below, ch.2, sects. I.2(*a*), (*b*), (*c*).
³⁰¹ *Yearbook of the UN*, 28 (1974), pp. 252–6; Ismael, *Iraq and Iran*, p. 20.

serious drain on Iraqi military and economic capabilities', and so in February 1974 Iraq requested the Security Council to intervene. A resolution calling for bilateral negotiations was passed and a ceasefire was arranged by the Security Council on 7 March 1974.[302] Negotiations were initiated, and at the Summit Conference of the Organization of Petroleum Exporting Countries, convened in Algiers in March 1975, the Shah of Iran and the President of Iraq held two meetings.[303] In the joint communiqué of 6 March 1975, also known as the Algiers Protocol of 1975, the two States agreed, *inter alia*, to 'proceed with the definitive demarcation of their land frontiers on the basis of the Constantinople Protocol of 1913 and the minutes of the Frontier Delimitation Commission of 1914'; and to 'delimit their river frontiers along the thalweg'.[304] Effectively, therefore, Iraq finally yielded to Iran's ancient demand, and abandoned the left-bank line. The communiqué went on to declare that both parties would commit themselves to exercising strict control along the frontier 'with a view to the complete cessation of all subversive infiltration from either side'. It appears that this provision constituted a *quid pro quo* for Iraqi abandonment of the left-bank frontier line and has important implications in the context of the boundary problem.[305] According to Ramazani, however, Iraq decided to agree to a thalweg line in the interest of greater domestic power and unity within OPEC.[306] At any rate, a Protocol embodying the principles of agreement was signed at Tehran on 17 March 1975 following meetings of the Foreign Ministers of Iran, Iraq, and Algeria.[307] In Baghdad on 13 June 1975, the Shah of Iran and the President of Iraq signed the Treaty Concerning the State Frontier and Neighbourly Relations.[308] Appended to this were three Protocols.[309] Article 2 of the Baghdad Treaty of 1975 confirmed that the

---

[302] *Iraq and Iran*, p. 20.

[303] Ibid; and Amin, *International and Legal Problems of the Gulf*, p. 81.

[304] Joint Communiqué between Iran and Iraq, 6 Mar. 1975. For text, see *UNTS* 1017, No. 1403, pp. 196–7 and Appendix 6 in Ismael, *Iraq and Iran*, pp. 60–2. Generally, see ibid., pp. 21–2; Amin, 'The Iran-Iraq Conflict', pp. 176–8; Pipes, 'A Border Adrift: Origins of the [Iran-Iraq] Conflict', in Tahir-Kheli (ed.), *The Iran-Iraq War: New Weapons, Old Conflicts*. (New York, 1983), p. 20. See Annexe 5 below.

[305] Below, ch. 2, sect. II.

[306] Ramazani, 'Iran's Search for Regional Cooperation', *Middle East Journal*, 30 (1976), p. 173 at 177; Amin, 'The Iran–Iraq Conflict', p. 177; Pipes, 'A Border Adrift', pp. 20–1.

[307] *UNTS* 1017, p. 198. See also Amin, 'The Iran–Iraq Conflict', p. 177; see also '*A Review of the Imposed War*', pp. xiii–xiv.

[308] For text, see *UNTS* 1017, No. 14903; and also see Annexe 1 in *A Review of the Imposed War*, loc. cit.; Appendix 9 and 10 in Ismael, *Iraq and Iran*, pp. 62–5. Another version of the Treaty appears in *International Legal Materials*, 14 (1975), p. 1133, and is a reprint from the *Baghdad Observer* of 23 and 24 June 1975. See below, Annexes 6 and 7 for both the Treaty and the Protocol on the Delimitation of the River Frontier.

[309] The three Protocols are: (i) Protocol on the Delimitation of the River Frontier; (ii) Redemarcation of the Land Frontier, and (iii) Protocol concerning Security on the Frontier between Iran and Iraq: see No. 14903 above, pp. 138, 140 and 190. Four more treaties were concluded on 26 Dec. 1975 and were concerned with frontier Commissioners, rules governing

frontier in the Shatt would be that which was delimited on the basis of the Protocol Concerning the Delimitation of the River Frontier. Article 4 stipulated that the provisions of the three Protocols would constitute an integral part of the treaty and would be final and permanent in character. Article 5 provided that, in keeping with the inviolability of the frontiers of the two States, the land and river boundaries would be inviolable, permanent, and final. In the Protocol regarding the redemarcation of the Land Frontier, Article 1 provided that the redemarcation had been conducted by the Iraqi-Iranian-Algerian Committee on the bases, *inter alia*, of the Protocol of 1913, the demarcation of 1914, the Teheran Protocol of 1975, and the record of the meeting of Ministers of Foreign Affairs on 20 April 1975 which adopted the record of the Committee to Demarcate the Land Frontier signed on 30 March 1975. Article 2 provided that the frontier line would follow the line specified in the descriptive record and in the maps referred to in Article 1, paragraph 6.

In the Protocol concerning the Delimitation of the River Frontier, the two States agreed in Article 2 that the 'frontier line in the Shatt . . . shall follow the thalweg, i.e. the median line of the main navigable channel at the lowest navigable level, starting from the point at which the land frontier between Iran and Iraq enters the Shatt . . . and continuing to the sea'. The latter point, or the Outer Bar Reach, at 48° 43' east longitude and 29° 50' north latitude, appears to have resolved the problem in the Marakats. As for the northern end of the Shatt boundary, it appears from the Treaty that the Mixed Technical Commission terminated the thalweg line at 48° 06' east longitude and 30° 27' north latitude, that is to say at the point at which the Khaiyin Canal enters the Shatt, and drew the line westwards from the latter point along the 'median water line' of the old Khaiyin Canal in the Shatt described in the Baghdad Treaty as the 'Nahr Al Khayin'. Apparently, the median line terminates at Boundary Mark No. 2 (48° 01' 27" east longitude and 30° 28' 40" north latitude) and coincides very nearly with Boundary pillar No. 2 placed in 1914. From this point the boundary begins its land territory delimitation in the north. It is clear that here the 1913–14 line or the local customary line observed by Lt. Wilson in 1910 has been retained virtually intact. This stretch, however, of the frontier is a short one and the major length of the line lies east of the narrow Khaiyin Canal. It was this subsector which had been the most contentious one, and by agreeing to a thalweg line division for the entire river, as opposed to the partial cessions of the river in 1913 and 1937 regarding Mohammara and Abadan, Iraq finally and officially abandoned the left-bank boundary and her sovereignty to the river. As a result of this develop-

---

navigation in the Shatt, transhumance, and the use of frontier water courses: see Nos. 14904, 14905, 14906, and 14907 in *UNTS* 1017 above.

The Boundary Problem

ment, the special boundary regimes set up in Abadan and Mohammara anchorages became superfluous and redundant. An examination of the maps annexed to the Baghdad Treaty shows the thalweg line within the Shatt running at times close to the Iraqi and at times close to the Iranian banks. In the upper and lower reaches of the river, the boundary also follows what is the approximate middle of the Shatt. Article 3 of the Baghdad Treaty provides that the river frontier is the line which was drawn on hydrographic charts by the Mixed Technical Commission and countersigned by the heads of the Iranian, Iraqi, and Algerian delegations to the Committee. This line was subsequently approved by the afore-mentioned meeting of the Ministers of Foreign Affairs.

With respect to land boundaries there appears to be some confusion as to which state benefited. According to Dr Amin, the Baghdad Treaty transferred about two hundred square miles to Iran,[310] while Heikal writes that two hundred square miles were allocated to Iraq.[311]

The Baghdad Treaty of 1975 was ratified by the parties on 22 June 1976 and 'its implementation went ahead with considerable smoothness'.[312] However, Iraq failed to reconcile herself to the loss of the Shatt and her claims that Iran supported the Kurdish insurgency within her borders complicated the issue. With the ascent to power of Ayatollah Khomeni in February 1979 in Iran, relations between the States deteriorated.[313] Iraq, dissatisfied with the frontier, now demanded a revision of the boundary treaty.[314] Hostilities broke out between the States in early September 1980 and have continued ever since. On 17 September 1980, Iraq purported to abrogate the Baghdad Treaty of 1975. The persistence of belligerency has precluded the resolution of the Shatt boundary question although it appears that the government of Iraq is inclined to annul the purported abrogation of the treaty in question and to 'accept' the 1975 line. A formal settlement, however, will have to await a cessation of hostilities.[315]

[310] Amin, 'The Iran–Iraq Conflict', p. 178; and *International and Legal Problems of the Gulf*, p. 82; see also Pipes, 'A Border Adrift', p. 25 n. 34.
[311] Heikal, *Iran: The Untold Story* (New York, 1982), pp. 205–6, as cited in Pipes, 'A Border Adrift', p. 25 n. 34.
[312] Amin, 'The Iran–Iraq Conflict', p. 178.
[313] *The Imposed War*, pp. xv–xx.
[314] Amin, 'The Iran–Iraq Conflict', p. 178; *The Imposed War*, op. cit.
[315] Below, ch. 2, Sect. III.

2
The Legal Analysis

An examination of the principal legal issues relating to the boundary dispute may conveniently be separated into two broad areas of enquiry, that is the legal regime of the boundary before and after 1975. The gradual westward expansion by Iran into Iraqi/Arab dominated territories over the course of the nineteenth and twentieth centuries culminated in 1975 when she concluded the Baghdad Treaty and acquired control of the Shatt up to the line of its thalweg. The treaty, hence, not only represents—at least before the war broke out—the latest phase, but also the logical conclusion of a process which had been evolving since ancient times, and thus merits consideration as a major juncture in the history of the frontier.

I THE LEGAL REGIME OF THE BOUNDARY BEFORE 1975

1. GENERAL

The examination of the historical and traditional facts of the dispute clearly showed that Ottoman rule existed to a considerable degree on either side of the Shatt and that with the passage of time the Pashas of Baghdad and Basra began to lose control over the territories on the left bank. They managed, however, to retain jurisdiction over the Shatt itself with the result that the left bank of the river became traditionally regarded as the frontier separating the dominions of the Ottoman rulers and the Persian kings.

The Treaty of Erzeroum of 1847 attempted to regularize the situation prevailing along the frontier. To that end each of the two parties recognized each other's mutually exclusive territorial control on the left and right bank of the Shatt respectively, with the proviso that the left bank of the river up to the sea was to be regarded as the frontier between them. It is to be noted that, on the strength of the facts on record, the analysis presented above ignores the Turkish interpretation of the 1847 treaty, namely that the frontier lay well to the east of the lands drained by the Karun, including Gabon. The attitude adopted by the Mediating Powers confirmed, by way of their attempts at demarcation, that the frontier established by the Treaty of Erzeroum in 1847 lay along the left bank and not the middle of the Shatt. While it is true that the line delimited by the Mediating Commissioners was not legally binding on either Party inasmuch as Turkey had failed to accept it, the merits of this line lie in the fact that it serves as evidence of the location of the boundary as perceived by the Mediating Commissioners; and it is significant that such perception was based not only on the plain facts of possession but also on a fair and reasonable interpretation of the terms of the treaty in question.[1] It is also legally significant that it was Iran (then Persia) which had initially challenged the left bank boundary and had agreed to accept the 1850 alignment determined by the Mediating Commissioners. Again, while this acceptance did not result in any legally binding allocation of territory and could not prejudice Iran's position *vis-à-vis* the 1850 line, it serves as evidence that on the balance of probabilities Iran recognized the fact that she had little or no valid claim beyond the left bank. Although the parties could not adopt a mutually acceptable demarcation, they agreed, in the Treaty of 1869, to preserve the status quo regarding the frontier 'such as was defined by the Commissioners of the four Powers'. This treaty, which was renewed in 1873, effectively precluded the development of a situation which would have prejudiced the legal rights of either party, and thus precluded the introduction of claims based on prescription, acquiescence, and recognition. The result, of course, was an entrenchment of the territorial status quo.

Notwithstanding the treaties of 1869 and 1873, and the objectives thereof, the evidence is clear that the status quo was indeed upset over a considerable period of time. By the first decade of the twentieth century, Persian officials had apparently consolidated their control over the territories on the left bank. Their unopposed activities right up to the middle of the Shatt began to acquire, at least on the local level and on the basis of repute, the colour of rightful authority, with the result that the boundary as observed locally came to be regarded as lying in the middle of the Shatt. Had Persia insisted then on a mid-line boundary on the basis of acquiescence, it is arguable that she might have made out a good case; she would, nevertheless, have had difficulty in reconciling her claims with the disclaimers contained in the treaties of 1869 and 1873. It may, at any rate, be futile to go into this particular issue in view of the conclusion of the Protocol of 1913 and the demarcation proceedings of 1914 wherein the parties agreed, once again, that the left bank of the Shatt was (to continue) to be the dividing line. Hence, even if Persia had been able to establish the claim that the alignment in the Shatt had shifted westwards along the half-way mark it would have been largely without legal relevance inasmuch as she, on the assumption that the locally observed line in the river had acquired a

[1] Above, ch. 1, sect. II.4(*b*).

degree of validity, ultimately abandoned it in favour of the left-bank frontier. In one sense, therefore, the 1913 treaty and the demarcation of 1914 reaffirmed the ancient frontier in the greater part of the Shatt, entrenching further the left-bank line, and nullifying all 'on-site' developments contrary to the left-bank boundary that had occurred in the period immediately preceding the 1913–14 agreements.

The Treaty of 1937 gave Iran a greater part of and rights to the Shatt; but the essential feature, which was that the greater part of the frontier ran along the eastern edge of the Shatt, remained constant. The thalweg line opposite the anchorage at Abadan was clearly seen as a derogation from the main lie of the alignment, and a concession to Iran. From the above analysis it is clear that the two States were agreed in principle on the 'true' location of the boundary, and there was accordingly no dispute, at least in law and theory, as to where the boundary was located. On this view of the matter, the boundary dispute was essentially political in nature. The difficulties did not lie in differing interpretations regarding the law governing the boundary regime, or where exactly the alignment ran along the bank, which, in principle, would have left the matter unsettled to some degree. The difficulties between the States lay in accepting and reconciling themselves to the boundary.

The legal effect of successive recognition of the left-bank boundary is not without importance. Such recognition implied that each State acknowledged title of the other State to the territory lying on either side of the frontier line and thus precluded the States from subsequently challenging the legality of the attribution of territory by the boundary. In the *Eastern Greenland* case,[2] the Permanent Court of International Justice took into consideration the fact that Norway had concluded a series of bilateral agreements with Denmark and that there were various multinational agreements to which both Norway and Denmark were contracting Parties and in which Greenland had been described as a Danish colony, or as forming part of Denmark, or in which Denmark had been allowed to exclude Greenland from the operation of the agreement. 'In accepting', the court held, 'these bilateral and multilateral agreements as binding upon herself, Norway reaffirmed that she recognised the whole of Greenland as Danish; and thereby she has debarred herself from contesting Danish sovereignty over the whole of Greenland, and in consequence, from proceeding to occupy any part of it'.[3]

In the *Temple* case,[4] one of the questions which fell to be considered by the International Court was that of Thailand's subsequent recognition and reaffirmation of the boundary depicted on the Annexe 1 map. It observed

---

[2] PCIJ Series A/B, No. 53 (1933).
[3] Ibid., pp. 68–9.
[4] *ICJ Reports* 1962, p. 6.

that Thailand had several opportunities of raising with the French authorities the question of the incorrect depiction on that map. In 1925 and 1937 she concluded two Treaties of Friendship, Commerce, and Navigation with France and although they were not boundary treaties as such, they provided for a general process of revision or replacement of previous agreements. However these treaties excluded the boundary settlements of 1893, 1904, and 1907 from their scope of operation.[5] 'Thereby', the court concluded, 'and in certain more positive provisions, the Parties confirmed the existing frontiers whatever they were'. It also held that it was difficult to overlook the fact that in the Treaty of 1937 Thailand (then Siam) had reaffirmed the established frontier.[6]

Similarly, in the *Rann of Kutch* arbitration[7] the question of successive recognition of a boundary arose in the context of a complex of official documentation, including governmental administrative records, gazettes, maps, and the like, published over a period spanning almost a century.[8] There was, however, no boundary treaty between the British Indian Provence of Sind, and the autonomous native State of Kutch. It was argued by India that this documentation constituted recognition of the northern edge of the Rann as the alignment between Kutch and Sind. The Chairman of the Court of Arbitration held in favour of India, and although he acknowledged the fact that there were many difficulties of interpretation and of facts in the documentation, he ruled that these statements and maps 'constitute acts of competent British authorities which—if viewed as being in response to claims by Kutch or other Indian States that the Rann was Indian state territory—may be interpreted as acquiescence in or acceptance of, such claims . . . '.[9] In respect of several series of wide-ranging maps, the Chairman, Judge Lagergren, observed that 'the cumulative effect of the publication of official maps, in conjunction with other acts or omissions by the British authorities, and the interpretation placed on the maps by those concerned at the time, might be such that the maps must be given decisive weight in determining the issues confronting the Tribunal'.[10]

In the *Beagle Channel* arbitration[11] both Argentina and Chile claimed title to the three disputed islands on the basis of the line delimited in the

---

[5] Ibid., pp. 27–8.
[6] Ibid., p. 27. See also the Separate Opinions of Judge Sir Gerald Fitzmaurice, p. 62, and Judge Alfaro, pp. 39–43. Cf. Oral Argument of Soskice, Counsel for Thailand, *ICJ Pleadings, Temple of Preah Vihear*, ii. 288, 320–3 regarding Thailand's non-recognition.
[7] 50 ILR, p. 1; 16 *RIAA* p. 1.
[8] ILR, ibid., pp. 217 *et seq.*
[9] Ibid., p. 500. See also the *Minquiers* case (*ICJ Reports* 1953, p. 47) regarding British reliance on several international instruments and correspondence as evidence of French recognition of Britain's sovereignty over the island groups: *ICJ Pleadings, Minquiers and Ecrehos Case*, i. 49–73 and 113–24.
[10] 50 ILR p. 1, at p. 486. See also p. 514.
[11] Award of 18 April 1977: HMSO 1977.

Boundary Treaty of 1881. While the Court of Arbitration was requested to interpret the treaty in order to determine the 'true' allocation, Chile also contended that several official Argentine decrees, which dealt with the administrative divisions of Argentine national territory and were issued in the period between 1883 and 1904, tended to confirm and corroborate her claims.[12] It was pointed out that none of the decrees showed the disputed islands as being under Argentine administrative control, notwithstanding the fact that they indicated specific boundaries. The court ruled in favour of Chile.[13]

In the same context, it is obvious that successive recognition by treaty can be seen as confirmation of the view that the States in question were disposed towards achieving a maximum degree of territorial stability and finality. Both Iraq and Iran were determined, it appears from the treaties, not to subject the established boundary to fundamental changes, and permit modifications only in small sectors of the line, namely at Mohammara and Abadan, with a view to accommodating the legitimate territorial problems of Iran. By and large, these States wished to maintain the location of the boundary and consequently to reaffirm the attribution of territory effected by the line in question. This point has particular significance in the context of the legal problem created by the alleged abrogation of the treaties of 1937 and 1975, and will be dealt with in some detail at the appropriate place.[14] It may be sufficient to note here that the doctrine of finality and stability of boundaries, which is one of the more fundamental principles relating to the international law of boundaries, places great emphasis on the conclusive nature of the resolution of all territorial and boundary-related problems.[15] States do not look kindly upon a system either of diplomacy or of law which continually challenges the location and validity of a boundary established on the basis of, and existing in, law. In the *Case concerning the Continental Shelf (Tunisian/Libyan Arab Jamahiriya)*[16] the International Court had the opportunity of referring to the status of the land frontier between the two States in order to determine the starting-

---

[12] Ibid., p. 102.
[13] Ibid., p. 106. See also the *Arbitral Award of the King of Spain* case, (*ICJ Reports* 1960, p. 192) wherein the International Court held that there had been 'repeated acts of recognition by Nicaragua' of the boundary Award of 23 December 1906 (p. 214) and that it was 'no longer open to Nicaragua to go back upon that recognition . . . ': p. 213. In the *Western Sahara* Advisory Opinion (*ICJ Reports* 1975, p. 12), Morocco contended that a series of international acts, including treaties, exchange of letters, and diplomatic correspondence constituted recognition of her title to territory extending to the south of the Noun and Dra'a. The court declined to uphold that view: pp. 49–57, but see the Separate Opinions of Judges Ammoun, pp. 87–92, and de Castro, pp. 161–4.
[14] Subsection 2(*b*). and section II below.
[15] Kaikobad, 'Some Observations on the Doctrine of Continuity and Finality of Boundaries', *BYIL* 54 (1983) p. 119 *et seq*.
[16] *ICJ Reports* 1982, p. 18.

point of the boundary on the coast. It observed that the boundary was initially settled by virtue of the Convention of 19 May 1910 between the Bey of Tunis, who had come under the protection of France, and the Ottoman Empire.[17] (The boundary was demarcated in the period 1910–11.[18]) The International Court went on to observe that the 1910 line had been 'expressly confirmed by the Treaty of Friendship and Neighbourly Relations concluded on 10 August 1955 between the French Republic (on behalf of Tunisia) and the United Kingdom of Libya, implicitly confirmed by the Treaty ... of 7 January 1957, which was amended and completed by the Establishment Convention of 14 June 1961, and expressly confirmed by an exchange of letters at the time of signing that Establishment Convention.'[19] It noted that the boundary had 'remained unchanged throughout the vicissitudes of the two World Wars', and that the principle declared in the 1964 Cairo Resolution of the OAU according to which 'all Member States pledge themselves to respect the borders existing on their achievement of national independence' was exemplified in the continuity of the boundary regime between the parties. Referring also to the principle of continuity of boundaries in the event of a succession of States predicated in Article 11 of the 1978 Vienna Convention on Succession of States in respect of Treaties, the court concluded that 'the permanence and stability of the land frontier is one of the points where the Parties are in full agreement'.[20]

The rule in question was a central feature in the judgment of the International Court in the *Temple* case. It was observed therein that in general where two States establish a frontier between themselves, one of the primary objectives is to achieve finality and stability. This would, it was ruled, be impossible if the line so established could at any given moment be called into question and its rectification claimed whenever any inaccuracy by reference to a clause in the parent treaty was discovered.[21]

State practice is consistent with this proposition of law. Reference may be made to the boundary dispute between Afghanistan and Pakistan. To some extent the facts are not altogether dissimilar in that the frontier, established by virtue of the Anglo-Afghan agreement of 12 November 1893 and demarcated in the period 1894–6, was confirmed in the Treaties of

---

[17] Ibid., p. 65.
[18] Brownlie, *African Boundaries: A Legal and Diplomatic Encyclopaedia* (London, 1979), p. 141.
[19] *ICJ Reports* 1982, p. 65.
[20] Ibid., p. 66.
[21] *ICJ Reports* 1962, p. 6 at p. 34. See also the *Grisbadarna* arbitration, (1909) 1 *Scotts Hague Court Reports*, p. 121 at p. 130; *State of South Australia v. State of Victoria* [1914] AC 283, at p. 310; *Costa Rica v. Nicaragua*, 2 *Moore's International Arbitrations*, p. 1945; *Costa Rica v. Panama*, 11 RIAA p. 528, regarding the existence of a traditional river boundary between the disputing States.

1905, 1919, and 1921, and in the exchange of notes of 1930. Afghanistan has since challenged the validity of the boundary on several grounds, including the non-applicability of the principles of continuity in the event of State succession, and *rebus sic stantibus* regarding the frontier agreements. In November 1947, three months after the transfer of power to Pakistan, Mr Gerald Fitzmaurice, (as he then was) who was Legal Adviser to the Foreign Office, advised the British government, in a joint opinion with Miss J. Gutteridge, that the boundary treaties and regime established by the treaties were valid and binding on Afghanistan.[22] In a statement to Parliament on 30 June 1949, Mr Philip Noel-Baker, the British Secretary of State for Commonwealth Relations, said that in the opinion of the British government, 'Pakistan is in international law the inheritor of the rights and duties of the old Government of India and of His Majesty's Government in the United Kingdom in these territories and that the Durand Line (that is, the Afghan–Pakistani frontier) is the international frontier.[23]

The above statement of the law warrants the conclusion that once States agree to allocate territory on the basis of a treaty, and thereafter implement its provisions by way of demarcation, and subsequently reaffirm the treaty and/or the location of the frontier with or without minor modifications to the alignment, it is reasonable to assume that the matter has, in principle, received its quietus and is not to be reopened. To the extent that a boundary agreement is the source of territorial and boundary-related obligations of both adjacent States, it may be seen as investing title to territory in favour of either State. The subsequent successive reaffirmation or confirmation of the alignment constitutes recognition of the conclusive nature of the boundary regime, which, in turn, precludes the States from subsequently contesting the validity of the boundary. It will be seen that each of those treaties (the treaties of 1847, 1913–14, and 1937) attributed territory to Iran and Iraq and were thus vestive of title. In another sense, the Treaty of 1913 and *procès verbaux* of 1914 made only modifications to the left-bank boundary and were to that extent reaffirming the prevailing alignment. They may be regarded as evidence of the conclusive nature of the allocation of territory made by the States. This implies, furthermore, that both Iran and Iraq were precluded from subsequently challenging the status of the left-bank boundary. The question of preclusion will be examined in the context of the unilateral abrogation of the boundary at a later

---

[22] Opinion of 5 Nov. 1947, in Ext. 8930/47, (File F4010/29SA), Collection 3/214 in L/P&S/12/1822. (File now withdrawn.)

[23] Hansard, 466 H.C. Deb, 5s. cols.1491–3 at col.1491. See also Prime Minister's statement to the House of Commons, 1 Mar. 1956, ibid., 549, col.1367; E. Lauterpacht, 'Contemporary Practice of the United Kingdom in the Field of International Law', *ICLQ* (1956) p. 421; and letter transmitted to UN by UK Permanent Representative, 26 Feb. 1965 in *Materials on Succession of States*, UN Legislative Series (New York, 1967) (ST/LEG/SER.B/14), pp. 186–7.

2. SPECIFIC ISSUES

(a) Mid-line or Thalweg in the Shatt

The question of the mid-line and/or the thalweg in the Shatt is perhaps central to a proper appreciation of the legal regime of the frontier and accordingly this matter, although familiar to students and writers of international law, needs to be examined in considerable detail. One of the arguments consistently put forward by Iran in earlier[24] as well as more recent times[25] was that the Shatt should be divided along either the middle of the river or the thalweg. In support of her claim, Iran has argued that it is a well-received rule of international law that when a river divides the territories of two or more States the boundary runs along either the thalweg or the median line, and not along either of the two banks of the river; and, hence, the left-bank alignment cannot be upheld in law. In his reply to the Iraqi representative's address to the Council of the League of Nations in February 1935, the Persian Minister, Mr Kazemi, claimed that the Treaty of Erzeroum '(did) not say a word about giving to the Porte the whole of the Shatt . . . in full sovereignty,' and concluded:

> It does not fix in direct, clear and categorical terms the frontier on the bank beyond the waters of the river; yet this should have been made quite explicit in absolute and formal terms, if the intention were to depart from the fundamental principle of the equal sovereignty of the two riparians as far as the middle of the river.[26]

At the outset, it is to be noted that although the concept of the median line is different from that of the thalweg, the two terms were apparently often employed interchangeably by officials of the government of Iran and the Foreign Office in Britain. While it is generally accepted that the term *medium filum aquae* is the line of geographic equidistance in the river, that is it divides the river lengthways in equal proportions, there is some difficulty in attributing an equally precise meaning to the term *thalweg*. Both

---

[24] See generally above, ch.1, sect.II. See also Melamid, 'The Shatt-al-Arab Boundary Dispute' *Middle East Journal*, 22 (1968), p. 351, at p. 354; Edmonds, 'The Iraqi-Persian Frontier, 1639–1938', *Asian Affairs*, 62 (1975), p. 147, at pp. 150–2.

[25] See Iran's letters to the President, Security Council, 1 and 9 May 1969 (including statements of 27 Apr. and 9 May 1969 by Ministry of Foreign Affairs, Iran): S/9190 and S/9200 and Add. 1, and letter of 2 Sep 1969: S/9425. See also Iraq's letters to President, Security Council, 29 Apr. 1969: S/9185; 13 May 1969: S/9205; 11 July 1969: S/9323 and Corr. 1: Yearbook of the United Nations 23 (1969) p. 246. See also Statement by Iraqi Minister of Foreign Affairs to General Assembly, 3 Oct. 1980: *Annexe to The Iraqi-Iranian Dispute: Facts and Allegations*, Ministry of Foreign Affairs, (Iraq, 1981); *Facts Concerning the Iraqi-Iranian Frontier*, 1960; *Comment on the Iranian Claims Concerning the Iraqi-Iranian Frontier Treaty of 1937*, ibid., 1969; and Ismael, *Iraq and Iran*, p. 26.

[26] *League of Nations Official Journal*, 16 (1935) p. 118; also see p. 120.

lawyers and geographers have observed that this term is susceptible of varying interpretations. Thus, the term thalweg can be understood as being either the median line in the main navigable channel, or the continuous line of deepest soundings, and according to some commentators even the axis of the safest and most accessible channel for the largest ships.[27] The precise meaning, however, of the term is of little or no consequence to this particular study inasmuch as nothing material turns on the question of the exact location of the thalweg, and it will therefore be sufficient to proceed on the understanding that, for purposes of this analysis, the term thalweg refers to the median line of the main navigable channel. This, at any rate, is the view that is most widely accepted. A question of greater importance is whether Iran was correct in claiming that there exists a fundamental principle of international law which requires the maintenance of a median-line boundary which could only be displaced by express agreement. This question requires some analysis of the law and practice of States relative to boundary lines in navigable rivers.

A discussion of frontier delimitation in respect of rivers may be appropriately prefaced by a brief historical survey. In so far as state practice is concerned, the development of the law has not, according to Professor Verzijl, been uniform: different regions in Europe have had diverse experiences.[28] In medieval times, the main rivers of Europe were governed by the legal regime of *stratae regiae* or, literally, the street of the Holy Roman Empire. Riparian 'states' (towns, areas, and so on) could only exercise rights appertaining to jurisdiction, navigation, fishery, and the like in broad rivers in so far as such rights had been expressly granted to them by the Empire. In the absence of such grant, the territorial rights of the riparians were limited by the bank of the river, while the Empire exercised exclusive sovereignty over it, up to and including its natural inundation area irrespective of the territorial claims of the riparians.[29]

However, in the Balkans the general trend, as seen in treaty provisions between Russia, Austria, and Turkey, was to leave either the entire river to one of the states or to fix their respective boundaries along both banks of the river, thus ascribing to the latter the status of 'no man's land'.[30] Verzijl observed that he 'did not find much indication which could support the

---

[27] Bouchez, 'The Fixing of Boundaries in International Boundary Rivers', *ICLQ* 12 (1963), p. 789 at p. 793; E. Lauterpacht, 'River Boundaries: Legal Aspects of the Shatt-al-Arab Frontier', ibid., 9 (1960), p. 208; McEwen, *International Boundaries of East Africa* (Oxford, 1971), pp. 78–9; Jones, *Boundary Making* (Washington, DC, 1945), pp. 114–17; Verzijl, *International Law in Historical Perspective* (1971), iii. 563–5; Cukwurah, *The Settlement of Boundary Disputes in International Law* (Manchester, 1967), pp. 51–4; Al-Izzi, *The Shatt-Al-Arab River Dispute*, pp. 70–3.

[28] Verzijl, *International Law*, pp. 540–1.

[29] Ibid. On a discussion of such medieval grants, see *The Twee Gebroeders*, 3 C.ROB. 336, at pp. 334–7.

[30] Verzijl, *International Law*, p. 563–5.

The Boundary before 1975

conscious acceptance in early times of the idea of a river condominium proper, and the express partition of a river into two strips divided by its median line, let alone divided along its thalweg, was still very rare'.[31] For other parts of Europe, he found no evidence of any 'fixed general customary rule' regarding the division of rivers. The view, therefore, that nations adhered at first to 'the principle of co-dominion, which assigned to the opposite riverain proprietors rights of sovereignty over the entire stream'[32] has to be tempered somewhat with the foregoing observations.

There is no doubt, however, that the concept of a median-line division did eventually gain greater currency among the states in Europe, and by the time Hugo Grotius wrote *De Jure Belli ac Pacis Libri Tres* in 1625 he could observe that 'in case of doubt the jurisdiction of two States bordering on the same river extends to the middle of the stream . . . '.[33] This technique, nevertheless, was found not to be free from difficulties in navigable rivers. The *medium filum aquae* did not necessarily correspond with the channel of navigation in the river, and a vessel following the main channel was likely to find itself on either side of the boundary in the course of its passage. Thus by the beginning of the nineteenth century States began to adopt the thalweg as their boundary in navigable rivers as opposed to a median-line division.[34] Gradually, the notion of the thalweg delimitation evolved as a principle of law. As Professor Hyde observed, 'The principal boundary treaties concluded (in this period) afford abundant evidence of the fact that States have generally taken great care to express their acceptance of the principle of thalweg and have avoided the use of words the literal meaning of which might encourage the inference that the contracting parties sought to retain the old method of establishing a frontier'.[35] In

---

[31] Ibid., p. 543. In this context, see the *Grisbadarna* case, (1909) 1 *Scott's Hague Court Reports*, p. 122 at p. 129; and below, n. 49.

[32] Hyde, *International Law Chiefly as Interpreted and Applied by the United States* (Washington, DC, 1947) Vol. 1, p. 443; see also *New Jersey* v. *Delaware*, 291 US 361, at p. 381; *Minnesota* v. *Wisconsin*, 252 US 273, at p. 282.

[33] *De Jure Belli ac Pacis Libri Tres* (translation by F. W. Kelsey, 1925), Carnegie Endowment for International Peace, Washington, 1964, Book II, Chap. 3, No. 18 (p. 218). Also see Vattel, *The Law of Nations* (1773) (Translation by J. Chitty), London, 1834, Book I, Chap. 22, No. 266; Pufendorf, *De Jure Naturae et Gentium Libri Octo* (1688) (translation by Oldfather, 1934), Carnegie Endowment for International Peace (New York, 1964), ii, Book IV, Chap. 7, p. 594.

[34] Hyde, *International Law*, p. 444; Verzijl, *International Law*, p. 553; Twiss, *The Law of Nations* (Oxford, 1884), pp. 249–50; Westlake, *International Law*, Part I, 'Peace' (Cambridge, 1904), p. 141. An interesting example of this change can be seen in part of the boundaries between the US and Canada. The 1783 Treaty and subsequent demarcation commissions of 1822 established the boundary in the geographical centre of the waters between the eastern terminus and the Neebish Falls situate in the water communication between Lakes Huron and Superior. However, the Webster–Ashburton Treaty of 1842 adopted the thalweg for the sector beginning from the Neebish Falls and ending at the Lake of Woods: Verzijl, *International Law*, p. 556, 1 *Moore's International Arbitrations*, pp. 162–95.

[35] Hyde, *International Law*, p. 445 n. 4.

general terms, the principle is that, in the absence of an agreement or evidence to the contrary, wherever a navigable river divides the territories of two (or more) States, the boundary lies, or is to be drawn, along the thalweg of the river.[36]

A notable feature of international jurisprudence is that there is a virtually complete absence of any detailed comment on the law of the thalweg and the *medium filum aquae*. This is especially conspicuous in view of the fact that tribunals *have* delimited boundaries along the thalweg of rivers in their judgments and arbitral awards. The explanation may be that in almost all the cases regarding river boundaries there have been no controversies regarding the extent of territorial sovereignty widthways in the watercourses: disagreement, more often than not, has been confined to the question of the location of the boundary on *terra firma*. Thus in the *British Guiana–Brazil Boundary* arbitration,[37] the arbitrator, King Victor Emmanuel of Italy, fixed the boundary in the thalweg of the rivers Ireng (Mahu) and Takutu.[38] Similarly, in the *North Eastern Boundary* arbitration,[39] between Great Britain and the United States, King William I of the Netherlands drew the 'line of convenience' along the thalweg of the St John and St Francis rivers, an alignment which neither of the parties had claimed.[40] In the *British Guiana–Venezuela Boundary* arbitration,[41] the tribunal, in an award delivered in October 1899, fixed the frontier along the midstream of a number of rivers.[42] It is noteworthy that Article 4(b) of the *Compromis* of February 1897 provided that 'The arbitrators may recognise and give effect to rights and claims vesting on any other ground whatever valid according to international law, and on any principles of international law which the arbitrators may deem to be applicable to the case.'[43]

In the *Alaska Boundary* arbitration, the tribunal was called upon to identify, *inter alia*, the 'true' Portland Channel along which part of the boundary was to run. According to the United States the inlet running south of Wales and Pearse Islands was the Portland Channel because, *inter alia*, 'the Channel contended for (by her) was the deepest, broadest and by

---

[36] Brownlie, *African Boundaries*, p. 17; Bouchez, loc. cit. n. 27 above, p. 799; McEwen, *East Africa*, pp. 78–84; E. Lauterpacht, loc. cit., n. 27 above, pp. 216–22; Cukwurah, *Boundary Disputes*, p. 51. For older authorities, see Hyde, *International Law*, pp. 444–9; and Hall, *International Law* (8th edn., London, 1924), p. 147; Wharton, *A Digest of the International Law of the United States* (Washington., DC, 1887), pp. 95–7, and Hackworth, *A Digest of International Law*, i (Washington, DC, 1940), pp. 570–4.

[37] 11 *RIAA* p. 21.

[38] Ibid., p. 23.

[39] 1 *Moore's International Arbitrations*, p. 127.

[40] Ibid., p. 134.

[41] 92 *BSFP* (1899–1900), p. 160.

[42] Ibid., p. 161. However, the boundary was drawn along the northern bank of the River Cuyuni.

[43] See 89 *BFSP* (1896–7), p. 57 at p. 60. See also the *Island of Timor* case: (1914) 1 *Scott's Hague Court Reports*, at p. 355.

far the most important because it is in fact the only really navigable and safe one'.[44] In her written argument, the US relied heavily upon the doctrine of the thalweg and controverted the British claim that the Channel lay along the northern side of the above-mentioned islands, describing it as a 'narrow rocky and really unnavigable channel'.[45] In his oral address, Sir Robert Finlay, Counsel for Great Britain, argued that the thalweg doctrine was irrelevant to the dispute inasmuch as the question was one of identity of the 'true channel, and not where the boundary lay in the undisputed channel'.[46] He admitted, however, that there was some confusion as to whether the United States regarded both the inlets as one channel separated by islands or whether there were two distinct channels. The Tribunal, which unanimously agreed that the boundary ran along the northern side of the Wales and Pearse Islands, based its decision entirely upon the intentions of the negotiators of the boundary treaty of 1825 and Admiral Vancouver's narratives of his journeys, and abstained from commenting upon the thalweg doctrine.[47] However, in his (individual) Opinion, Lord Alverstone remarked that in his view 'there is no foundation for the [US] argument in favour of the thalweg doctrine'.[48]

The question of the thalweg was also raised in the *Grisbadarna* arbitration[49] wherein the Permanent Court of Arbitration accepted this method of delimitation as a 'rule' of international law but failed to apply it to the case at hand on the basis of the restrictions imposed by the principles of intertemporal law. For similar reasons, the Permanent Court rejected the claims to a median-line division.[50]

It is the *genus* of decisions of national courts which has played the major part in developing the doctrine of the thalweg in boundary rivers. In the earlier part of this century, the Supreme Court of the United States of America was seised from time to time of a number of cases which were concerned with disputes regarding boundaries in rivers between the various States of the Union. Its decisions have thus become the chief English language source of judicial opinion on this question.[51] In the cases before it, the court has consistently ruled in favour of the thalweg principle. In *Iowa* v. *Illinois*, one of the earlier cases on this matter, Justice Field ruled:

[44] 15 *RIAA* p. 491.
[45] *Argument of the United States Before the Tribunal* (Washington, 1903), pp. 41–2.
[46] *Alaska Boundary Tribunal, Minutes of Proceedings*, 17 Sept. 1903, pp. 2–6 at pp. 4–5.
[47] 15 *RIAA*, p. 492–3, 495, 501–2, 512–13, 521–23.
[48] Ibid., p. 495.
[49] (1909) 1 *Scott's Hague Court Reports*, p. 122.
[50] Ibid., p. 129. Also see the judgment in *Zurich* v. *Schaffhausen*, below text at nn. 63 and 64.
[51] See *Iowa* v. *Illinois*, 147 US 1; *Louisiana* v. *Mississippi*, 202 US 1; *Arkansas* v. *Tennessee*, 246 US 158; *Arkansas* v. *Mississippi*, 250 US 39; *Minnesota* v. *Wisconsin*, 252 US 273; *New Jersey* v. *Delaware*, 291 US 361; *Washington* v. *Oregon*, 211 US 127; *Handly's Lessee* v. *Anthony et al.*, 5 Wheat. 374; *Buttenuth et al.* v. *St. Louis Bridge Co.*, Scott's Cases on International Law (Washington, DC, 1922), p. 206 (123 Ill. 535; 17 NE Rep. 439).

When a navigable river constitutes the boundary between two independent States, the line defining the point at which the jurisdiction of the two separates is well established to be the middle of the main channel of the stream. The interest of each State in the navigation of the river admits of no other line. The preservation by each of its equal right in the navigation of the stream is the subject of paramount interest. It is, therefore, laid down in all the recognised treaties on international law of modern times that the middle of the channel of the stream marks the true boundary between the adjoining States up to which each State will on its side exercise jurisdiction.[52]

In *Louisiana* v. *Mississippi*,[53] Chief Justice Fuller went on to hold that on occasion the principle of the thalweg was applicable in respect of water boundaries to sounds, bays, straits, gulfs, estuaries, and other arms of the sea.[54] In *New Jersey* v. *Delaware*,[55] the Supreme Court observed that the underlying rationale of the doctrine of the thalweg was one of equality and justice and gave prominence to the fact that if the dividing line were to be placed in the centre of the stream rather than in the centre of the channel the whole track of navigation might be thrown within the territory of one State to the exclusion of the other.[56]

The point, which is particularly worthy of note, but frequently overlooked in commentaries relating to these cases, is that in none of the disputes did any of the states of the Union lay claim to the entire width of the river which separated them; and that, therefore, the question to which the Supreme Court was confined was whether or not the thalweg boundary, as claimed by one state, was, in principle, to be given precedence over the median-line division, as claimed by another. Indeed, in some of these cases, the Federal Enabling Acts, which described, *inter alia*, the territorial extent of the States joining the American Union, stipulated that the boundaries of the states in question lay along the middle of certain rivers.[57] Furthermore, in several cases, the delimitation of boundaries along the middle of certain rivers was expressly provided for in treaties concluded between the British, French, Spanish, and US governments in the eighteenth and nineteenth centuries in respect of their North American territories.[58] Accordingly, it is important to be reminded of the context in which the

[52] 147 US 1, especially p. 7.
[53] 202 US 1.
[54] Ibid., p. 50.
[55] 291 US 361.
[56] Ibid., p. 380. See Garner, 'The Doctrine of the Thalweg as a Rule of International Law', *AJIL* 29 (1935), p. 309.
[57] See *Iowa* v. *Illinois*, 147 US, at pp. 10–11, 13–14; *Arkansas* v. *Tennessee*, 246 US, p. 160 et seq.; *Arkansas* v. *Mississippi*, 250 US at pp. 41–46; *Nebraska* v. *Iowa*, 143 US 359, at pp. 359–60; *Missouri* v. *Nebraska*, 196 US 23, at pp. 23–35; *Buttenuth* v. *St. Louis Bridge Co.*, loc cit. n. 51 above.
[58] See *Louisiana* v. *Mississippi* 202 US 1; *Arkansas* v. *Tennessee*, 246 US 158; *Iowa* v. *Illinois*, 147 US 1; *Vermont* v. *New Hampshire*, 289 US 593.

Supreme Court made its decisions in favour of the thalweg principle and to note that it was not faced with claims of title to the entire width of the river. It can, therefore, hardly be contended that the Supreme Court accepted the proposition that the rule of the thalweg had to be applied without qualification to all boundary rivers. On the contrary, it is manifest that the court did not approve of this interpretation of the rule in question. In *Washington* v. *Oregon* the matter before the court was whether the boundary in the Columbia River, which separated the two states, lay along the 'middle of the north ship channel of the Columbia River'. The territorial extent of Oregon was described in the Act of 14 February 1859 which admitted the state into the Union and provided that part of the boundary lay in the middle of the said north ship channel. It was contended by counsel on behalf of Washington that the 'true boundary line is the varying centre or middle of that channel of the river which is best suited and ordinarily used for the purposes of navigation',[59] and thus the boundary ran along the centre of the southern, or main, channel of navigation. In response to the arguments advanced by Washington, the court referred, *inter alia*, to some of the earlier decisions passed by it in favour of the thalweg principle, and in distinguishing them, observed:

But in these cases the boundary named was 'the middle of the main channel of the river' or 'the middle of the river' and it was upon such a description that it was held that in the absence of avulsion the boundary was the varying centre of the channel. But there is no fixed rule making (the thalweg) the boundary between States bordering on a river ... Now, if Congress in establishing the boundary between Washington and Oregon had simply named the middle of the river, or the centre of the channel, doubtless it would be ruled that the centre of the main channel, varying as it might from year to year through the process of accretion, was the boundary between the two States ... However, ... when Congress came to provide for the admission of Oregon ... it provided that the boundary should be the middle of the north channel. The Courts have no power to change the boundary thus prescribed and establish it at the middle of some other channel.[60]

The Supreme Court, moreover, has recognized in certain *obiter* passages that the thalweg rule cannot be applied in every case. In *Iowa* v. *Illinois*, it remarked that the reason for and necessity of the thalweg rule may not be as cogent in interstate disputes in the United States as it is among European States where there is no central government, 'yet the same rule will be held to obtain unless changed by statute or usage of so great a length of time as to have acquired the force of law'.[61] The same precept was adopted in *New Jersey* v. *Delaware* when the court held that unless prescription or

[59] *Washington* v. *Oregon*, 211 US at p. 129.
[60] Ibid., pp. 134–5.
[61] 147 US at p. 10. See also *Vermont* v. *New Hampshire*, 289 US 593.

convention had entrenched another rule, the court was to utilize the formula that would make equality prevail.[62]

Reference may also be made to the decision of the Swiss Federal Court rendered on 9 November 1897 regarding the boundaries of the cantons of Zurich and Schaffhausen along the Rhine.[63] In this case the Federal Court was seized of claims and facts not entirely dissimilar to the ones obtaining in the Shatt boundary dispute. Schaffhausen claimed that the boundary ran along the left bank of the Rhine leaving the entire width of the river under her jurisdiction. She based her claim on the Confederate Award of 1555 which resolved the dispute between the two cantons by attributing territorial sovereignty over the entire width of the relevant sector of the Rhine to Schaffhausen. Zurich contested this by arguing that the modern concepts of international law were in favour of a median-line division and therefore the alignment between the parties lay not along the left bank but in the middle of the Rhine. The Federal Court was not convinced by the arguments of Zurich and in a passage which has particular relevance to the present study observed:

> The circumstance that now, in accordance with the development of objective law, more importance is attached to the doctrine of international law, according to which the boundary of two States divided by a river is usually found in the middle of the said river, and less importance is attached to the actual possession and events of feudal law, cannot now effect any change in the juridical condition determined in such an authentic way any more than it could have done so previously. For the principal question to be decided today is whether the present dispute has not already been decided, at least to a certain extent, in a legally binding manner, and whether thereby a condition has been created which must be guarded according to the principles of acquired rights, regardless of how the dispute would be decided according to the now prevalent norms and conceptions.[64]

---

[62] 291 US at p. 383. See also *Handly's Lessee* v. *Anthony*, 5 Wheat. 374, at pp. 378–84; *Regina* v. *Mat Erat* (1872) 2 Ky. (Cr.) 86; 8 CILC 379; *In re Village of Fort Erie and Buffalo and Fort Erie Public Bridge Co*, (1927) 61 OLR 502; 4 ILR 121; 8 CILC 433; *Buttenuth et al.* v. *St. Louis Bridge Co.*, *Scott's Cases on International Law* (1922), p. 212.

[63] See Schindler, 'The Administration of Justice in the Swiss Federal Court in International Disputes', *AJIL* 15 (1921) p. 149 at pp. 167–8.

[64] Ibid., pp. 167–8. Translation by Schindler. In another case in respect of a different sector of the boundary, the claims were reversed. Zurich argued that by virtue, *inter alia*, of prescription and *usucapio*, her sovereignty extended up to the northern (or right) bank of the Rhine, while Schaffhausen claimed a median line. The Federal Court held that Zurich had failed to establish her claims in law, and declared that the line lay in the middle of the Rhine. Decision of 28 May 1907, cited in Schindler, ibid., pp. 168–9. See also, in passing, Venezuela's arguments in the *British Guiana* v. *Venezuela* arbitration in respect of the middle distance and natural boundaries. Referring generally to watersheds, she argued: 'Before the rule of the middle distance can be used, it must be found that there is no line of right; that neither party has a superior right to the whole or any determinate part of the disputed territory.' *Printed Argument on Behalf of the United States of Venezuela* (New York, 1898), i. 757. In the *Barotse Kingdom* boundary arbitration, part of the boundary between (Portuguese) Angola and (British Northern Rhodesia) Zambia was located along the left bank of the Kwando river: Brownlie, *African Boundaries*, pp. 1067–70.

The Boundary before 1975

The point which emerges clearly from the above discussion is that the thalweg rule in boundary rivers is not an absolute principle, that is, a 'rule' to be followed whenever a navigable river separates two or more States. The thalweg doctrine is applicable only in certain circumstances, and one of these circumstances, apart, of course, from incidents of express agreement between the parties, is a situation in which neither of the parties can adduce evidence in the form either of a treaty, municipal instruments, acquiescence, or otherwise, regarding the location of the line in a navigable river. In other words, in such situations, the boundary will, in all the appropriate circumstances, be located in the thalweg of the river and neither in the middle of or along one of the banks of the navigable river. It amounts to this, therefore, as Professor Brownlie observed that the principles of the thalweg and of the *medium filum aquae* in non-navigable rivers are essentially presumptions,[65] which may be rebutted by either party upon submission of evidence to the contrary. There is considerable support for this view among the earlier and more contemporary writers on international law.[66] Indeed, in reference to the Shatt question itself, both Sir E. Davidson and Cecil Hurst (later Sir), Legal Adviser and Assistant Legal Adviser to the Foreign Office in 1912, were able to advise the British Foreign Secretary of the day, Sir Edward Grey, to the effect that 'under normal conditions there is no doubt a presumption that each riparian owner owns on his side of the river "*usque ad medium filum aquae*", but that, in the present case, that presumption has by implication undoubtedly been swept away by the Treaty of Erzeroum (1847) the effect of which was to give Turkey the whole waterway'.[67] Equally, and this is a concomitant of the foregoing, there is no presumption in favour of exclusive title to both sides of the boundary rivers. Thus in *The Twee Gebroeders* case, the judge, Sir William Scott, observed, in the context of the status of the Groningen Watt, a river running along the Groningen (Dutch) coast that there was, in principle, a presumption in favour of a communal use of the rivers flowing through the territories of States. He added that while it may be that a State

---

[65] Brownlie, *African Boundaries*, p. 17. In respect of river estuaries and bays, see Verzijl, *International Law*, pp. 593-4.

[66] Adami, *National Frontiers in Relation to International Law* (Oxford, 1927), pp. 15, 17, 20-1; G. F. Martens, *The Law of Nations* (Cobbett translation) 4th edn., London, 1829, pp. 159-60; Travers Twiss, *The Law of Nations*, pp. 249-51, esp. n. 33, p. 250; Wheaton, *Elements of International Law* 6th edn. by Keith, London, 1929, pp. 384-5; Westlake, *International Law*, i. 142; Hall, *International Law*, p. 147; Moore, *A Digest of International Law* (Washington, DC, 1906), i. 616-17; Lindley, *The Acquisition and Government of Backward Territory in International Law*, (London, 1926), pp. 272, 276-7; Cukwurah, *Boundary Disputes*, pp. 47-9; Verzijl, *International Law*, iii. 561; Al-Izzi, *The Shatt-al-Arab River Dispute*, pp. 72-3.

[67] For references to advice given by Davidson and Hurst see FO to IO, 31 May 1912, Letter No. 22934/12 in conjunction with Parker's comments to Cox letter to IO of 21 May 1912: PCP 25042, 12 June 1912, Reg. P2184, 7 June 1912, in L/P&S/10/266.

may have, by way of prior settlement, secured possession of the bank of a river, 'the general presumption certainly bears strongly against such exclusive rights, and the title is a matter to be established, on the part of those claiming under it, in the same manner as all other legal demands are to be substantiated, by clear and competent evidence'.[68]

State practice affords corroboration of the view that delimitation by thalweg in navigable boundary rivers is not an absolute principle. Although it is true that the greater number of treaties stipulate for either a median-line or thalweg delimitation, the attribution of the entire width of the river to one of the parties is by no means unknown. Thus, examples of international boundaries which run along the banks of navigable rivers are to be found in Europe, America, and Africa.[69] By virtue of the Franco-Liberian Treaty of 18 September 1907, the boundary between Liberia and the Ivory Coast was drawn along the right, or western, bank of the River Cavally, thereby placing the entire course of the river south of its confluence with the River Nuon under French/Ivory Coast sovereignty.[70] The 1907 line, it may be added, was a modification of the thalweg regime established by an earlier agreement of 1892. No dispute regarding this sector exists between the States today.[71] In Europe, the Chiers, a tributary of the Meuse, was ceded by Austria in its entirety to France pursuant to Article 21 of the Treaty of 16 May 1769.[72] Certain sectors of the French–Swiss boundary between Mont Delont and Lake Geneva were, by virtue of the agreement signed on 10 June 1891, delimited along the left bank of the L'Eau Noire and the right banks of La Barberine and La Morge, attributing the entire width of the streams to France.[73] In South America, the frontier line between Surinam and (French) Guyana runs, on the basis of an agreement signed by Dutch and French governors on 9 November 1836, along the

[68] 3 C. ROB. 336; 165 ER 485; (SC 1 Eng. Pr. Cas. 323) at p. 339 and pp. 346–7; Lindley, *Acquisition and Government*, p. 276.

[69] See generally, Bouchez, loc. cit. no. 27 above, p. 791; and 'The Netherlands and the Law of International Rivers', in Panhuys (ed.) *International Law in the Netherlands* (The Hague, 1978), i. 215 *et seq.*; Brownlie, *African Boundaries*, *passim*; Menon, 'International Boundaries: A Case Study of the Guyana-Surinam Boundary', *ICLQ* 27 (1978), p. 738, at pp. 753–4; Adami, *National Frontiers*, at pp. 21–2; Verzijl, *International Law*, pp. 545–7; Cukwurah, *Boundary Disputes*, p. 47; McEwen, *East Africa*, pp. 78–9.

[70] Brownlie, *African Boundaries*, pp. 358–70; McEwen, *East Africa*, pp. 85–6.

[71] Brownlie, *African Boundaries*, p. 369. See also the boundary along the eastern bank of Ngobwe Creek between Kenya and Tanzania by virtue of the Anglo-German Protocol of 1900: McEwen, *East Africa*, pp. 84–5. For disputed river boundaries see the Mali–Mauritanian frontier along the Senegal river: Brownlie, *African Boundaries*, pp. 407–15; and the sector of the River Falémé between Mali and Senegal, ibid., pp. 423–6.

[72] Verzijl, *International Law*, p. 545; see generally, pp. 545–7, 590–610.

[73] Adami, *National Frontiers*, p. 22. For disputed river boundaries, see the Ems–Dollard estuary problem between West Germany and the Netherlands. The former claims the entire breadth of the Ems estuary on the ground of historic title, while the Dutch government argues in favour of the thalweg boundary: Bouchez, 'The Netherlands and the Law of International Rivers', p. 282.

right bank of the Maroni River, although, for purposes of navigation in the estuary, the limits, according to the Treaty of 30 September 1915, lie along the median line.[74]

In view of the above discussion of the law and practice on the question, two conclusions may now be drawn. First, it was not unlawful for either Iraq or Iran to have concluded an agreement (or agreements) which adopted the left bank of the Shatt, as opposed to the thalweg or median line, as the boundary between them. There is clearly no prohibition in international law against the conclusion of a frontier agreement which attributes the entire width of a river to one of the contracting States, and consequently the objections raised by Iran and other commentators were misconceived. Secondly, no presumption in favour of a thalweg or median-line boundary can arise in the Shatt. Iran had assented in three separate agreements concluded in 1847, 1913–14 and 1937 to an alignment which ran, save the Abadan and Mohammara sectors, along the left bank of the river. Even if a presumption existed at any point in favour of a thalweg division, it could easily be rebutted by reference to the treaties mentioned above and the demarcation proceedings of 1914. In the final analysis, therefore, Iran's objections and representations made prior to the conclusion of the Baghdad Treaty of 1975, which challenged the validity of the left-bank boundary on the ground that international law recognized only the thalweg/median line in navigable rivers, were based on a misunderstanding of the position in law.

(b) *The abrogation of the Treaty of* 1937

Iran unilaterally abrogated the Treaty of 1937 in April 1969. Several arguments were raised in support of abrogation, one of which was that the boundary stipulated in the treaty ran along the left bank and was therefore invalid. The question of validity of the left-bank alignment has been examined above. The doctrine of *rebus sic stantibus* was also relied upon by Iran, which claimed that, in as much as there had occurred a fundamental change of circumstances between the parties, the Treaty of 1937 had stood terminated. Accordingly, the line established by it had ceased to exist. In order to appreciate the validity of this action and the arguments submitted in support of it, a survey of the relevant law is essential.

Before examining the role of the *rebus sic stantibus* doctrine, a brief statement regarding the general theory of executed boundary provisions and related matters will be in order. Generally speaking, alignments

[74] Day (ed.), *Borders and Territorial Disputes* (London, 1982), pp. 376–7. The Dutch governors' agreement of 1799 in respect of the boundaries of Berbice (now in Guyana) and Surinam settled the frontier along the west, or left, bank of the Corentyne river: See Menon, loc. cit. n. 69 above, pp. 748–55. The Franco-Portuguese frontier agreement of 10 Aug. 1797 delimited the line along the right bank of the Oyapec: see Bouchez, op. cit. n. 27 above, p. 791.

between States are to be viewed in terms of a maximum degree of continuity on account, *inter alia*, of the fact that boundary treaties have 'dispositive' characteristics, that is to say, they have the effect of creating permanent rights which run and remain with the territory acquired by either State under the terms of the frontier treaty.[75] The logical basis for this proposition is that the delineation of the boundary by treaty constitutes a kind of conveyance of territory between States who thereafter acquire valid title to territory in accordance with the terms of the boundary settlement. Once the treaty is concluded and ratified, the respective rights relating to territory and boundaries are considered transferred and the treaty stands executed. It continues, nevertheless, to serve as evidence of the transfer of territory and location of the alignment. To some extent, the treaty functions not unlike a title deed to land transferred under municipal law. In the words of the late Sir Humphrey Waldock, 'it may be argued that a boundary treaty has constitutive effects and establishes a legal and factual situation which thereafter has its own separate existence . . . .'.[76] An attempt to state the law on the matter was made by the International Law Association at its biennial conference in Buenos Aires in 1968. At that conference, the Committee on the Succession of New States to Treaties passed a series of resolutions, one of which, No. 8, stated that when a treaty which provided for the delimitation of a national boundary had been executed in the sense that the boundary had been delimited and no further action needed to be taken, the treaty had spent its force and what was succeeded to was not the treaty but the extent of national territory so defined.[77]

It is in this context that the law relating to the doctrine of *rebus sic stantibus* and international boundaries needs to be examined. It is generally accepted that the doctrine of *rebus sic stantibus* is not applicable to those treaties which by definition create situations intended to be permanent in character and duration, such as, *inter alia*, agreements in respect of the delimitation and demarcation of frontiers. Thus the exclusion of frontier treaties from the operation of the doctrine in question constitutes an exception to the general rule. Some of the rationale behind the existence of this

---

[75] O'Connell, *International Law* (2nd edn. London, 1970), 373–4; and *State Succession in Municipal Law and International Law*, (Cambridge, 1967), ii. p. 273; McNair, *The Law of Treaties* (Oxford, 1961), pp. 655–64; Haraszti, 'Treaties and the Fundamental Change of Circumstances', *Recueil des Cours*, 146 (1975-III) pp. 65–72; Vallat, in *Yearbook of the International Law Commission*, 1974, ii, Part I, p. 83; Lester, 'State Succession to Treaties in the Commonwealth', *ICLQ* 12 (1963), p. 475, at pp. 492–5; Udokang, *Succession of New States to International Treaties* (New York, 1972), pp. 377–402; Tyranowski, 'State Succession: Boundaries and Boundary Treaties', *Polish Yearbook of International Law*, 10 (1979–80), p. 115; Fischer-Williams, 'The Permanence of Treaties', *AJIL*, 22 (1928), p. 89.

[76] *YILC*, 1972, ii. 54. See below in the context of the doctrine of *rebus sic stantibus*.

[77] Report of the 53rd Conference (1968), London, 1969, p. 589, at p. 598. Commentary, p. 603. But cf. below, sect. II. See also ILA Handbook, *The Effect of Independence on Treaties* (London, 1965), pp. 352–5.

proviso was elicited in the preparatory work conducted by the International Law Commission on the Law of Treaties. In his Second Report on the Law of Treaties, the Special Rapporteur, Sir Humphrey Waldock, introduced a proviso to the principle of *rebus sic stantibus* in favour of boundary treaties.[78] By and large there was general agreement among members of the Commission regarding the inclusion of such proviso.[79] 'Clearly', stated Professor Jiménez de Aréchaga the Chairman of the Commission at its fifteenth session, 'territorial rights established by a treaty would not be affected by the doctrine of a change in circumstances, because the parties would have no further interest in securing the termination of a treaty already executed.[80] At the session in January 1966, the member from Austria, Verdross, pointed out that the proviso to the *rebus sic stantibus* doctrine 'was not a special rule, but simply the application of a more general rule to the effect that the *clausula rebus sic stantibus* was not applicable to a treaty which had already been fully executed, for reliance on that clause always presupposed the continued existence of obligations flowing from the treaty'.[81] Where a treaty, he added, had been fully executed it ceased to produce any obligation and the clause was inoperative. However, Waldock reminded members of the Commission that the reason for the exclusion of boundary treaties from the *rebus sic stantibus* rule was not that the provisions of those treaties were executed provisions but that treaties of that type were intended to create a stable position.[82] 'It would', he said, 'be inconsistent with the very nature of those treaties to make them subject to the *rebus sic stantibus* rule'.[83] In its definitive form as Article 62, paragraph 2(a) of the Vienna Convention on the Law of Treaties,[84] the rule is formulated thus:

A fundamental change of circumstances may not be invoked as a ground for termination or withdrawing from a treaty:

(a) If the treaty establishes a boundary . . .

Furthermore, the question of *rebus sic stantibus* and boundary treaties can

---

[78] *YILC*, 1963, ii. 79–85.

[79] See generally, ibid., i. 136–63. For views of State governments, see ibid., 1966, ii. 39–42.

[80] Ibid., 1963, i. 150. See also his remarks, ibid., 1966, i. 83–4. For commentary on this provision, see Lissitzyn, 'Treaties and Changed Circumstances', *AJIL* 61 (1967), p. 895.

[81] *YILC*, 1966, i. Part I, p. 76.

[82] Ibid., p. 86. See below in reference to war, boundary treaties, and the views of Sir Cecil Hurst, p. 103.

[83] Ibid. See also the observations of Mr De Luna, Member, Sixth Committee, General Assembly, *General Assembly Official Records* 18th Session, 792nd meeting, p. 56, para. 10.

[84] UN Document A/CONF. 39/27.*United Kingdom Treaty Series*, No. 58 (1980): Cmnd, 7964. References to the Convention are made strictly on the basis of the fact that it constitutes evidence of the accepted law on treaties in the international community. Apart from the fact that Article 4 of the Convention precludes retroactive application, Iraq has neither signed nor ratified and Iran, who has signed, has failed to ratify the Convention.

be seen in light of the general rule against the unilateral abrogation of boundary treaties. The views expressed in the preceding paragraphs in respect of the proviso to the *rebus sic stantibus* principle are cognate with and constitute part of the rationale for the general rule against the unilateral abrogation of boundary treaties. Inasmuch as a boundary agreement creates permanent rights in favour of either party regarding the territorial limits of two (or more) States, it no longer remains within the province of any one State to attempt to deprive the other of the rights vested lawfully in that State. It is the case that States view matters of territory and frontiers with considerable care and caution, and hence if the law were to support a State in attempts at unilateral denunciation of a valid frontier on whatever grounds, it would create uncertainty and instability in the international community. It is not inconceivable and that States dissatisfied with the allocation of territory would be tempted to initiate new contestations over territory or to challenge existing frontier regimes. Clearly, the law cannot, and does not, give countenance to such claims and supports the position that a valid boundary treaty is conclusive of all relevant questions and the alignment established cannot be modified or denounced without agreement, express or otherwise, with the coterminous State. Emphasis here is on the word 'valid', and thus a boundary treaty which has never been accepted as valid does not fall within the ambit of this rule.

Considerations of this nature were predicated in draft article 17, paragraph 4, in the Second Report on the Law of Treaties submitted by Sir Humphrey Waldock, the Special Rapporteur.[85] Draft article 17 dealt with the question of the denunciation and termination of treaties which contained no provisions regarding their duration or termination. While it enumerated four kinds of treaties which could in certain specified circumstances be denounced, it provided in paragraph 4:

A treaty shall continue in force indefinitely with respect to each party where the treaty—

(*a*) is one establishing a boundary between two States, or effecting a cession of territory or a grant of rights in or over territory.

---

[85] *YILC*, 1963, ii. 64. cf. draft article 4, Fitzmaurice, 2nd Report (1957), ibid., 1957, ii. 22–3, 38–9, which was predicated on the rule that 'silence means, in principle, no termination except by general consent': p. 38; and Harvard draft article 34 which is based on similar premisses, *AJIL* 29 (1935), Supplement, pp. 1173–83. For a general review on unilateral denunciation of treaties see McNair, *The Law of Treaties*, pp. 493–505, 539–71, esp. 494, 531–3 (on executed territorial treaties); Brierly, *Law of Nations* (6th edn., Oxford, 1963), pp. 327–40; Nahlik, 'The Grounds of Invalidity and Termination of Treaties', *AJIL* 65 (1971) p. 736, at 746–51; Sinha, *Unilateral Denunciation of Treaty Because of Prior Violations of Obligations by Other Party* (The Hague, 1966); Widdows, 'The Unilateral Denunciation of Treaties containing no Denunciation Clause', *BYIL* 53 (1982), p. 83, esp. p. 109. Also see Indian Memorial, ICJ Pleadings, *Appeal Relating to the Jurisdiction of the ICAO Council* (1973), pp. 38–44.

In his commentary, Waldock explained that paragraph 4, which listed five types of treaty,[86] was based on the premiss that 'the intention of the parties must be presumed to be to establish a permanent treaty regime, in the sense of a regime which will continue indefinitely until revised or terminated by subsequent agreement'.[87] The draft article was presented as Article 53 to the Committee of the Whole at the Vienna Conference in 1968 by which time the reference to frontier agreements had been deleted and the article had undergone substantial changes.[88] In the preparatory Meetings of the Committee of the Whole, several amendments to Article 53 were tabled.[89] The main thrust of these amendments was to incorporate reference to the nature and character of the treaty in the provision, a reference which the International Law Commission had decided to exclude from its draft, as one of two grounds on the basis of which alone a State could denounce or withdraw from the treaty. From the records of the Meetings of the Committee it is clear that certain Members were particularly inclined in favour of the stability of boundary treaties.[90] Accordingly, Article 53 was redrafted and the text adopted by the Committee of the Whole and the Plenary Meeting emerged as the definitive Article 56 of the Vienna Convention.[91] It provided:

---

[86] i.e. those establishing a special international regime for a particular area, territory, river, waterway, or airspace; a treaty of peace, disarmament, or maintenance of peace; one effecting a final settlement of an international dispute; a general multilateral treaty providing for the codification or development of international law. Cf. the dictum of the Swiss Federal Court in *Luzern* v. *Aargau* (1882), wherein the court observed that a State servitude may be annulled unilaterally under certain circumstances, including *rebus sic stantibus*. Schindler, 'The Administration of Justice in the Swiss Federal Court', pp. 164–5; but see below, n. 94 for views on general principle.

[87] *YILC*, 1963, ii.69. See also draft Article 28: unless the treaty provides otherwise the unilateral termination of a treaty shall not affect the validity of any act performed or of any right acquired under the provisions of the treaty prior to termination. See Minutes of the ILC, ibid i. 234–6, esp. Mr Lachs who emphasized the importance of permanent rights, p. 235.

[88] Draft article 17 was criticized by members on the basis, *inter alia*, that it was more liberal in terms of the right to denounce or withdraw from treaties than was generally admitted under customary law, particularly the *pacta sunt servanda* rule: see Minutes of the ILC, ibid., i. 99–107, and 239–41. See also Commentary to draft article 39 in the Report of the Commission to the General Assembly, 1963, in ibid., ii. 200–02.

[89] See Reports of the Committee of the Whole on its work at the first session of the Conference: A/CONF.39/14 in *Official Records of the UN Conference on the Law of Treaties (first and second sessions), Documents of the Conference*: A/CONF.39/11/Add. 2, p. 177–8.

[90] See observations of Messrs Alvardo (Peru); Martinez Caro (Spain); Kovalev (USSR); Makarewicz (Poland); Myslil (Czechoslovakia); and cf. Alvarez Tabio (Cuba); 59th Meeting, May 1968, ibid., *first session, Summary Records of the plenary meetings and of the meetings of the Committee of the Whole*: A/CONF.39/11, pp. 336–43.

[91] See also draft Article 39 of 1963 which referred, *inter alia*, to the 'character of the treaty': ibid., p. 200. For comments by governments on draft Article 39, see *YILC*, 1966, ii. 25–7. Although draft Article 53 of 1966 did not refer to either the nature of character of the treaty in question, the commentary observed: 'Treaties of peace and treaties fixing a territorial bound-

90   *The Legal Analysis*

1. A treaty which contains no provision regarding its termination and which does not provide for denunciation or withdrawal is not subject to denunciation or withdrawal unless:

   ... (*b*) a right of denunciation or withdrawal may be implied by the nature of the treaty ...

The problem of unilateral abrogation of boundary treaties was also raised and commented upon by the Commission in its preparatory work on the Law of State Succession to Treaties. In his first report as Special Rapporteur, Sir Francis Vallat observed that there was a 'practical need' to make an exception to the clean-slate principle in order to deal with boundary and territorial regimes. Otherwise, he said, in every case of succession, States would have a unilateral right to repudiate existing boundaries and territorial rights and obligations created by treaty. He wrote: 'The disturbance to international relations that might follow from such a right of unilateral repudiation is not one that could be lightly contemplated ... Indeed, the disturbance of existing boundaries is much more likely to create chaos than their maintenance'.[92] Accordingly, Article 11 of the Vienna Convention on Succession of States in respect of Treaties provides that

A succession of States does not as such affect
   (*a*) a boundary established by a treaty; or
   (*b*) obligations and rights established by a treaty and relating to the regime of a boundary.[93]

In *Costa Rica* v. *Nicaragua* the Central American Court of Justice was seised of the rights of Costa Rica regarding navigation and other facilities over the San Juan River, which she alleged had been prejudiced owing to the conclusion of the US–Nicaragua Treaty of 5 August 1914. In its judgment the Court observed *obiter* that 'the Cañas–Jerez Treaty (The Treaty of Limits) has preserved its full obligatory force and effect down to the present day, as well by virtue of the categorical holdings in the Cleveland Award [of March 1888] ... as by virtue of the permanent character of its stipulations. Wherefore, in the absence of mutual consent by the contracting parties, the treaty cannot be lawfully

---

ary are examples of such treaties': ibid., 1966, ii. 250. Cf. Briggs who refers to the 'nature' and 'character' of perpetual treaties as 'a pseudo-scientific notion which refers not to the nature of treaties but to their content and political purpose': 'Unilateral Denunciation of Treaties: The Vienna Convention and the International Court of Justice', *AJIL*, 68 (1974), p. 51, at p. 64. See Widdows, op. cit. n. 85 above, p. 93.

[92] *YILC*, 1974, ii. Part I, p. 1 at p. 83. See also pp. 73–83; and Waldock Report, ibid., 1968, ii. 92–3, and ibid., 1972, ii. 44–59.

[93] UN Document A/CONF.80/31 (22 Aug. 1978); *International Legal Materials*, 17 (1978), p. 1488. See also Brownlie, *Principles of Public International Law* (3rd. edn., Oxford, 1979), p. 667.

The Boundary before 1975

denounced or held to be dead, nor can the agreements therein stipulated be avoided . . .'[94]

The question of the alleged 'lapse' or 'cancellation' of the Treaty of 1859 between Britain and Guatemala has some bearing on the matter. In Article 1 of the Treaty, Guatemala effectively acknowledged British sovereignty over, and ceded large tracts of land to, the British Settlement and Possessions in the Bay of Honduras, the areas of which were also defined in the said article. In Article 7, both parties 'conjointly' agreed to use their 'best efforts' to establish a line of communication between the capital of Guatemala and 'the fittest place on the Atlantic'. An agreement was concluded in August 1863 with a view to clarifying the obligations of the parties relative to Article 7; but owing to the failure of ratification of the treaty Britain declared herself released from the obligations imposed by Article 7 of the 1859 Treaty. After over fifty years of fruitless negotiations, Guatemala indicated in September 1939 that the 1859 Treaty had lapsed in view of Britain's failure to build the line of communication; that therefore the 'cession' of territory to Great Britain was invalid and that the title to the territory had accordingly reverted to Guatemala.[95] Mr Luis Anderson, writing on behalf of the government of Guatemala, recognized the problem of declaring the treaty lapsed or terminated, for he wrote that the treaty had already been executed by way of demarcation of the ceded territory which was in the possession of Great Britain.[96]

The government of the United States had occasion to comment upon the question under consideration in the context of the frontier dispute between Peru and Ecuador.[97] In 1960, the latter unilaterally denounced the frontier agreement of 1942, also known as the Rio Protocol, on grounds of invalidity. The United States, one of the four guarantor States, advised Ecuador against such a course of action and in a telegram to her government observed:

It is a basic principle of international law that the unilateral will of one of the Parties is not sufficient to invalidate a boundary treaty nor to liberate it from the

---

[94] 11 *AJIL* (1919) p. 181 at p. 194. In *Luzern* v. *Aargau*, the Swiss Federal Court observed that treaties which created 'concrete juridical relations' could not be unilaterally denounced: 'such treaties remain binding for both parties as long as no special juridical reasons for their annulment has arisen': as cited in Schindler, 'The Administration of Justice in the Swiss Federal Court', p. 164.

[95] For a review of the dispute see Anderson, *The Belize Question: Continuation of White Book: Controversy between Guatemala and Great Britain relative to the Convention of 1859 on Territorial Matters*, Ministry of Foreign Affairs (Guatemala, CA, 1940); Mendoza, *Britain and her Treaties on Belize . . .* , Ministry of Foreign Affairs (Guatemala, CA, 1946); Bloomfield, *The British Honduras–Guatemala Dispute* (Toronto, 1953).

[96] Luis Anderson, loc.cit., pp. 57–8. For views similar to these, see Bloomfield, loc.cit., pp. 116–19. Of course, Britain does not concede that the treaty was one of cession, rather it was an acknowledgment by Guatemala of the validity of Britain's existing title.

[97] Whiteman, *Digest of International Law*, iii. (Washington, DC, 1964), pp. 676–80.

obligations imposed therein. Only mutual agreement by both Parties can modify its provisions or attribute competence to an international tribunal to judge questions which may arise regarding such an instrument.[98]

On 8 December 1941, China declared war on Japan and announced the (unilateral) abrogation of the Treaty of Shimonoseki of 1895, which had ceded Formosa (Taiwan) and the Pescadores to Japan. In a debate on the status of Formosa in the House of Lords, it was queried whether the islands had, in view of the abrogation, reverted in principle to China. The joint Parliamentary Under-Secretary of State for Foreign Affairs, the Marquess of Lansdowne, replied: 'According to international law, a State cannot merely by unilateral declaration regain rights of sovereignty which it has formally ceded by treaty. China, therefore, could not and did not regain sovereignty over those territories by the unilateral denunciation of this treaty in 1941.'[99]

The conclusions which may be drawn are clear. The unilateral abrogation of the Treaty of 1937 was not a lawful course of action on the part of the government of Iran and the arguments advanced in support of the abrogation of the boundary treaty are legally not persuasive. Consequently, the abrogation did not affect the boundary regime: the alignment in the Shatt continued to run along the left bank save at the ports of Mohammara and Abadan where it ran in the middle and along the thalweg of the river. The territorial and boundary-related rights and obligations of both Iran and Iraq continued to exist in law and to bind the States.

(c) General conclusions

The conclusions which may be drawn regarding the specific issues of the boundary dispute are that before 1975 the boundary line in the Shatt sector was formed by the left-bank boundary, except for the sections opposite Mohammara and Abadan which were divided along the median line and thalweg respectively. Both parties were bound to observe this frontier which existed on the basis of a series of treaties and protocols, beginning

---

[98] Ibid., p. 679. See also above, text at nn. 22 and 23, in reference to the Afghan abrogation of the 1893 boundary treaty, and the statement of the British government to the Secretary-General of the UN: 26 Feb. 1965: Materials on Succession of States, (UN Leg. Series, ST/LEG/SER.B/14), pp. 186–7. See Wright in reference to the continuity of ceasefire lines (acting as international boundaries) upon the termination of the relevant treaty: 'The Termination and Suspension of Treaties', *AJIL* 61 (1967), p. 1000 at 1002.

[99] Hansard, 212 H.L. DEB. 5s. cols. 497–9, at col. 497, (13 Nov. 1958). See E. Lauterpacht, 'The Contemporary Practice of the United Kingdom in the Field of International Law: Survey and Comment, Part VII, 1958', in *ICLQ* 8 (1959) p. 193. See also the British statement of 13 Nov. 1962 in the seventeenth session of the Fourth Committee of the General Assembly protesting against Venezuela's unilateral decision to regard the boundary arbitral Award of 1899 (between the latter and British Guiana) as null and void: E. Lauterpacht, ibid., 1962, Part II, pp. 161–75, at p. 163, esp. 173.

with the Treaty of 1847 and ending with the Treaty of 1937. There was in principle and in strict legal terms no question or dispute regarding a median or thalweg boundary: Iran had claimed a mid-line/thalweg alignment but had over the years settled for a left-bank boundary. Her representations in favour of a median-line division were motivated by political considerations and had little, if any, support in law.[100] Similarly, the abrogation of the Treaty of 1937 was an act carried out primarily for political purposes, and had no legal consequences.

Nevertheless, it remains a prerogative of a sovereign State to *request* (as opposed to demand) coterminous States to consider the revision of an alignment which may appear to be less than satisfactory to herself, or to all or any one of them. Boundaries may not be altered *unilaterally*: but there is no objection to agree mutual revision. It follows therefore that it was perfectly lawful for Iran to have approached Iraq for a revision of the boundary in the Shatt sector, not on the basis of legal obligation, but on political expediency, goodwill and/or reciprocity.[101] At the same time, it was open to Iraq to accept or reject the overtures made by Iran; Iraq's insistence on the left-bank boundary was, under the circumstances, not invalid. In the event, however, Iraq accepted a modification in the frontier and thereby changed the status of the waters of the Shatt. The following section attempts to analyse the post-1975 status of the boundary regime.

II THE LEGAL REGIME OF THE BOUNDARY AFTER 1975

The location of the boundary in the Shatt region changed radically after the conclusion of the Algiers Protocol and Baghdad Treaty of 1975. Article 2 of the Protocol Concerning the Delimitation of the River Frontier stated clearly that the boundary ran along the thalweg, 'i.e. the median line of the main navigable channel at the lowest navigable level', and accordingly there were no legal, as opposed to technical, problems in appreciating either the location or status of the alignment between the two States thereafter. Legal problems, however, were created in September 1980 when the government of Iraq abrogated the treaty on the basis of arguments which constituted a mix of legal and political considerations. One of these arguments was that the Shatt and the adjacent province of Ahwaz in Iran were in fact Iraqi territories, and that the Ottoman Empire had relinquished its sovereignty over them and ceded them to Iran.[102] It was also contended

---

[100] Cf. the observations made in the Conclusion to this work, below.
[101] See Conclusion, below.
[102] Ismael, *Iran and Iraq*, p. 26; Amin, 'The Iran–Iraq Conflict', p. 168.

that the majority of the inhabitants of Ahwaz were Arabs who had dominated the area ever since Islam had spread in the Mesopotamian region.[103]

Another argument put forward by Iraq in support of her abrogation was that Iran had herself 'terminated' the agreement 'by word and deed' prior to Iraq's more formal abrogation. The line of reasoning here was that Iran had secured the thalweg boundary in the Shatt, a cession of considerable importance to her, by agreeing to desist from fomenting, provoking, or aiding the Kurdish rebellion in Iraq. It was contended that Iran's guarantee regarding the Kurdish insurgency was in the nature of a *quid pro quo* in respect of the cession of the thalweg line extended by Iraq. The latter argued that Iran had disregarded this obligation and provided Kurdish rebels with the facility of using parts of Iranian territory as bases for operations against the national integrity and internal security of Iraq.[104] It was alleged that Iran's leaders were trying to export the Iranian revolution to Iraq. Article 3 of the Baghdad Treaty, it may be noted, provides that the parties 'undertake to exercise strict and effective permanent control over the frontier in order to put an end to any infiltration of a subversive nature from any source on the basis of and in accordance with the provisions of the Protocol [and annexe] concerning frontier security . . . '. Iraq concluded: 'The elements of the 1975 agreement constituted an indivisible whole, a violation of one aspect rendered the entire treaty null and void.'[105]

These representatives may be analysed on two levels. First, it is true that the inhabitants of the region are Arabs, and there is evidence to support the claim that the Shatt and adjacent territories had, at a certain epoch in history, been under the control of the Ottoman Empire. Nonetheless, as the government of Iraq has itself admitted, the lands were ceded to Persia, and a latter-day examination of the validity or otherwise of a transfer of title to territory which (*a*) took place over a century ago; and (*b*) was accepted as a valid transfer by the contracting parties at that time, is precluded in principle. The point, which has been explained and emphasized in

---

[103] Ismael, *Iran and Iraq*, p. 26. See also, *A Review of the Imposed War*, Legal Department, Ministry of Foreign Affairs, Iran 1983, pp. xvii–xviii, xx, 5, 77, 92–120; Akhtar, 'The Iraqi-Iranian Dispute over the Shatt-al-Arab', *Pakistan Horizon*, 22 (1969), p. 213, at 216, 217–18.

[104] See Iraqi letters to President, Security Council, 21 May 1980: A/35/268; 20 June 1980: S/14020; 22 and 24 Sept. 1980: S/14191, S/14192; 25 Nov. 1980 (with Annexes): S/14272; The Iraqi-Iranian Dispute, Ministry of Foreign Affairs, Iraq, p. 4; Iraqi Ministry of Foreign Affairs to Iranian Embassy, Baghdad, 17 Sept. 1980: Annexe to letter of 25 Nov. 1980: S/14272. Cf. Iranian claims of Iraqi subversion: letters to President, Security Council: 23 July 1980, S/14070; 1 Oct. 1980: S/14206 and 10 Nov. 1980 (with Annexe: Iranian Ministry of Foreign Affairs to government of Iraq): S/14249. Yearbook of the United Nations, 34 (1980) p. 318–19. See generally, Al-Mukhtar, 'The Iraqi Position', in Dessouki (ed.), *The Iraq–Iran War: Issues of Conflict and Prospects for Settlement* (Princeton, 1981), p. 16.

[105] Ismael, *Iran and Iraq*, p. 26.

a preceding section of this work,[106] is that the law does not in principle look favourably upon a re-examination of well-settled incidents of territorial attribution and boundary allocation; and it will not hence be necessary here to analyse the legal implications of the Iraqi representations in greater detail. It may, at any rate, be added that the question of ethnicity of the disputed regions is largely irrelevant to the status of both the territorial and boundary regimes in view of the clear provisions of the Treaties of 1847, 1913–14, and 1937 which attributed the territories on the left bank of the Shatt to exclusive Persian control and jurisdiction. Similarly, although Iraq's argument to the effect that the Shatt has historically been Iraqi territory is, in principle, correct, her claim has to be seen in light of the fact that over a period of more than half a century, Iraq and her predecessors had ceded progressively greater parts of, and control over, the river to Iran. In 1913–14, she ceded half the breadth of the river opposite Mohammara, and a cession along the thalweg line was made in respect of Abadan in 1937. Ultimately, the whole river was divided along the thalweg in 1975. The Baghdad Treaty of 1975, which constitutes, in fact, the latest development in a history of receding Iraqi control over the Shatt, cannot be adjudged as invalid merely on the ground that it establishes the thalweg and not the left bank as boundary. Iraq, as the lawful sovereign of the river, had, in principle, the legal right to dispose of any degree of territorial or jurisdictional control over the river to Iran, the party who was ready and willing to accept such transfer of control and title. The previous status of the river, not unlike the earlier status of the adjacent Arab-inhabited regions, cannot by itself invalidate or vitiate the Baghdad Treaty of 1975; it became, in fact, an irrelevance to the general question of the status and location of the boundary once the Baghdad Treaty of 1975 had been concluded.[107]

The question which has to be approached next is whether Iraq was legally justified in abrogating the treaty, the provisions of which had not been observed and respected by Iran. The burden of Iraq's grievance is that the abrogation of the treaty had only the appearance of being unilateral, and that the treaty was effectively a dead letter at the time of its abrogation by the government of Iraq in September 1980. Iran was obliged not to aid the Kurdish insurgency in Iraq, a matter of central importance to her, and, having transgressed Article 3, she had forfeited the right to expect Iraq to continue to observe those provisions which placed obligations upon her. The Baghdad Treaty of 1975 had, as it were, ceased to be the basis on which the boundary regime between the two States rested.

On the fact of it, there appears to be some truth in Iraq's general representations. For one thing, it is true that Article 3 of the Baghdad Treaty

---

[106] Above, sect. I.1.
[107] See below, regarding recognition.

did have the character of *quid pro quo*, in the absence of which it is doubtful whether Iraq would have agreed to a thalweg boundary. The Kurdish revolt had proved to be a source of considerable disquiet in Iraq and the costs of mounting counter-insurgency operations, in terms of men and *matériel*, were high.[108] She had hoped to gain peace by destroying the insurgents' sources of supply and succour, and with a view to securing this objective had agreed to meet one of Iran's most valued claims: a thalweg boundary in the Shatt. The latter agreed to cease aiding the insurgency and the outcome was seen in Article 2, which effectively provided for a thalweg boundary, and Article 3, which contained a general obligation on both parties to desist from subversive activities against each other.[109]

In any case, the importance which the two parties ascribed to these articles is reflected in Article 4 of the treaty, which stated:

The High Contracting Parties confirm that the provisions of the three Protocols and the Annexes thereto,[110] referred to in articles 1, 2 and 3 above and attached to this Treaty as an integral part thereof shall be final and permanent. They shall not be infringed under any circumstances and shall constitute the indivisible elements of an overall settlement. Accordingly, a breach of any of the components of this over-all settlement shall clearly be incompatible with the spirit of the Algiers [Protocol].

The Algiers Protocol or Joint Communiqué, of 6 March 1975 provides similar clues. Paragraph 2 of the Protocol provides that the two contracting parties have decided to delimit their river frontiers along the thalweg line, and accordingly in Paragraph 3 the parties committed themselves, *inter alia* to exercising a strict and effective control over their frontiers with a view to the complete cessation of all subversive infiltration from either side. The two parties also agreed in Paragraph 4 to consider the arrangements referred to above as indivisible elements of an overall settlement. '[A]ccordingly', the Protocol stated, 'a breach of any of its component parts would clearly be incompatible with the spirit of the Algiers Agreement.'

It is clear, therefore, that there is a strong link between Articles 2, 3, and 4 of the Baghdad Treaty of 1975 and that they together constitute the core of the arrangements embodied in it. It may be argued, therefore, that any infringement of the obligation 'to put an end to any infiltration of a sub-

---

[108] Al-Mukhtar, 'The Iraqi Position', p. 16; Pipes, 'A Border Adrift', p. 20; Hunseler, 'The Historical Antecedents of the Shatt al Arab Dispute', in El-Azhary (ed.), *The Iran–Iraq War*, pp. 18–19.

[109] Clearly, the obligation to desist from subversive activity had to be a mutual one.

[110] The three protocols attached to the Baghdad Treaty were: The Protocol concerning the Delimitation of the River Frontier between Iran and Iraq, the Protocol concerning the Redemarcation of the Land Frontier between Iran and Iraq; and the Protocol concerning Security on the Frontier between Iran and Iraq.

versive nature from any source' destroyed the basis of the understanding on which Iraq had agreed to a thalweg line in the Shatt. On this view of the matter, one aspect of the problem can be studied by reference to a question of fact, namely whether Iran did in fact give aid to the Kurdish insurgents or carry out any other acts which constituted infiltration of a subversive nature. If, on the one hand, evidence cannot be adduced to support the claim that Iran gave aid to the Kurdish insurgency, it would be clear that Iraq's accusations were unfounded and her principal argument in the case for abrogation would fail. If, on the other hand, it can be established that Iran had indeed infringed Article 3, it will have to be seen whether such infringement had any legal effects upon the boundary regime and, if so, what these legal effects are.

To begin with, the law as it stands is that a material breach of a bilateral treaty invests the other state with a right either to terminate or to suspend the agreement in whole or in part.[111] Article 60 of the Vienna Convention, which may be perceived as being declaratory of the law on the matter, defines, in paragraph 3, a material breach as consisting, *inter alia*, of 'the violation of a provision essential to the accomplishment of the object or purpose of the treaty'. There can be little doubt that Article 1, 2, 3, and 4 of the Baghdad Treaty fall within this class. The proposition, however, that Iraq therefore has the right to terminate the treaty has, on this view of the matter, to be seen in light of the following considerations.

First, reference may be made to the text of Article 4. It provides, *inter alia*, that 'a breach of any of the components of this overall settlement shall clearly be incompatible with the spirit of the Algiers agreement'. However, neither Article 4 nor the Algiers Protocol of 1975 defines precisely the meaning of the 'spirit' of this agreement. While it is clear that it is an indirect reference to the *quid pro quo* character of the treaty, it is equally clear that the phrase is inconclusive and vague in substance. The important point is that it fails to state the precise legal position of the parties in the event of a breach of any of the 'components' of the Baghdad Treaty, that is whether the Baghdad Treaty will be regarded as terminated *ipso facto*, or whether the innocent party will thereafter have, at its option, the right either to terminate or to suspend the treaty in whole or in part. Moreover, it is clear that the parties contemplated the possibility of infringement of the said articles but were content to leave the resultant situation unclarified. In

---

[111] McNair, *The Law of Treaties* (Oxford, 1961), pp. 539–71; Sinha, *Unilateral Denunciation of Treaty*; Nahlik, 'The Grounds of Invalidity and Termination of Treaties', *AJIL* 65 p. 736; draft Article 20, 2nd Waldock Report, 1963, *YILC*, 1963, ii. 72–7; Harvard draft Article 27 on the Law of Treaties, *AJIL* 29 (1935), Supplement, pp. 1077–96; Garner and Jobst, 'The Unilateral Denunciation of Treaties by one Party Because of Alleged Non-Performance of Another Party or Parties), ibid., 29 (1935), p. 569, in reference mainly to the German attempts to terminate her obligations under Part v of the Treaty of Versailles. Cf. Brierly, *The Law of Nations*, pp. 327–8.

view of the importance of these legal alternatives to both States, their omission suggests that at the time of the negotiations both Iraq and Iran had agreed not to adopt them in Article 4. In other words, the failure, on the one hand, to state the precise legal position of the parties and the boundary regime in the event of infringement, and the inclusion, on the other, of a reference to the 'spirit of the Algiers Agreement' indicates that the parties did not admit the right of unilateral abrogation of the Baghdad Treaty: *expressio unius est exclusio alterius*.

This view, secondly is supported by the fact that Article 5 provides: 'In keeping with the inviolability of the frontiers of the two States and strict respect for their territorial integrity, the High Contracting Parties confirm that the course of their land and river frontiers shall be inviolable, permanent and final.' This article, importantly, appears immediately after Article 4, which, it is submitted, had the effect of entrenching Articles 1, 2, and 3 in the Baghdad Treaty. The clear reference to permanence and finality of the land and river frontiers can in one sense be regarded as a clarification of the stipulations contained in Article 4, namely that nothing in Article 4 should be interpreted as having the effect of rendering the boundary void or voidable or terminable for any reason whatever. Article 6(1) provides that in 'the event of a dispute regarding the interpretation or implementation of this Treaty, the three Protocols or the annexes thereto, any solution to such a dispute shall strictly respect the *course* of the Iraqi-Iranian frontier . . . and shall take into account the need to maintain security on the Iraqi-Iranian frontier in accordance with article 3 . . . .'.[112] Hence, it is clear that the parties henceforth can, in an issue which involves the interpretation or implementation of the Baghdad agreements, dispute or question only the *location* of the frontier, namely the exact or technical determination of the median line in the thalweg, and cannot question the legal status of the regime. In other words, they are precluded from raising any issue which involves questions of the fundamental validity of the general boundary regime. Clearly, Iraq's abrogation has provoked a series of legal problems which relate essentially to the latter position. Furthermore, Article 6 goes on to set out the procedure which the parties are required to adopt in the event of a failure of bilateral negotiations, that is the processes of mediation (Article 6(3)) and of arbitration (Articles 6(4), (5), and (6)). Evidently, the parties attached great importance to the resolution of the more technical problems regarding the location of the line in the thalweg and were antipathetic to leaving these issues unresolved. Accordingly, it appears inconceivable that the parties would agree to contemplate the possibility of unilateral abrogation of the treaty, an abrogation which would serve to heighten rather than reduce the legal and

[112] Emphasis added.

political complications and uncertainty following infringements of Articles 1, 2, or 3.

Finally, and this point is of some significance, reference may be made to that section of this analysis which examined the matter of the unilateral abrogation of boundaries, and to the conclusions drawn therefrom.[113] The function of a boundary treaty is to define with relative precision the territorial limits within which the contracting parties may exercise their sovereign powers of control and jurisdiction, and once this has been done, the States acquire real and permanent territorial rights independent, to some extent and in certain circumstances of the treaty in question. Thus Article 70 of the Vienna Convention on the Law of Treaties provides that in the absence of an agreement to the contrary, the termination of a treaty 'does not affect any right, obligation or legal situation of the parties created through the execution of the treaty prior to its termination'.[114] Furthermore the International Law Commission, in its Commentary to draft article 57, which subsequently appeared as the definitive Article 60 of the Vienna Convention, cautioned against the termination or suspension of a treaty on the basis of mere allegations of a material breach of the provisions thereof.[115] This, in conjunction with Article 65, would require a State to exercise extreme restraint before deciding to abrogate a treaty.

The conclusion, therefore, is that notwithstanding Iran's alleged actions in promoting the Kurdish insurgency in Iraq, the latter had, in view of all the circumstances of the case no right to abrogate the Baghdad Treaty of 1975. It follows that the boundary in the Shatt continued in law to run along the thalweg.

III WAR AND THE BAGHDAD TREATY OF 1975

The hostilities which broke out between Iran and Iraq in September 1980 are still continuing and have succeeded in adding a new dimension to the boundary problem. The factual political situation, as opposed to a legal

---

[113] Above, pp. 85–93.
[114] Also see Introductory Note to Chapter 5 in *Restatement of the Law: Foreign Relations Law of the United States*, 2nd edn., American Law Institute (St Paul, 1965), p. 476.
[115] *YILC*, 1966, ii. 254–5. Articles 65 and 66 of the Convention provide 'procedural safeguards against the possibility that the nullity, termination or suspension of the operation of a treaty may be arbitrarily asserted as a mere pretext for getting rid of an inconvenient obligation': Commentary to draft article 62 in ibid., p. 262. See also draft articles 18–20 of the Second Report by Fitzmaurice wherein he leaned heavily in favour of a cautious approach to the question of termination of treaties on the grounds of a fundamental breach: ibid., 1957, ii. 52–6; and Harvard draft article 27, and commentary, loc. cit. n. 111 above, p. 1077, 1089, 1091–2.

one, prevailing in the Shatt is relatively easy to describe. The Shatt is closed to navigation and parts of both banks are under the control of either Iraq or Iran. Control of the river, it may be reasonable to presume, fluctuates in proportion to the degree of power either of the States can exercise against the other at any given time. The legal position, however, is, relatively speaking, more complex, and the material question here is whether the war has in law affected the status of the territory in the borderlands or the location of the 1975 line. This question can be approached in two forms: first, whether the Iran–Iraq war has had in principle any effect or effects on the Baghdad Treaty; and second, whether the war has invested either of the belligerents with the right to make changes in and modifications to the frontier. Both levels of investigation, however, are interrelated and the division is primarily one of convenience.

The first issue can be understood in light of the problem relative to the question whether the outbreak of hostilities between States abrogates bilateral treaties existing between them. The earlier view, held by jurists and States alike, was that all treaties were *ipso facto* abrogated upon the occurrence of war between States.[116] The consensus of opinion today is more sophisticated. It is generally agreed that the universal abrogation of treaties between belligerents has no place either in the law or in the practice of States. The continuation or abrogation of treaties depends not only upon the intention of the contracting States, but upon the nature and content of the treaties as well. It is clear that multilateral treaties and bilateral agreements dealing, for example, with the conduct of war will not become inoperative on account of the outbreak of hostilities between the co-signatories; but this aspect of the matter is of little or no concern to this study. The point relevant here is that boundary agreements are recognized as belonging to that category of treaties which are not annulled upon the occurrence of war between two or more States.[117] Although a frontier

---

[116] For commentaries on the law see McNair, *Law of Treaties*, pp. 695–728; and 'The Functions and Differing Legal Character of Treaties' *BYIL*, 11 (1930), pp. 100, 101–5; R. Rank, 'Modern War and the Validity of Treaties', *Cornell Law Quarterly*, 38 (1952–3) pp. 321–55; O'Connell, *International Law* 268–71; La Pradelle, 'The Effect of War on Private Treaties', *International Law Quarterly*, 2 (1948), p. 555; Hurst, 'The Effect of War on Treaties, *BYIL*, 2 (1921–2) pp. 37–47; Harvard Draft Article 35, *AJIL* 29 (1935, Supplement), pp. 1183–1204; Verzijl, *International Law*, vi (1973), pp. 371–91; Hackworth, *Digest of International Law* (Washington, DC, 1943, v., 377–90; Whiteman, *A Digest of International Law*, (Washington, 1970), xiv. 490–510; Delbrück, 'Effect of War on Treaties' in Bernhardt (ed.), *Encyclopaedia of Public International Law* (Instalment 4 (Amsterdam, 1982), pp. 310–15); Fitzmaurice, 'The Contribution of the Institute of International Law to the Development of International Law', *Receuil des Cours*, 138 (1973-I), pp. 235–6.

[117] McNair, *Law of Treaties*, p. 705; Verzijl, *International Law* pp. 371–2; Wheaton, *International Law*, pp. 504–6; Moore, *A Digest of International Law*, v. 377–86; Hall, *International Law*, pp. 453, 456–7; Westlake, *International Law*, Part II: 'War' (Cambridge, 1907), p. 30; Oppenheim, *International Law*, Lauterpacht, 7th edn., London, 1952, ii. 302–6; Coleman Phillipson, *Termination of War and Treaties of Peace*, (New York, 1916), pp. 250–4, 261–7.

agreement is deemed to be 'suspended' in certain respects for the duration of the war, it remains valid and the frontier continues to mark the limits of true sovereignty until changed by a peace or other treaty. The importance of the continuation in law of boundaries and boundary treaties during hostilities was acknowledged by Sir Robert Phillimore who, in his treatise on international law, observed that a treaty which contained a final adjustment of a particular question, such as the fixing of a disputed boundary, did not lapse at the commencement of hostilities.[118]

There is a singular lack of substantial international jurisprudence relating to the question of the effect of war on boundary or territorial treaties. However, in the *Jaworzina* Advisory Opinion,[119] the Permanent Court remarked *obiter* that when, as a result of the European Great War and the dissolution of the Austro-Hungarian Empire, Poland and Czechoslovakia were re-established as independent States, their frontiers were, generally speaking, indicated by historical and ethnological factors which 'pointed naturally' to the former frontier between Galacia and Hungary. 'With the exception', it said, 'of certain disputed sectors . . . this frontier seems, indeed, to have been adopted by the two States from the very outset as being the natural outcome of these circumstances.'[120]

In the Anglo-American dispute in respect of fisheries along the North Atlantic coast, Britain argued, *inter alia*, that whatever rights and liberties the United States enjoyed by virtue of the Treaty of 1783 in respect of fisheries along the coasts of Newfoundland had been terminated as a result of the War of 1812.[121] The United States contended that these rights were permanent by virtue of the nature of the treaty in question and could not therefore be abrogated.[122] In a letter to Lord Bathurst, the British Secretary of State for War and the Colonies, Mr John Quincy Adams, the American envoy in Britain, reasoned, by way of analogy, that the treaty of 1783 also contained provisions relative to the boundaries of the United States.[123] He argued that if Britain were to declare that the frontier line could not now be observed,

is it not obvious that the answer would have been that the United States needed no

---

[118] *Commentaries upon International Law* (London, 1873: 2nd edn.), iii. 796. See also Vattel, *The Law of Nations*, Book II, Ch. 12, No. 192, p. 208.

[119] PCIJ, Series B. No. 8 (1923).

[120] Ibid., p. 20.

[121] *Case of Great Britain, Proceedings in the North Atlantic Coast Fisheries* arbitration, Washington, 1912, Vol. 4, pp. 43–4; and *Case of the United States*, ibid., i. 14–31.

[122] *Case of the United States*, ibid. i. 14–31. See also the *Oral Argument* of Mr Turner, Counsel of the United States, in *Oral Arguments*, ix. 493–507, where a right of servitude was claimed. For British reply, see Sir William Robson, *Oral Arguments*, xi. 1655–1721.

[123] Letter of 25 Sept. 1815, *Appendix to the Case of the United States*, (Part I), ii. 268–73. See also Adams to Monroe, 19 Sept. 1815, p. 266; and Adams to Castlereagh, 22 Jan. 1816, pp. 279–84.

new acknowledgement of their independence, nor any new grant of a boundary line?—that if . . . the boundary line [was to be] curtailed, it could only be by their own acts of renunciation, or of cession, and not by the declaration of the intentions of another Government?'[124]

The dispute came before the Permanent Court of Arbitration at the Hague in 1910. The court failed to give any detailed comments on the effect of war on treaties in its examination of the case, namely the *North Atlantic Coast Fisheries* arbitration,[125] and confined itself to the observation: 'International law in its modern development recognises that a great number of Treaty obligations are not annulled by war, but at most suspended by it . . .'.[126]

The Supreme Court of the United States has had occasion to review the question of the effect of war on treaties. In *Society for the Propagation of the Gospel* v. *New Haven and Wheeler* (1823),[127] the court was concerned with the proprietary rights of a British corporation situate in Vermont. It was argued that (Articles 6 and 9 of) the Anglo-American Treaty of November 1794 (the Jay Treaty) protected such rights and that the War of 1812 had not abrogated the said treaty. In the course of its judgment the court observed that it was true that certain treaties, on account of their object and import, were annulled by war. It added that where treaties contemplate a permanent arrangement of territorial and other national rights, it would be against every principle of just interpretation to hold them extinguished by the event of war. 'If such', it held, 'were the law, even the Treaty of 1783, so far as it fixed our limits, and acknowledged our independence, would be gone, and we should have had again to struggle for both upon original revolutionary principles. Such a construction was never asserted, and would be so monstrous as to supersede all reasoning.'[128]

In *State* v. *Reardon*[129] the question before the Supreme Court was whether German citizens could inherit property in the United States as provided in Article 14 of the US–Prussian Treaty of 1828. The State of Kansas argued that the treaty had become inoperative on account, *inter alia*, of the Great War between Germany and the US. In an *obiter* passage the court observed: 'It is too clear for controversy that not all treaties are annulled by a state of war. A treaty which establishes a permanent status—

---

[124] Letter of 25 Sept. 1815, ibid., pp. 271–2. In his reply to Mr Adams, Lord Bathurst conceded that, 'It is by no means unusual for treaties containing recognitions and acknowledgements of title, in the nature of permanent obligations to contain . . . grants of privileges liable to revocation. The treaty of 1783 . . . contained provisions of different characters—some of their own nature irrevocable . . .': Letter of 30 Oct. 1815, *Appendix*, ibid., p. 275.
[125] 11 *RIAA* p. 173.
[126] Ibid., p. 181.
[127] 8 Wheaton 464.
[128] Ibid., p. 494.
[129] 120 Kansas 614; 245 Pacific Reporter 158.

such for instance as one fixing a boundary—plainly is not intended to be affected, and is not affected by war.'[130]

The theory behind this rule is that the conclusion of a boundary treaty results in the mutual conveyance and acquisition of territorial and boundary-related rights, the enjoyment of which ceases thereafter to exist exclusively on the bases or the continuance of the boundary treaty alone. The rights subsist on the basis of the rationale that a boundary treaty allocates territory to either side in a permanent and conclusive manner and neither State can be allowed to suffer a diminution of territory on account merely of the occurrence of war between the parties. Effectively, therefore, as the Supreme Court of Canada said in *Francis* v. *The Queen*,[131] treaties dealing, *inter alia*, with the recognition of independence and the establishment of boundaries are deemed executed and the treaty becomes a muniment or evidence of the political or proprietary title.[132] While he acknowledged the fact that it was the entire set of acquired rights flowing from the treaties which was permanent, Sir Cecil Hurst emphasized the point that boundary treaties 'cease to be in force, i.e. they are no longer operative, from the moment when the arrangements which they contemplate are carried into effect'.[133] With respect, it may be said that although the views are in substance correct, less emphasis should be given to the view that the treaties cease to be in force, or that they are no longer operative *once carried into effect*. It is submitted that the treaties remain in force and are operative, and that the transfer of territorial rights does not depend upon the execution or implementation of the treaty but upon the valid conclusion thereof. The nub of the matter is that territorial and boundary related rights stand transferred to either of the States and exist *independently but on the basis of the treaty*. Issue may also be taken with the term 'suspension

---

[130] Ibid., p. 159 (Pacific Reporter). In *Techt* v. *Hughes* (229 NY 222; 128 North Eastern Reporter 185) Judge Cardozo said: 'Treaties of alliance fall [in war]. Treaties of boundaries and cession, "dispositive" or "transitory" conventions survive': North Eastern Reporter, p. 191. In *Karnuth* v. *US* (279 US 231), Mr Justice Sutherland held: ' . . . there seems to be fairly common agreement that, at least, the following treaty obligations remain in force [in war] . . . treaties of "cession", boundary and the like . . . ', p. 236. In *Sutton* v. *Sutton* (1830) (1 R & M 663; 4 BILC 362) the British Court of Chancery was concerned with the continuance of proprietary rights of American and British citizens in Britain and the US, as protected under Art. 9 of the Jay Treaty and implemented in 37 Geo. 3, c.97. Counsel arguing in favour of title queried: 'Were the boundaries so fixed to cease to be the boundaries, the moment that hostilities broke out?': pp. 672-3. See also the *Trademark Registration* case, Federal Patent Court, Federal Republic of Germany, 27 Sept. 1967: 59 ILR (1980) p. 490, at 492.

[131] (1956) 3 DLR (2d) 641.

[132] Ibid., p. 647.

[133] Loc. cit. n. 116 above, p. 46. Wheaton wrote: 'The extinction of the treaties would no more extinguish the title to real property acquired or secured under their stipulations than the repeal of a municipal law affects rights of property vested under its provisions': *International Law*, p. 505. See also Keeley, 'The Effect of End of War on Pre-War Treaties between the Belligerents', *Transactions of the Grotius Society*, 12 (1927), pp. 7, 8.

of boundary treaties', which, it is submitted, is neither adequate nor comprehensive in nature. The fact of the matter is that a boundary treaty is but one medium out of several through which States mutually convey and acquire territorial and boundary-related rights and obligations, and that it is this body of rights and obligations which is paramount. International law recognizes that it is not essential for a frontier to exist exclusively on the basis of a treaty or protocol: a valid alignment may be founded on a set of municipal instruments; or upon a complex of official documentation including gazetteers, maps, and governmental records and archives; or upon the evidence of State activity, acquiescence and recognition; and/or on a combination of any two or more of these factors. The boundary, for example, between Vietnam and Cambodia is based not upon a treaty but upon the erstwhile internal provincial limits established by the French government in Indo-China between 1869 and 1942. Thus when Vietnam invaded Cambodia in 1979, there was no boundary treaty as such to suspend. It would, accordingly, be more appropriate, in terms of comprehensiveness, to speak of territorial and boundary-related rights rather than boundary treaties as such. As for suspension, it appears illogical to describe the legal situation as one of 'suspension' of boundary and territorial rights, one of which is the inviolability of and mutual respect for an alignment, the moment they are transgressed. There would, effectively, be no legal protection if the suspension of the right to secure frontiers could be effected by the violation of that very frontier: the *raison d'être* of rights and obligations between States would be defeated.[134] It would, on this view of the matter, be more accurate, therefore, to describe the legal situation as one of violation, whether mutual or otherwise, of territorial and boundary rights and obligations. To the extent, however, that the term 'suspension' is employed in juxtaposition to 'abrogation' of treaties during war, it is recognised that the term is not without merit.

Finally, it is noteworthy that the rule against abrogation of boundaries and boundary treaties is one of several different manifestations of the doctrine of finality and continuity of boundaries. Reference to this doctrine has been made in an earlier part of this study[135] and need not be repeated here. Suffice it to say that several incidents in the history of war and diplomacy give support to the principle in question. The western frontiers of Germany with France, Belgium, Luxembourg, and the Netherlands, which were settled on the basis of agreements concluded in the nineteenth century,[136] survived the war of 1939–45. Notwithstanding the fact that these

---

[134] On annexation of territory during or after the war, see below.
[135] Above, pp. 72–5.
[136] Treviranus, 'Boundary Settlements between Germany and her Western Neighbours after the Second World War', in Bernhardt (ed.), *Encyclopaedia*, Instalment 3 (1982), pp. 71–4 at 71.

States entertained major territorial claims against Germany, it was agreed in a joint communiqué issued by the Western Powers on 26 March 1949 to make only provisional 'minor modifications' along the Western frontiers of Germany.[137] Thus, the greater part of the frontier was maintained with a loss only of 52 square miles (135 square kilometres) of German territory.[138] It is of some interest that the minor adjustments to the frontier were 'justified [on grounds of] administrative necessities and by conditions affecting communications along Germany's western frontier':[139] no reference to the war was made in this regard. These rectifications were subsequently implemented by British and French Ordinances; and Germany concluded treaties confirming these alignments, albeit with further minor changes, with Belgium, Luxembourg, and the Netherlands.[140] There was a similar restoration of boundaries after the termination of the 1971 Indo-Pakistan war. Article 4(1) of the Simla Agreement of 3 July 1972 provided that the 'Indian and Pakistani forces shall be withdrawn to their side of the international border.'[141] The Uganda–Tanzanian boundary, which is also not based on any international agreement, was violated on account of the hostilities which broke out between the two States in early 1979. After Kampala, the capital of Uganda, fell to combined Tanzanian and Uganda Liberation Front troops in April 1979 the war ended;[142] and Uganda's boundary and territorial rights, especially those relating to the location of the alignment, were restored without change.

However, on a great many occasions in history, the more successful and powerful belligerents have been known to take the opportunity provided by the outcome of the war to effect major or minor changes in the status of the territories of the defeated State by way of annexation, transfer to third state, or simple boundary modification. It is this aspect of the matter, that

---

[137] Ibid, pp. 71–2. For text, see Whiteman, *International Law*, iii (1964) 398–99. The joint communiqué was preceded by a protocol concluded by the Western Powers in London.

[138] Joint Communiqué, op. cit. Treviranus, loc. cit, n. 136 above, p. 71. France gained only 6.9 kilometres of German territory. While Alsace-Lorraine, which had been transferred to her by virtue of the Versailles Peace Treaty, was retained, France relinquished the Saar in 1959.

[139] Joint Communiqué, paragraph 2; also see paragraph 7. See Article 1 of the Belgian–German Frontier Treaty of 24 Sept. 1956: 'With a view to establishing, between the two countries, a rational frontier line which will eliminate anomalies and thus conform to local conditions and meet the needs of traffic . . . '. For text, see Whiteman, *International Law*, iii. 420–2.

[140] British Ordinance No. 184, 23 Apr. 1949: text in Whiteman, *International Law*, iii. 399–401; French Ordinance, 23 Apr. 1949, ibid., pp. 401–2; Belgian–German frontier treaty of 24 Sept, 1956 in ibid., pp. 420–2. For reference to German–Dutch and German–Luxembourg Treaties of 1960 and 1959, see ibid., pp. 423–4. See Treviranus generally, pp. 72–4.

[141] For text, see *International Legal Materials*, 11 (1972), pp. 954–7. See also Joint Statement of Indo-Pakistan Officials on Implementation of the Simla Agreement, 30 Aug. 1972, paragraph 3 (ii) in ibid., pp. 958–62.

[142] Chatterjee, 'Some Legal Problems of Support Role in International Law: Tanzania and Uganda', *ICLQ*, 30 (1981), p. 755 at 756–77.

is whether or not the war has invested, or is capable of investing, either of the belligerent States with the right to effect changes (either unilateral or bilateral) in the boundary, which constitutes the second level of investigation. To an extent the issue can be resolved by reference to the rule stated above, namely that a boundary line is not abrogated *in toto* at the outbreak of hostilities and that it continues in law to govern the territorial limits of the parties. Accordingly, any unilateral act which, by way of annexation, transfer to third state, or boundary modification, deprives the defeated belligerent state of territory to which she had legal title, is invalid.

Approaching the issue on a more general plane, the threat or use of force by states as an instrument of national policy, or as a medium for the settlement of international disputes, is prohibited in international law,[143] and consequently unilateral changes made by a belligerent state in the status of territory during[144] or after the war by way of annexation or otherwise are unlawful.[145] The outlawry of war, which is a relatively recent development in the history of the law of nations, is based on various considerations, one of which is *ex iniuria jus non oritur*. This rule was reflected partly in the Stimson doctrine, that is the non-recognition of title acquired by conquest and the use of force. Latterly, several multilateral treaties and other instruments have not only condemned the use of force but have reiterated the importance of territorial integrity and the inviolability of frontiers. Article 2(4) of the Charter of the United Nations, which obliges Member States to refrain from the threat or use of force against the territorial integrity or political independence of States, is clearly of the first

---

[143] On the general outlawry of the use of force see Brownlie, *International Law and the Use of Force by States* (Oxford, 1963), pp. 66–122; Lauterpacht, Special Rapporteur, Report on the Law of Treaties, *YILC*, 1953, ii. 147–9; Waldock, ibid., 1963, ii. 51–2. Schwarzenberger, *International Law as Applied by International Courts and Tribunals*, ii: *The Law of Armed Conflict* (London, 1968), pp. 37–58, esp. pp. 50–8; de Aréchaga, 'General Course in International Law', *Recueil des Cours*, 159 (1978-I), pp. 86–92; Falk, 'The New States and International Legal Order', *Recueil des Cours*, 118 (1966-II), pp. 44–6; Jennings, *The Acquisition of Territory in International Law* (Manchester, 1963), pp. 52–67; Oppenheim, *International Law*, ii. 151–9, 177–97. See also article 9 of the Draft Declaration on the Rights and Duties of States, *YILC*, 1949, ii. 287–8. Cf. Castren, *The Present Law of War and Neutrality* (Helsinki, 1954), pp. 40–7, 50–6, esp. 56–7.

[144] Jennings, *The Acquisition of Territory*, p. 52; Schwarzenberger, *International Law*, pp. 166–73.

[145] Brownlie, *International Law and the Use of Force*, pp. 410–23; Jennings, *Acquisition of Territory*, pp. 52–68; Greig, *International Law* (London, 1976), pp. 160–1; Bowett, *Self-Defence in International Law* (Manchester, 1958), pp. 29–38; Garner, 'Non-Recognition of Illegal Territorial Annexation and Claims to Sovereignty', *AJIL* 30 (1936), pp. 679–88; Lauterpacht, op. cit. n. 143 above, p. 148; Kelsen, 'The Draft Declaration on Rights and Duties of States', *AJIL* 44 (1950), p. 259, at 272–4; Shihata, 'Destination Embargo of Arab Oil: Its Legality Under International Law', *AJIL* 68 (1974), pp. 591, at 598–608. Cf. Fitzmaurice, 'The Juridical Clauses of the Peace Treaties', *Recueil des Cours*, 73 (1948-II) p. 279; Briggs, 'Non-Recognition of Title by Conquest and Limitations on the Doctrine', *Proceedings of the American Society of International Law*, 34 (1940), pp. 80–2; O'Connell, *International Law*, p. 432.

importance.¹⁴⁶ The Charter of the Organization of American States, signed in Bogota in April 1948, provided, in Article 17, that the territory of a State is inviolable and that it could not be the object, even temporarily, of military occupation or of other measures of force taken by another State.¹⁴⁷ The Conference of the Heads of State and Governments of Non-Aligned Countries, assembled at Cairo in 1964, adopted a Declaration, Principle 5, Section 4 of which stipulated:

> States must abstain from all use or threat of force directed against the territorial integrity and political independence of other States; a situation brought about by the threat or use of force shall not be recognised and in particular the established frontiers of States shall be inviolable.¹⁴⁸

In 1970, the General Assembly of the United Nations adopted the Declaration on Principles of International Law Concerning Friendly Relations and Co-operation among States. Paragraph 4 of Article 1 provides:

> Every State has the duty to refrain from the threat or use of force to violate the existing international boundaries of another State or as a means of solving international disputes, including territorial disputes and problems concerning frontiers of States.¹⁴⁹

On 1 August 1975, the Conference on Security and Co-operation in Europe, attended by delegates from thirty-four European States and the United States of America, adopted the Final Act in Helsinki. Article 2 of Section 1 bound the States against the threat or use of force in their mutual and international relations, and Articles 3 and 4 obliged the States to respect the frontiers and territorial integrity of the participating States.¹⁵⁰

Finally, reference may be made to paragraph 10, Article 1 of the Declaration on Principles of International Law concerning Friendly Relations and

---

¹⁴⁶ For commentary, see Brownlie, 'The Use of Force in Self-defence', *BYIL*, 37 (1961), pp. 232–7. See also Article 1 of the General Treaty for the Renunciation of War, *United Kingdom Treaty Series*, 29 (1929), Cmd. 3410; and Article 10 of the Covenant of the League of Nations, *AJIL* 15 (1921, Supplement), p. 4.

¹⁴⁷ Text in *AJIL* 46 (1952, Supplement), p. 43. For other multilateral American agreements, see the Anti-War Treaty of Non-Aggression and Conciliation, 1933, Article 11 of the Convention on Rights and Duties of States, 1933. The Buenos Aires Declaration, 1936; The Lima Declaration, 1938. Second Meeting of the Ministers of Foreign Affairs of the American Republics, Habana, 1940; see Brownlie, *International Law and the Use of Force*, pp. 95–107; Whiteman, *International Law*, v (1965), pp. 874–6.

¹⁴⁸ For the text, see *Indian Journal of International Law*, 4 (1964), p. 599, at 609. See also Charter of the Organization of African Unity, Sections 3 and 5 of Article 3; and the 1964 Cairo Declaration: Brownlie, *Basic Documents on African Affairs* (Oxford, 1971), pp. 2–9 and 360–1 respectively.

¹⁴⁹ Annexe to Resolution 2625 (XXV) in *International Legal Materials*, 9 (1970), p. 1292; Brownlie, *Basic Documents in International Law* (Oxford, 1983: 3rd edn.) p. 35.

¹⁵⁰ *International Legal Materials*, 14 (1975), p. 1292. On the development of the principle of the inviolability of frontiers and the content of this principle in reference to the Helsinki Declaration, see Movchan, 'Problems of Boundaries and Security in the Helsinki Declaration', *Recueil des Cours*, 154 (1977-I) pp. 14–17; 18–27.

Sections 2 and 3 of Article 5 of the General Assembly Resolutions on the Definition of Aggression, adopted on 14 December 1974,[151] both of which stipulate in terms that the territory of a State cannot be the object of acquisition by another State resulting from the threat or use of force or from aggression.[152] Both articles, furthermore, stipulate that acquisition of territory in such circumstances will not be recognized as lawful.

It is clear that the weight of the opinions of writers and the legal materials is against any unilateral alteration of the status of a territory *durante bello* or following the termination of the war. Fine questions of lawful or unlawful use of force are of no legal consequence to the general principle.[153] It is to be noted that in the opinion of Professor Julius Stone there is no rule of law 'requiring (the) automatic withdrawal by a military occupant who lawfully entered in (the) course of self defence'.[154] In his commentary on the proceedings of the Special Committee regarding the question of the definition of aggression, Professor Stone has been less than precise regarding the *acquisition of title* to territory occupied in self-defence. Nevertheless, he has supported, on grounds of principle, the rejection of Article 8 of the Thirteen Power draft, which stipulated against any territorial acquisition irrespective of the nature of the measures of force used by the acquiring State. 'Such an unqualified rule', he added, 'would obviously involve the drastic, and in policy incomprehensible, departure from existing international law . . . '[155] It is submitted, with respect, that this view of the law is difficult to justify.

On this view of the matter, notwithstanding the fact that the war may well be the outcome of a legitimate use of force, as for example self-defence, *unilateral* changes in the status of a territory are to be regarded as unlawful. Certain anomalies in the law would present themselves if there were no provision in favour of universal disqualification. For one thing, the condition of mutual agreement and consent, given *expressis verbis* or otherwise, has always been regarded in contemporary international law as an essential feature in territorial arrangements and allocation between

---

[151] General Assembly Resolution 3314 (XXXIX), General Assembly Official Records, 29th Session, Supp. 31; *International Legal Materials*, 13 (1974), p. 710.

[152] While the former does not distinguish between the nature of the force employed, Article 5 of the latter Resolution is confined to the acquisition of territory by aggression. (On the significance of the question of lawful use of force and acquisition of territory, see below (main text).) The Six-Power draft of 1970 on the question of defining aggression proposed, *inter alia*, in draft article 4, that the diminishing of territory or altering of boundaries of a State by the use of illegal force constituted aggression: see UN Document A/AC.134/L.17, annexe to Report of the Special Committee, 25th Session, Supp. No. 19, A/8019, July–Aug. 1970. See also 1971 Draft (A/AC.134/L.32), Annexe II to Report, ibid., 26th Session, Supp. No. 19, A/8419, Feb.–Mar. 1971.

[153] Jennings, *Acquisition of Territory*, pp. 54–6. In respect of treaties and lawful use of force see below. See also Greig, *International Law*, pp. 895–6.

[154] Stone, *Conflict Through Consensus* (Baltimore, 1977), p. 59.

[155] Ibid., p. 62.

States. Unilateral changes, by definition, give no countenance to the wishes of the affected State and cannot, in principle, be accepted as valid. The mere fact that a State has exercised force in support of law cannot, on this view of the matter, be regarded as a licence to effect unilateral changes in the admitted status of the territory concerned. In his memorandum on the matter of Israel's right to develop new oil fields in Sinai and the Gulf of Suez, the Legal Adviser to the US Department of State, Mr Monroe Leigh, wrote, *inter alia*, that belligerent occupation rights were limited by the criteria related to the requirements of orderly government sufficient to meet the needs of military occupation. These limitations, he wrote, were consistent with, if not compelled by, the limited purposes for which force may be used under the Charter of the United Nations. 'It is difficult', he added, 'to justify a rule that the use of force in self-defence may, during any resulting occupation, give the occupant rights against the enemy sovereign not related to the original self-defence requirement or not required as concomitants of the occupation itself and the occupant's duties. A rule holding out the prospect of acquiring unrestricted access to and use of resources and raw materials, would constitute an incentive to territorial occupation by a country needing raw materials, and a disincentive to withdrawal.'[156] The Legal Adviser's comments are equally valid in respect of changes in title. There appears, therefore, to be no reason in general to grant greater legal importance to the fact of the legality of the use of force, used or threatened, as opposed to the fundamental requirement of mutuality in matters of territorial arrangements and allocation. Moreover, although the concept of self-defence is in principle capable of legal determination[157] the concept is not entirely free from controversy in terms of interpretation and application.[158] Apart from that, it is vulnerable to abuse

[156] *Digest of the United States' Practice in International Law* (1976), pp. 700–6. See also Report of the Special Committee (on the definition of aggression), 26th Session, op. cit. n. 152 above: 'No one could deny that territorial acquisition resulting from the unlawful use of force was illegal; a State could not annex the territory or part of the territory of another State in the exercise of its right of self-defence, a principle which had long been recognized': p. 10. Also see statement of Pakistan's representative Mr M. Mahmud, in this respect: A/C.6/ SR.1477, p. 2; Stone, *Conflict through Consensus* p. 64. Cf. Schwebel, 'What Weight to Conquest?' *AJIL* 64 (1970), pp. 346–7; and Jennings, *Acquisition of Territory*, who gives importance to the role of recognition by the international community exercising its will in a legislative or quasi-legislative capacity in respect of territorial changes effected by a State at the end of a war of self-defence: p. 56.
[157] Lauterpacht, *The Function of Law in the International Community* (Oxford, 1933), pp. 179–82; Brownlie, 'The Use of Force in Self-Defence', pp. 195, 207–9; Bowett, *Self-Defence*, *passim*; Greig, *International Law*, pp. 876–900, esp. 877, 883–7, 892–7.
[158] See references cited above. The main differences of opinion involve questions of anticipatory self-defence and armed attack. For varying interpretations see Waldock, 'The Regulation of the Use of Force by Individual States', *Recueil des Cours*, 81 (1952-II), pp. 497–98; Brownlie, 'The Use of Force in Self-Defence', pp. 242–4; and *International Law and the Use of Force*, pp. 257–61, 269–75, 275–80; Bowett, *Self-Defence*, pp. 184–93; and 'Reprisals Involving Recourse to Armed Force', *AJIL* 66 (1972), p. 4; Higgins, *The Development of*

The Legal Analysis

and, as Professor Charles De Visscher said, 'its exercise in concrete cases always runs into contradictions, owing either to opposing political views or to the uncertainties surrounding the conditions of fact that justify its use'.[159] In view of the general outlawry of the use of force, it is not uncom-

International Law through the Political Organs of the United Nations (London, 1963), pp. 197–210; Kelsen, *Principles of International Law* 2nd edn., New York, 1966, pp. 62–3, 70–2; Stone, *Conflict through Consensus*, pp. 47–50; Greig, *International Law*, p. 893; O'Connell, *International Law*, pp. 316–18; Farer, 'Law and War', in Black and Falk (eds.), *The Future of International Legal Order* (Princeton, 1971), iii. 30–6, (regarding nuclear warfare). See also the *Questionnaire and Replies on Some Aspects of the Principle of Self-Defence and the Legality of the Use of Force*, Part III, International Law Association proceedings on the UN Charter, Report of the 48th Session (New York, 1958), pp. 593–621. On whether self-defence includes rights of intervention, self-help, reprisals, etc. see Brownlie, *International Law and the Use of Force*, pp. 265–8, 272–5, 430, 433–6; Bowett, *Self-Defence*, p. 29 *et seq*; Kelsen, *International Law*, pp. 73–80; Greig, *International Law*, pp. 878–83; Dugard, 'The OAU and Colonialism: An Inquiry into the Plea of Self-Defence as a Justification for the Use of Force in the Eradication of Colonialism', *ICLQ* 16 (1967), p. 157; Fonteyne, 'Forcible Self-Help by States to Protect Human Rights', in Lillich (ed.), *Humanitarian Intervention and the United Nations* (Charlottesville, 1973), pp. 209–16 (regarding the differing views of members of the Special Committee on Principles of International Law Concerning Friendly Relations . . .). See British Prime Minister's Statement in Parliament regarding British intervention in the Suez and subsequent debate: Hansard, 588. H.C. DEB. 5s Cols. 1446–1572 (30 Oct. 1956); E Lauterpacht, 'Contemporary Practice of the U.K. in the Field of International Law, III', *ICLQ* 6 (1957), pp. 325–7; Israeli Representative Herzog's Statement in the Security Council following the Entebbe Raid, 9 July 1976: UN Doc. No. S/PV.1939, 9 July 1976, *International Legal Materials*, 15 (1976), pp. 1228–31; and Statement of Acting Secretary of State Rush to Professor Rostow, 29 May 1974 regarding the difference between self-defence and reprisals: *Digest of US Practice in International Law*, 1974, p. 700.

[159] *Theory and Reality in Public International Law*, (rev. edn. trans. P. E. Corbett) (Princeton, 1968), p. 121; Jennings, *Acquisition of Territory*, pp. 55–6, 64–5, 66–7, 69–87; Falk, 'The Legal Control of Force in the International Community' in Falk and Mendlovitz (eds.), *The Strategy of World Order*, ii: *International Law* (New York, 1966), p. 306; Kelsen, *International Law*, pp. 73–5; Stone, *Legal Controls of International Conflict* (New York, 1954), pp. 243–4. Major abuses of the plea of self-defence include: the German invasion of Norway and the USSR: see *International Military Tribunal (Nuremberg)*: Judgement and Sentences: 1 Oct. 1946, in *AJIL* 41 (1947), p. 172 at pp. 203–7 and 211–13; the Italian invasion of Ethiopia: see Report of the [Committee of the] Council of the League of Nations, 5 Oct. 1935, in *AJIL* 30 (1936, Supplement), p. 1: 'The Italian Government informed the Council that the warlike and aggressive spirit in Ethiopia had succeeded in imposing war against Italy . . . ', p. 15; and the American War in Vietnam: see Legal Memorandum of the Legal Adviser to the US Department of State, L. C. Meeker, 4 Mar. 1960: 'The Legality of US Participation in the Defence of Vietnam', in *AJIL* 60 (1966), pp. 565–85; and cf. Wright, 'Legal Aspects of the Vietnam Situation', ibid., 60, pp. 750–69. One of the difficulties regarding self-defence and aggression is the controversy regarding the 'priority principle' versus the universal approach. It featured in the proceedings of the 6th Committee of the General Assembly and the Special Committee commissioned to define aggression: see the Reports of the 25th to 28th Sessions (1970–3) of the Special Committee: No. 19, A/8019, July–Aug. 1970; No. 19, A/8419, Feb.–Mar. 1971, No. 19, A/8719, Jan.–Mar. 1972, No. 19, A/9019, Apr.–May 1973. The Western Powers initially opposed the priority principle inasmuch as 'it was often impossible to determine who had acted first . . . [A] minor first use of armed force might have been provoked or falsified as a pretext for massive retaliation . . . ': Ferencz, *Defining International Aggression, The Search for World Peace: A Documentary History and Analysis* (New York, 1975), ii. 31; Stone, *Conflict through Consensus*, pp. 44–7. See also 1970 Report of the 6th Committee to the General Assembly: General Assembly Official Records, 25th Session, A/. 8171, p. 4 (19 Nov. 1970).

mon today for both belligerents genuinely to claim and adduce evidence in support of a lawful use of force. Indeed, both Iran and Iraq claim to be acting out of self-defence.[160] Where territorial claims are the basis of the hostilities, it is not inconceivable that at times questions of self-defence may be intricately tied up with those of title to territory, with the result that a judicial or arbitral decision regarding self-defence will ultimately turn upon questions of title to territory. In other words, at times a tribunal may have to decide the central issue of title before it can rule on an issue of self-defence.[161] At any rate, the question of title to territory cannot, speaking in broad terms, be seen to be dependent upon a decision pertaining to whether or not a state has exercised force consistent with the principles of the Charter, but upon the more substantive issues of law and facts of the dispute in question.

Furthermore, if the law were to allow the unilateral acquisition of title to territory, provided only that the State in question used force consistent with the principles of the Charter, it would leave a way open for States either to characterize or disguise acts of aggression as those of self-defence with a view to the legitimization of their status in occupied territory. It is recognized, however, that the plea of self-defence cannot be understood on the basis of the *ipse dixit* of the claiming State, and that the veracity of such a plea is determined by reference to a set of precise legal criteria.[162] Nevertheless, given the inadequacies prevalent in the international legal order, exemplified by the tendency of *de facto* territorial situations to consolidate over a period of time and the absence of an agency for purposes of enforcement of international law in general or decisions of international tribunals in particular, a State may be tempted to employ this subterfuge for her adventures. Finally, it is the case that unilateral changes in boundaries and territories tend to exacerbate rather than resolve the fundamental problems between States and consequently generate further uncertainty and greater instability not only in the region but also in the system as a whole. A rule conducive to instability is to be deprecated.

---

[160] See Iraqi letters of 22 and 24 Sept. 1980 to the President of the Security Council: S/14191, S/14192 and Iranian President's letter to id., 1 Oct. 1980: S/14206.

[161] O'Connell writes that where the frontier violated is itself the object of dispute, measures taken by either side cannot be regarded as measures of self-defence within the meaning of Article 51: *International Law*, p. 319. See also Bowett, *Self-Defence*, pp. 34–8. Writing of the Goa invasion by India, Wright observes: '[I]f a State were free to occupy territory in the *de facto* possession of another State to which territory it believes it has legal title, attacks would be permissible in every boundary dispute, and the barriers by which the Charter seeks to protect territorial sovereignty would be broken down': 'The Goa Incident', *AJIL* 56 (1962), p. 623.

[162] Article 51 of the UN Charter provides that the inherent right of individual or collective self-defence comes into play if an *armed* attack occurs against a Member of the UN, and until the Security Council has taken measures necessary to maintain international peace and security. For commentary, see Brownlie, 'The Use of Force in Self-Defence', and Bowett, pp. 184–99.

The important point, hence, it that of mutuality regarding changes in the status of territory and the location of boundary alignments. It may, however, be argued that the dominant State, having won the war, is in a position to seek to extract consent for any agreement from the defeated State with the result that changes effected by a post-war frontier treaty arguably constitute unilateral measures. An argument along such lines takes the analysis into the field of essential validity of treaties, and, in particular, to that of coercion by States in the conclusion of treaties. It is clear that such an analysis lies outside the purview of this work. Nevertheless, in the interest of completeness, some observations in this regard are necessary. The legal issue here is whether a boundary treaty, concluded at the end of hostilities where one of the States is left in a position to dominate and extract territorial concessions from the other, (and does so) may be regarded as a valid agreement capable of creating and transferring legal title.

A preliminary answer to this question lies in Article 52 of the 1969 Vienna Convention on the Law of Treaties, which is declaratory of customary international law.[163] It provides: 'A treaty is void if its conclusion has been procured by the threat or use of force in violation of the principles of international law embodied in the Charter of the United Nations.' The emphasis here is on the legal nature of the use of force. Speaking in general terms, this implies that where the threat or use of force is lawful, the treaty concluded after the termination of hostilities cannot be challenged on the grounds of coercion.[164] Thus, Article 75 of the Vienna Convention stipulates that the provisions of the Convention are without prejudice to any obligation in relation to a treaty which may arise for an aggressor State in consequence of measures taken in conformity with the Charter of the United Nations with reference to that State's aggression. Similarly, the use of force in self-defence, as protected and provided in Article 51 of the Charter, will be legally relevant in any subsequent challenge to the treaty regime. These provisions in favour of the legitimate use of force are a logical outcome of the general outlawry of force employed as an instrument of national policy: they reflect a departure from the earlier position of the writers on this aspect of the law who sought, *inter alia*, to protect peace treaties in general from being challenged on the ground of coercion, but

---

[163] See generally, Commentary to the Final Draft Article 49, *YILC*, 1966, ii. 246–7; Lauterpacht, Special Rapporteur, Report on the Law of Treaties, *YILC*, 1953, ii. 147; Waldock, Special Rapporteur, ibid., Second Report, ibid., 1963, ii. 51–2; McNair, *Law of Treaties*, pp. 206–11; Brownlie, *International Law and the Use of Force*, pp. 404–5, 408–9; but he recommends the supervision of the Security Council, p. 408; Schwarzenberger, *International Law* pp. 736–40.

[164] Lauterpacht, op. cit., p. 150; Waldock, p. 52; Brownlie, *International Law and the Use of Force*, pp. 408–9; De Visscher, *Theory and Reality*, p. 254. Cf. Stone, *Legal Controls of International Conflict*, pp. xxxi–xxxiii; Grewe, 'Peace Treaties', in Bernhardt (ed.), *Encyclopaedia*, Instalment 4 (1982), p. 106: 'Whether the international legal order will be more disturbed than improved by the provision [of Article 52] is also in doubt.'

failed to distinguish between treaties concluded by a successful defending State and those dictated by a successful aggressor.[165] It is submitted that a simplistic recourse to Article 52 is unsatisfactory. Some of the difficulties mentioned earlier in respect of lawful use of force and unilateral allocation of territory have equal relevance here. Thus where there are competing claims to territory it may at times be difficult to determine, without going into questions of title, which of the belligerents did, as a matter of fact, use force consistent with principles of international law. A treaty concluded in circumstances where the validating criterion, that is the lawful nature of force, is obscure will at best be open to doubt and at worst vulnerable to challenge by the dissatisfied State at any unspecified time in the future. Depending, of course, on all the circumstances, a treaty affecting changes in the status of territory may constitute a garb of legitimacy adopted by the successful aggressor claiming the right of self-defence.

Second, although the proviso in favour of lawful use of force is based essentially on the thesis that '[a] State which tramples underfoot the fundamental norm of the present international legal order is fully responsible for its actions' and that the 'validity of such treaties is not affected by the fact that the treaty is applied as a sanction against the aggressor State',[166] there is, on this view of the matter, an underlying and unexpressed assumption that the State threatening or using force consistent with the principles of international law embodied in the Charter will elect to treat the defeated State in a just and fair manner. This is not necessarily true in every case. Without attempting to cast doubt on the validity of the series of peace treaties concluded in the period 1919–20, the experience of all the defeated belligerent States—Germany, Austria–Hungary, and the Balkan States—bears this fact out. The attitude of the dominant State is in fact dependent upon a host of political factors, only one of which is the fact that the force in question was lawfully employed. Clearly, an important factor influencing the attitude of such States will be the role played by territorial issues in the war between the parties.

---

[165] See Hall, *International Law*: ' . . . Unless a considerable degree of intimidation is allowed to be consistent with the validity of contracts, few treaties made at the end of a war or to avert one would be binding, and the conflicts of States would end only with the subjugation of one of the combatants or the utter exhaustion of both': p. 382; also see Wheaton, *International Law*, p. 503; Keeton, 'Extraterritoriality', *Recueil des Cours*, 72 (1948-I) pp. 350–2; Fitzmaurice, Special Rapporteur, Third Report on the Law of Treaties, *YILC*, 1958, ii. 38: ' . . . if peace is a paramount consideration, it must follow logically that peace may, in certain circumstances, have to take precedence for the time being over abstract justice . . . '; Castren, *War and Neutrality*, p. 135; Coleman Phillipson, *Termination of War*, pp. 162–3; cf. Brierly, *Law of Nations*: pp. 318–19; and Van Der Molen, *Symbolae Verzijl*: (The Hague, 1958): Illegal war cannot be legalized by a peace treaty to retain advantages accruing from such war, pp. 247–8. Generally, see Detter, 'The Problem of Unequal Treaties', *ICLQ* 15 (1966), p. 1069.

[166] Haraszti, 'Reflections on the Invalidity of Treaties', in Haraszti (ed.), *Questions of International Law* (Budapest, 1977), p. 59 at 67.

The difficulties attendant upon this approach emphasize the complexity of the question. In principle neither an aggressor nor a State which has taken action in self-defence has the *right* to obtain title as a consequence of the use of force. Hence, a defeated aggressor State, as authoritatively determined by the General Assembly, may nevertheless challenge a treaty which purports to acquire territory on the exclusive justification that the defending State used force consistently with international law. Clearly the plea of self-defence is not a licence to exact territorial concessions by treaty. The essential criterion in such cases is the requirement of some form of general recognition, such recognition historically normally involving a multilateral peace settlement not confined to the actual parties gaining or losing territory. In this connection, an act of recognition by the United Nations Organization of the new territorial settlement as a contribution to a just and durable peace without reference to questions of lawful or unlawful use of force may be regarded as being essential to the legal and political survival of the treaty itself. An *imprimatur* of the Security Council or an *ad hoc* international or regional Convention will constitute evidence of the reasonableness of the terms of the treaty and conclusive nature of the settlement. Professor (as he then was) Jennings gave great importance to recognition by the international community exerting its will in a legislative or quasi-legislative capacity in respect of territorial changes effected at the end of a war of self-defence.[167]

The merit of this solution is that it seeks to resolve, to some extent, difficulties connected with peace treaties. It is not improbable that pleas of self-defence may well be advanced by both States and that claims of coercion will be made in order to cast doubt on the validity of treaties concluded after the termination of hostilities. A treaty recognized by a body of States as representing a final settlement of all issues is less likely to be challenged in the future, and international recognition will make claims to self-defence irrelevant to the treaty regime.

Recapitulating briefly, it is to be observed that in a state of war between two (or more) States, boundary rights may be mutually transgressed, but not abrogated. Thus, war may affect the realities of the border situation but it cannot *ipso facto* modify the status of the territories on either side of it: it cannot affect either title to territory or the location of the frontier in the absence of an agreement between the States concluded after the termination of the armed conflict. Unilateral measures adopted by a State which affect the status of territory or location of the line either *durante bello* or after the end of the war are without legal effect and cannot create or transfer valid title. It follows that bilateral treaties involving general multilateral recognition are essential if territorial adjustments after a war are to be regarded as valid.

[167] Jennings, *The Acquisition of Territory*, p. 56.

In the light of these observations, it is clear that the rights created in favour of Iran and Iraq by virtue of the Baghdad Treaty of 1975 are being mutually transgressed on account of the war, but this has not affected title to territory on either side of the alignment, namely the thalweg in the Shatt. Unilateral measures adopted by either Iraq or Iran incorporating territory on either side of the thalweg boundary will not affect the territory allocated by the Baghdad Treaty. At the end of the war, and in the absence of an agreement to the contrary, the thalweg line will once again become operational as the international boundary between the parties. Both states will be free to conclude an agreement which either modifies the Baghdad Treaty of 1975 in terms of relocation of the frontier or reiterates the continuing validity of the said agreement, or to conclude no agreement regarding boundaries at all. Recognition of the peace treaty by the United Nations or a regional body of States will no doubt contribute towards the continued acceptance of the treaty by the parties as a conclusive and final settlement of the boundary questions and all outstanding issues.

Conclusion

A brief commentary on some of the general and specific principles of law elicited in the study will be in order. First, in reference to the question of the thalweg, the law as it stands is that there is no absolute rule in favour of the thalweg line wherever a navigable river separates two (or more) States. States are free in principle to adopt any alignment which is mutually acceptable to all the coterminous States. In the absence, however, of evidence to the contrary, the thalweg in a navigable river will be the dividing line. The rule, thus, is essentially a rebuttable presumption in favour of the thalweg and cannot be put any higher than that. Evidence of a line different from that of the thalweg may include boundary provisions in a treaty and acts signifying acquiescence and recognition. A rule of law which compels the delimitation of frontiers along the thalweg of navigable rivers would be quite impracticable. It would be capable of coming into conflict with situations sanctioned in boundary agreements, rules relative to acquiescence, and the historical evolution of frontiers. Moreover, while it would inhibit the freedom of States from seeking to adopt alignments of their own choosing, a rule of this kind has no merits in terms of either securing any higher ideals or alleviating more imperative problems between States.

Second, there is no principle of international law which justifies the unilateral abrogation of valid frontier agreements. Boundary treaties create real territorial rights which stand permanently transferred in favour of either State, and cannot be terminated either by unilateral abrogation or on ground of *rebus sic stantibus*. Although allegations of violations of the terms of a boundary treaty cannot in principle serve as grounds for its unilateral abrogation by one of the parties, the interpretation of the terms of the treaty will be relevant to a proper appreciation of the problem.

Third, war may affect, but cannot abrogate, either a boundary regime or a frontier agreement. It is preferable, on this view of the matter, not to speak of a 'suspension' of boundary treaties, but to refer simply to a transgression of boundary and territorial rights, whether mutual or otherwise. It follows that no title can in principle pass in favour of either party through occupation, annexation, or otherwise, either *durante bello* or subsequent to the termination of hostilities. The rationale behind this proposition of law is twofold. First, there are considerations relative to permanent territorial rights vested in either State by virtue of the 'dispositive' character of boundary agreements. This constitutes the more classical or traditional approach to the continuity of frontiers. The second and relatively more recent consideration is that the use of force as a method of settlement of international disputes or as an instrument of national policy is categorically prohibited by international law. Thus, treaties which attempt to modify the status of territories after the conclusion of a war of aggression are invalid, and incapable of creating or transferring valid title. However, if such a treaty were concluded at the end of a legitimate use of force, and were recognized by an international body, such as the General Assembly of the UN, as representing fair and reasonable terms for the conclusive settlement of all issues, it would not be considered invalid.

The politico-historical provenance of a frontier question is perceived as assuming considerable legal significance. It is important not only because it provides perspective to the dispute, but also because details of the political history tend to reveal the incidents and distribution of power between the parties and the role played by it in the development of the frontier. Both sets of facts, namely, the questions of power and of the historical sources of difficulties, tend to create problems for the legal analysis.

As regards the former, although it is in principle external to the legal system, power tends to exercise a degree of influence over it by determining, *inter alia*, the nature and performance of certain rights and obligations between States. The history of the Shatt question has shown that the unequal distribution of power between Iran and Iraq had frustrated a final and conclusive settlement of *all* the issues, and had on every occasion prompted an agreement the weaker State was least inclined to accept. Yet in legal terms there were no outstanding problems: the alignment had, in every case, been 'conclusively' settled.

Second, the facts have shown that despite the impracticable nature of the left-bank boundary Iran had, up to 1975, been unable to secure a line which would have resolved her genuine difficulties in the Shatt. From her perspective, it could be argued that laws which do not take into consideration the equitable needs of a State, rooted not in territorial aggrandizement but genuine sources of difficulties, inhibit change and are not in touch with political reality. *A fortiori*, a rule of law which accommodates such claims would contribute towards the easing of tension between adjacent States.

Inasmuch as law is a creature of custom and State practice it cannot ignore the evolution of political facts and ideals and must respond to the needs and interests of States. Wherever the law diverges from these needs and interests, its efficacy may either be lost or reduced. The application hence of the law in different situations must be tempered with flexibility in order to strike a balance between the rules of law and the exigencies of States.

Although generally correct, these observations merit qualification. First, it is not the rigidity of the law, but the rigidity in the attitude adopted by

States which is ultimately a bar to the accommodation of genuine grievances. Second, it may not be at times impossible to define the term 'genuine', but the resolution of such grievances may well depend upon an infinite range of political criteria far too extensive to be provided for or enumerated in law.

Third, a provision for change will inevitably lead to a periodic review of boundary agreements which in turn will engender rather than resolve, problems of territorial instability. Indeed the Iran–Iraq war is an apt illustration of the difficulties States would be vulnerable to if a periodic review of alignments were sanctioned by law.

Finally, the law is not totally oblivious to the imperatives of change. The reconciliation between law and fact is facilitated at times by the doctrine of finality of boundaries. One of the objectives of the principles of acquiescence, estoppel, and recognition is to give due weight to situations which, while they may not be totally coincidental with certain treaty provisions, are predominant on the ground. Nor does the law ignore the fact that in certain circumstances the relevance of the principle of equity may be compelling, alleviating as it does the rigours imposed by a strict application of the law. Yet, it is in principle reasonable to deny a continuously available process whereunder calls for revision of boundary regimes in light of difficulties or changed circumstances may be made. There is, at any rate, no legal bar to the resolution of the problem by way of diplomacy.

ANNEXE I

Second Treaty of Erzeroum, 31 May 1847[1]

[Ratifications exchanged at Constantinople, March 21, 1848.]

ART. I. Les 2 Puissances Musulmanes arrêtent que les réclamations pécuniaires qu'elles avaient élevées jusqu'à présent, l'une à charge de l'autre, soient totalement abandonnées; mais que nulle atteinte ne soit portée par cet arrangement aux dispositions (prises) pour le règlement des réclamations insérées dans l'Article IV.

II. Le Gouvernement de Perse s'engage à abandonner au Gouvernement Ottoman tous les terrains plats, c'est-à-dire, les terrains de la partie occidentale de la province de Zohab; et le Gouvernement Ottoman s'engage de son côté à abandonner au Gouvernement Persan la partie orientale, c'est-à-dire, tous les terrains montagneux de la province de Zohab, avec la vallée de Kerrind.

Le Gouvernement Persan se désiste de toute espèce de prétention relative à la ville et à la province de Suleimanié, et s'engage formellement à ne jamais exercer nulle espèce d'immixtion ni d'empiètement par rapport au droit de souveraineté du Gouvernement Ottoman sur ladite province.

Le Gouvernement Ottoman s'engage formellement à ce que la ville et l'échelle de Mohammara, l'île de Khizr, le lieu d'ancrage, et aussi les terrains de la rive orientale, c'est-à-dire, de la rive gauche du Schatt-ul-Arab, qui sont en la possession des tribus reconnues comme relevant de la Perse, soient dans la possession du Gouvernement Persan en pleine souveraineté. Outre cela, les navires Persans auront le droit de naviguer en pleine liberté sur le Schatt-ul-Arab, depuis l'endroit où ce fleuve se jette dans la mer jusqu'au point de contact des frontières des 2 parties.

III. Les 2 Parties Contractantes ayant par le présent Traité abandonné leurs autres réclamations territoriales, s'engagent à nommer immédiatement des 2 côtés des Commissaires et des Ingénieurs, afin que ceux-ci déterminent les frontières entre les 2 États d'une manière conforme à l'Article précédent.

IV. Il est respectivement décidé que des Commissaires seront immédiatement nommés de part et d'autre, pour juger et régler d'une manière équitable les questions des dommages essuyés des 2 côtés depuis l'acceptation des propositions amicales tracées et communiquées par les 2 grandes Puissances médiatrices au mois de Djémaziy-ul-evvel, 1261: ainsi que celles des droits de pâturage depuis l'année où leur paiement a été arriéré.

V. Le Gouvernement Ottoman promet de fixer à Brousse le domicile des Princes Persans fugitifs, et de ne pas permettre qu'ils s'absentent dudit lieu, ni qu'ils entretiennent des relations clandestines avec la Perse. Et les 2 Hautes Puissances s'engagent à ce que, conformément au précédent Traité d'Erzeroum, les autres transfuges soient tous rendus.

VI. Les négociants Persans paieront en nature ou en argent comptant les droits de

[1] *Source*: *BFSP* 45 (1847–8), p. 874.

douane pour leurs marchandises, selon la valeur actuelle et courante desdites marchandises, et de la manière indiquée dans l'Article relatif au commerce du Traité d'Erzeroum conclu en 1238. On ne demandera rien (pas une pièce de monnaie) en sus de montant fixé dans ledit Traité.

VII. Le Gouvernement Ottoman promet d'accorder les privilèges nécessaires pour que, en conformité des Traités précédents, les pélerins Persans puissent visiter, en toute sûreté et à l'abri de toute espèce de vexation, les lieux saints qui se trouvent dans les États Ottomans. Et, de plus, désirant raffermir et consolider les liens de l'amitié et de la concorde qui doivent subsister entre les 2 Puissances Musulmanes et entre leurs sujets respectifs, il s'engage à prendre les mesures les plus convenables à ce que, de même que les pélerins Persans jouissent de tous les privilèges dans les États Ottomans, les autres sujets Persans aussi en participent, et que, tant pour leur commerce que sous d'autres rapports, ils soient mis à l'abri de toute sorte d'injustice, de molestation, ou d'incivilité. Outre cela, le Gouvernement Ottoman promet de reconnaître les Consuls qui seront nommés par le Gouvernement Persan dans tels endroits des États Ottomans où les intérêts commerciaux et la protection des sujets et négociants Persans l'exigeraient, à l'exception de la Mecque la vénérée, et de Medine la resplendissante; et d'observer à l'égard desdits Consuls tous les privilèges dûs à leur caractère officiel et qui sont observés envers les Consuls des autres Puissances amies.

De son côté, le Gouvernement Persan s'engage à user en toute chose de procédés réciproques, soit envers les Consuls qui seront nommés par le Gouvernement Ottoman dans tels endroits de la Perse où ils seront jugés nécessaires, soit à l'égard des sujets et négociants Ottomans qui fréquenteraient la Perse.

VIII. Les 2 Hautes Puissances Musulmanes s'engagent à adopter et à mettre à exécution les mesures nécessaires pour empêcher et réprimer les vols et les brigandages des tribus et des autres peuplades établies sur les frontières; auquel effet, elles placeront des troupes dans les lieux convenables. Et elles s'engagent à s'acquitter de leur devoir quant à toute espèce d'actes d'agression, tels que pillage, déprédation, ou meurtre, qui auraient lieu sur leurs territoires respectifs.

Les 2 Hautes Puissances laisseront une fois pour toutes à la libre volonté des tribus qui, leur Suzerain n'étant pas connu, sont contestées, la faculté de choisir et de désigner les endroits où dorénavant elles demeureront toujours; et il est arrêté que les tribus dont la dépendance est connue, seront forcées de rentrer dans le territoire de l'État dont elles relèvent.

IX. Tous les points et les Articles des Traités précédents, et particulièrement ceux du Traité conclu à Erzeroum en 1238, qui ne sont pas spécialement modifiés ou annulés par le présent Traité, sont confirmés dans toute leur force et dans toutes leurs dispositions, comme s'ils eussent été insérés mot-à-mot dans cette pièce. Il est convenu entre les 2 Hautes Puissance qu'après que ce Traité aura été échangé, elles l'accepteront et le signeront, et que les ratifications en seront échangées dans l'espace de 2 mois, ou plus tôt.

16 Djemazil Akhir, 1263.

(L.S.) ENVARRE EFFENDI.
(L.S.) MIRZA TAKKEE KHAN.

ANNEXE 2

Agreement Relative to Frontier Delimitation between Persia and Turkey, signed at Tehran, 21 December 1911[1]

Les Gouvernements Persan et Ottoman, mus par un égal désir d'écarter désormais tout sujet de controverse à l'endroit de leurs frontières communes, ayant chargé d'une part le Ministre des Affaires Étrangères de Perse et d'autre part l'Ambassadeur de Turquie à Téhéran d'établir les bases de négociations et la procédure à suivre pour la délimination desdites frontières, les soussignés, après délibération, sont tombés d'accord sur les points suivants:

1. Une commission composée d'un nombre égal de délégués de part et d'autre devra se réunir dans le plus bref délai possible à Constantinople.
2. Les délégués des deux Gouvernements, munis de tous les documents et preuves à l'appui de leurs réclamations, seront chargés d'établir dans un esprit de sincère impartialité, la ligne frontière séparant les deux pays après quoi une Commission technique aura simplement à appliquer sur place la délimination définitive sur les bases arrêtées par les travaux de la première Commission.
3. Les travaux de la Commission mixte qui se réunira à Constantinople auront pour bases les clauses du traité dit d'Erzeroum conclu en 1263.
4. Dans le cas où les délégués des deux parties ne tomberaient pas d'accord sur l'interprétation et l'application de certaines clauses de ce traité, au bout d'une période de six mois de négociations, pour solutionner complètement la question de la délimination des frontières, il est entendu que tous les points sur lesquels il y aurait divergence seront soumis ensemble à la cour arbitrale de la Haye afin que la question entière soit ainsi définitivement tranchée.
5. Il va sans dire qu'aucune des deux parties ne pourra se prévaloir de l'occupation militaire des territoires en litige pour s'en servir comme argument de droit.

[1] *Source*: Parry, *Consolidated Treaty Series*, 215 (1911–12), p. 138.

ANNEXE 3

Protocol Signed at Constantinople 17 November 1913[1]

The undersigned: His Excellency Sir Louis Mallet, Ambassador Extraordinary and Plenipotentiary of His Britannic Majesty to His Majesty the Sultan; His Excellency Mirza Mahmud Khan Kajar 'Ahd-i-Shāmus Saltaneh, Ambassador Extraordinary and Plenipotentiary of His Majesty the Shah of Persia to His Majesty the Sultan; His Excellency M. Michel de Giers, Ambassador Extraordinary and Plenipotentiary of His Majesty the Emperor of Russia to His Majesty the Sultan; His Highness Prince Said Halim Pasha, Grand Vizier and Minister for Foreign Affairs of the Ottoman Empire; have met for the purpose of recording in the present Protocol the Agreement concluded between their respective Governments with regard to the Turco-Persian boundary.

They began by recapitulating the progress, up to date, of the negotiations recently instituted among them.

The Joint Commission provided for in Article 1 of the Protocol signed at Teheran between the Imperial Ottoman Embassy and the Persian Minister for Foreign Affairs with a view to determining the bases for the negotiations relating to the delimitation of the Turco-Persian boundary held eighteen meetings, the first on May 12th (25th) and the last on August 9th (22nd), 1912.

On August 9th (22nd), 1912, the Imperial Russian Embassy at Constantinople addressed to the Sublime Porte, under No. 264, a note stating that 'the Imperial Government considers that too much emphasis cannot be laid on the necessity of putting into effect without delay the explicit stipulations of the Treaty of Erzeroum, which are tantamount to the restoration of the *status quo* of 1848.'

The Imperial Embassy at the same time forwarded to the Imperial Ottoman Government a memorandum showing in detail the frontier-line in conformity with the stipulations of the treaties in force.

The Imperial Ottoman Government replied to this communication by a note dated March 18th(31st), 1913, No. 30469/47. It stated that 'the Sublime Porte, being anxious to comply with the desire expressed by the Imperial Russian Government by eliminating any cause of difference in its cordial relations with the latter, and wishing, further, to demonstrate to the Persian Government its entire good faith in regard to the dispute existing on the subject between the two countries, had decided to accept the line mentioned in the aforesaid note and memorandum of the Ambassador of His Majesty the Emperor of Russia for the delimitation of the

[1] *Source: League of National Official Journal*, 16 (1935), p. 201.

Annexe 3

northern part of the Turco-Persian frontier from Serdar Bulak to Bane—that is to say, down to the 36th parallel of latitude.'

Nevertheless, the Imperial Ottoman Government suggested a number of modifications in the line proposed in the memorandum annexed to the note of the Imperial Russian Embassy dated August 9th (22nd), 1912, No. 264.

The Imperial Ottoman Government also appended to its note 'an explanatory note on the situation of the Zohab boundaries and the arrangement that it would be able to accept in order to reach a final and equitable understanding with the Persian Government on that part of the frontier.'

The Imperial Russian Embassy replied by a note dated March 28th (April 10th), 1913, No. 78. It noted the statement 'by which the Imperial Ottoman Government recognizes as a principle for the delimitation of the Ararat-Bane section the exact sense of Article 3 of the Treaty of 1848, known as the Treaty of Erzerum, as set forth in the note of August 9th (22nd), 1912, No. 264.' As regards the modifications proposed by the Sublime Porte, the Imperial Embassy stated (with a reservation on the question of Egri-chai) that it could not sufficiently emphasize the necessity of making no change in the line established in its note of August 9th (22nd), 1912.

As regards the question of Zohab, the Imperial Russian Embassy, while reserving the right to submit its detailed observations concerning that frontier, expressed 'its opinion on the whole of the Ottoman draft, which does not seem to it to guarantee sufficiently, for the future, the maintenance of order and peace on the frontier.'

On April 20th (May 3rd), 1913, the Russian and British Embassies addressed an identic note to his Highness Prince Said Halim Pasha, accompanied by a memorandum summarizing their point of view regarding the delimitation of Zohab and the regions situate south of that district.

This exchange of notes was followed by conversations between Their Excellencies M. de Giers and Sir Gerald Lowther, of the one part, and His Late Highness Mahmud Shefket Pasha, of the other part. The result of these conversations was recorded in an *aide-mémoire* presented by His Excellency the Russian Ambassador to His Highness the Grand Vizier on June 6th, 1913, and in a note from the Sublime Porte addressed on June 26th (July 9th), 1913, No. 34553/95, to the Russian Embassy, and on July 12th, 1913, to the British Embassy.

On July 29th, 1913, a 'declaration' was signed in London by Sir Edward Grey and His Highness Ibrahim Hakky Pasha concerning the demarcation of the southern boundary between Persia and Turkey.

The Imperial Russian Embassy then proceeded to recapitulate the principles of delimitation established in the correspondence concerning the Turco-Persian boundary. It addressed to the Sublime Porte a note dated August 5th (18th), 1913, No. 166. An identic note was addressed to the Sublime Porte by the British Embassy on the same date.

The Sublime Porte replied to these communications by identic notes dated September 23rd, 1913, No. 37063/113.

As a result of the subsequent negotiations, the four plenipotentiaries of Great Britain, Persia, Russia and Turkey, agreed on the following provisions:

Annexe 3

I

It is agreed that the boundary between Persia and Turkey shall be defined as follows:

The boundary in the north shall start from boundary-mark No. XXXVII on the Turco-Russian frontier, situate close to Serdar Bulak, on the crest between Little and Great Ararat. It shall then drop southwards by way of the ridges, leaving on the Persian side the valley of Dambat, Sarnvitch, and the water system of Yarym-Kaya, which rises to the south of mount Ayubeg. The boundary shall then leave Bulakbashi, in Persia, and shall continue to follow the highest ridge, the southern extremity of which is situate at about 44° 22' longitude and 30° 28' latitude. Then, skirting the west side of the marsh which extends to the west of Yarym-Kaya, the boundary shall cross the Sary-Su stream, pass between the villages of Girde-baran (Turkish) and Bazyrgan (Persian), and, ascending to the ridge to the west of Bazyrgan, follow the watershed formed by the Saranli, Zenduli, Gir-Kelime, Kanly-baba, Geduki-Khasineh, and Deveji ridges.

After Deveji, the line shall cross the valley of Egri-chai at the place to be designated by the Delimitation Commission in conformity with the *status quo*, leaving the villages of Nado and Nifto in Persia.

The ownership of the village of Kyzyl-Kaya (Bellasor) shall be established after an examination of the geographical situation of the village, the western side of the watershed in that region being allocated to Turkey, and the eastern side to Persia.

Should the final boundary line leave outside Ottoman territory a section of the road which passes close to Kyzyl-Kaya and connects the district of Bayazid with the province of Van, it is understood that the Persian Government shall give free passage over this section of the road to the Imperial Ottoman Posts and to travellers and goods, other than military troops and convoys.

The frontier shall then ascend to the ridges forming the watershed: Kyzyl-Ziaret Sarychimene, Dumanlu, Kara-burga, the hill between the reservoirs of Ayry-chai (Persian) and of Jelli-gol (Turkish), Avdal-dashi, Reshkan, the hill between Akhurek and Tavin Bevra-begzadan, Gevri-Mahine, Khydyr-baba, Avristan.

As regards Kotur, the Protocol of July 15th (28th), 1880, known as the Protocol of Sary-Kamiche, shall be applied in such a way that the village of Kevlik shall remain in Turkey, and the villages of Bilejik, Razi, Gharatil (Haratil), the two Jelliks, and Panamerik shall remain in Persia.

The frontier following the Mir-Omar ridge shall ascend the mountain of Surava, and leaving Khanyga on the Turkish side, shall pass by way of the watershed formed by the pass of Borush-Khuran, the mountain of Haravil, Beleko, Shinetal, Sardul, Gulamli, Kepper, Bergabend, Peri-Khan, Iskander, Avene, and Kotul. The valley of Bajirga shall remain in Turkey, and the villages of Sartyk and Sero in Persia, and the frontier shall pass from the southern extremity of Kotul over the ridge rising to the west of the Persian village of Behik, and, following the peaks of Seri-Baydost, shall join the crest of Mount Zont.

From Mount Zont the frontier shall follow continuously the watershed between the Persian districts of Tergever, Desht, and Mergever, and the Turkish sanjak [district] of Hakkiari—that is to say, the crests of Shiveh-Shishali, Chil-Chovri,

Chel-Berdir, Kuna-Koter, Kazi-beg, Avukh, Mai-Helaneh, the mountains to the west of Binar and Delamper; then, leaving on the Persian side the basin emptying by way of Ushnu into the lake of Urumiya, including the sources of the Gadyr river known as Abiserigadyr (the valley of which is situated to the south of Delamper and to the east of Mount Girdeh), it shall reach the pass of Keleh-Shin.

To the south of Keleh-Shin the frontier shall leave on the Persian side the reservoir of Lavene, including the valley of Chumi-Geli (situate to the east of Zerdegel and to the south-west of Spi-rez), and on the Turkish side the waters of Revnaduz, and shall pass by the following peaks and passes: Siah-Kuh, Zerdeh-Gel, Boz, Barzin, Ser-shiva, Kevi-Khoja-Ibrahim. Thence the frontier shall continue to follow towards the south the main chain of Kandil, leaving on the Persian side the basin of the affluents of Kialu on the right side: the streams Purdanan Khydyrava and Talkhatan.

It is understood that the Turkish tribes which are in the habit of spending the summer in the said valleys at the Gadyr and Lavene springs shall still have the use of their pastures under the same conditions as in the past.

Having reached the summit of Seri-Kele-Kelin, the line shall pass over Zinvi-Jasusan and the pass of Bamin, and shall cross the Vezne river near the Purde-Berdan bridge. The Delimitation Commission will have to decide as to the future of the village of Shenieh, on the basis of the general principle of the *status quo*.

After Purde-Berdan, the frontier shall ascend over the chains of Foka-baba-kyr, Berde-spian, Berde-Abul-Fath and the pass of Kaniresh. It shall then follow the watershed formed by Lagav-Ghird, Donleri, the pass of Khan-Ahmed, and the southern extremity of Tepe-Salos. The frontier will thus pass between the villages of Kandol (Turkish) and Kesh-keshiva and Mazynava (Persian), and reach the course of the Kialu river (the Little Zab).

After joining the course of the Kialu river, the frontier shall follow it upstream, leaving on the Persian side the right bank (the Alani-ajem) and on the Turkish side the left bank of that river. On reaching the mouth of the Khileh-resh river (an affluent of the Kialu on the left side), the frontier shall follow the course of that river upstream, leaving on the Persian side the villages of Alot, Kovero, etc., and on the Turkish side the district of Alani-Mavont. At the south-western extremity of Mount Balu, the frontier shall leave the course of the Hileh-resh river, and, ascending over the north-west extremity of the Surkew chain, extending to the south of the Hileh-resh river, shall pass over the Surkew ridge, leaving the districts of Siwel and Shive-Kel on the Turkish side.

On reaching the astronomical point of Surkew almost at latitude 35° 49', the frontier shall pass in the direction of the village of Champar-aw, the future of which shall be decided by the Delimitation Commission on the basis of the accepted principle of the *status quo*. The line shall then ascend over the chain of mountains which form the frontier between the Persian district of Baneh and the Turkish district of Kyzyieja; Galash, Berdi-Kechel, Pusht-Hangajal, Du-bera, Parajal, and Spi-Kana, after which it shall reach the pass of Now-Khuvan. Thence, still following the watershed, the frontier shall turn southwards and then westwards, passing by way of the summits of Vul-Guza, Pushti-Shehidan, Hazar-Mal, Bali-Keder, Keleh-

Melaik, and Kuhi-Koce-resha, separating the Turkish district of Teretul from the Persian district of Merivan.

From there, the frontier shall follow the course of the Khalil-Abad brook downstream as far as its confluence with the Chami-Kyzylja, and then this last-named river upstream as far as the mouth of its left affluent flowing from the village of Bnava-Suta; it shall follow this Bnava-Suta brook upstream and, by way of the passes of Keli-Naveh-Sar and Keli-Piran, shall reach the pass of Surene, known, it appears, by the name of Chigan (or Chakan).

The main chain of Avroman, extending in the direction north-west–south-east, shall then form the frontier between Persia and the Ottoman district of Shehrisor. On reaching the peak of Kemadjar (south-east of Kala-Selm and north-west of Sheri-Avroman), the frontier shall continue to follow the main ridge as far as its ramification on the western side, rising to the north of the valley of Dere-Vuli, leaving the villages of Khan-Germela and Nowsud on the Persian side. For the remainder of the frontier as far as Sirvan, the Commission shall—by way of exception—delimit the ground, taking into consideration such changes as may have occurred there between the year 1848 and the year 1905.

South of Sirvan, the frontier shall begin close to the mouth of the Chami-Zimkan, shall pass by way of the Beyzel (Bezel) mountain, and shall descend to the Chemi-Zerishk watercourse. Next, following the watershed between this last-named watercourse and the river which, rising in the Bend-Bemo, bears, according to the identic map, the name of Pushti-Gherav (Arkhevendu), it shall ascend to the summit of Bend-Bemo.

After following the ridge of Bamu (Bemo), the frontier, on reaching the defile of Derbendi-Dehul (Derbendi-Hur), shall follow the course of the Zengeneh (Abba-san) river as far as the point nearest to the summit of the Shevaldir (astronomical point) and situate below the village of Mamyshan. It shall ascend this summit and shall next pass by way of the crests of the hills forming a watershed between the plains of Tileku and Serkaleh, then by way of the chains of Khuli-Baghan, Jebel-Ali-Beg, Bender-Chok-Chermik, Sengler, and Asengueran, as far as the point in the Tengi-Hammam defile situate opposite the northern extremity of the Karawiz mountains.

Thence the frontier shall follow the course of the river Kuretu as far as the village of that name. The future of the village of Kuretu shall be decided by the Delimitation Commission on the basis of the nationality of its inhabitants. Thence the frontier shall pass by way of the road between the villages of Kuretu and Kush-Kurrek, then along the crests of Mounts Kishka and Ak-Dag, and then, leaving Kala-Sebzi in Persia, it shall turn southwards as far as the Ottoman post of Kani-bez. Thence it shall follow the course of the Elvend river upstream as far as the point of a quarter of an hour's distance downstream from its confluence with the Gilan watercourse; from that point it shall continue as far as the Naft-Su, skirting the Ab-Bakhshan in accordance with the line agreed upon with the late Mahmud Shefket Pasha and shown roughly on the map annexed to the note of the Imperial Russian Embassy dated August 5th (18th), 1913, and leaving Naft-Mukataasy to Turkey. Thence, the frontier-line, following the Naft-Deressi, on reaching the point where the Kassri Shirin road cuts that waterway, shall continue along the mountains of Varbulend, Koherigh-Keleshuvan, and Jebel-Gerebi (the extension of the Jebeli-Hamrinach in).

The Delimitation Commission shall draw up a special agreement for the distribution of the Gengir (Sumar) waters between the parties concerned.

The part of the frontier between Mendeli and the northern point of the line indicated in the declaration made in London on July 29th (Shuaib) between Hakky Pasha and Sir E. Grey not having yet been discussed in detail, the undersigned leave the establishment of that part of the frontier to the Delimitation Commission.

As regards delimitation from the region of Hawizeh as far as the sea, the frontier-line shall start from the place called Umm-Shir, where the Khor-el-Duvel divides from the Khor-el-Azem. Umm-Shir is situate east of the junction of the Khor-el-Muhaisin with the Khor-el-Azem, nine miles north-west of Bisaitin, a place situated at latitude $31° 43' 29''$. From Umm-Shirr, the line shall turn south-westwards as far as longitude $45°^2$ at the southern extremity of a small lake known also by the name of Azem and situate in the Khor-el-Azem some distance north-west of Shuaib. From this point the line shall continue to the south along the marsh as far as latitude $31°$, which it shall follow directly eastwards as far as a point northeast of Kushk-i-Basra, so as to leave this place in Ottoman territory. From this point the line shall go southwards as far as the Khayeen canal at a point between the Nahr-Diaiji and the Nahr-Abu'l-Arabid; it shall follow the *medium filum aquae* of the Khayeen canal as far as the point where the latter joins the Shatt-al-Arab, at the mouth of the Nahr-Nazaileh. From this point the frontier shall follow the course of the Shatt-al-Arab as far as the sea, leaving under Ottoman sovereignty the river and all the islands therein, subject to the following conditions and exceptions:

(*a*) The following shall belong to Persia: (1) the island of Muhalla and the two islands situate between the latter and the left bank of the Shatt-al-Arab (Persian bank of Abadan); (2) the four islands between Shetait and Maawiyeh and the two islands opposite Mankuhi which are both dependencies of the island of Abadan; (3) any small islands now existing or that may be formed which are connected at low water with the island of Abadan or with Persian *terra firma* below Nahr-Nazaileh.

(*b*) The modern port and anchorage of Muhammara, above and below the junction of the river Karun with the Shatt-al-Arab, shall remain within Persian jurisdiction in conformity with the Treaty of Erzerum; the Ottoman right of usage of this part of the river shall not, however, be affected thereby, nor shall Persian jurisdiction extend to the parts of the river outside the anchorage.

(*c*) No change shall be made in the existing rights, usages and customs as regards fishing on the Persian bank of the Shatt-al-Arab, the word 'bank' including also the lands connected with the coast at low water.

(*d*) Ottoman jurisdiction shall not extend over the parts of the Persian coast that may be temporarily covered by water at high tide or by other accidental causes. Persian jurisdiction, on its side, shall not be exercised over lands that may be temporarily or accidentally uncovered when the water is below the normal low-water level.

---

[2] This should read $47° 45'$ (. . .)

(e) The Sheik of Muhammara shall continue to enjoy in conformity with the Ottoman laws his rights of ownership in Ottoman territory.

The frontier-line established in the declaration is shown in red on the map annexed hereto.[3]

The parts of the frontier not detailed in the above-mentioned frontier-line shall be established on the basis of the principle of the *status quo*, in conformity with the stipulations of Article 3 of the Treaty of Erzerum.

II

The frontier-line shall be delimited on the spot by a Delimitation Commission, consisting of commissioners of the four Governments.

Each Government shall be represented on this Commission by a commissioner and a deputy commissioner. The latter shall take the commissioner's place on the Commission in case of need.

III

The Delimitation Commission, in the performance of the task devolving upon it, shall comply:

(1) With the provisions of the present Protocol;

(2) With the Rules of Procedure of the Delimitation Commission annexed (Annex [A]) to the present Protocol.[4]

IV

In the event of a divergence of opinion in the Commission as to the boundary-line of any part of the frontier, the Ottoman and Persian commissioners shall submit a written statement of their respective points of view within forty-eight hours to the Russian and British commissioners, who shall hold a private meeting and shall give a decision on the questions in dispute and communicate their decision to their Ottoman and Persian colleagues. This decision shall be inserted in the Minutes of the plenary meeting and shall be recognized as binding on all four Governments.

V

As soon as part of the frontier has been delimited, such part shall be regarded as finally fixed and shall not be liable to subsequent examination or revision.

[3] Not annexed to the Iraqi request.
[4] Not reproduced here.

Annexe 3

VI

As the work of delimitation proceeds, the Ottoman and Persian Governments shall have the right to establish posts on the frontier.

VII

It is understood that the concession granted by the Convention of May 28th, 1901 (9 sefer, 1319, of the Hegira), by the Government of His Imperial Majesty the Shah of Persia to William Knox D'Arcy and now being worked, in conformity with the provisions of Article 9 of the said Convention, by the Anglo-Persian Oil Company (Limited), having its registered office at Winchester House, London (the said Convention being referred to hereunder as 'the Convention, in the Annex [B] to the present Protocol),[5] shall remain in full and unrestricted force throughout the territories transferred by Persia to Turkey in virtue of the provisions of the present Protocol and of Annex [B] thereto.

VIII

The Ottoman and Persian Governments will distribute among the officials on the frontier a sufficient number of copies of the delimitation map drawn up by the Commission, together with copies of translations of the statement provided for in Article XV of the Commission's Rules of Procedure. It is understood, however, that the French text alone shall be regarded as authentic.

(signed) Louis Mallet
Ehtechamos-Saltaneh Mahmud
Michel de Giers
Said Halim

---

[5] Not reproduced here.

ANNEXE 4

No. 4423.—Boundary Treaty Between The Kingdom of Irak and The Empire of Iran. Signed at Teheran, July 4th, 1937.[1]

HIS MAJESTY THE KING OF IRAQ, of the one part,
and
HIS IMPERIAL MAJESTY THE SHAHINSHAH OF IRAN, of the other part,
Sincerely desirous of strengthening the bonds of brotherly friendship and good understanding between the two States, and of settling definitively the question of the frontier between their two States, have decided to conclude the present Treaty and have to that end appointed as their Plenipotentiaries:

HIS MAJESTY THE KING OF IRAQ:
    His Excellency Dr. NADJI-AL-ASIL, Minister for Foreign Affairs;
HIS IMPERIAL MAJESTY THE SHAHINSHAH OF IRAN:
    His Excellency Monsieur Enayatollah SAMIY, Minister for Foreign Affairs;

Who, having communicated their full powers, found in good and due form, have agreed as follows:

ARTICLE I.

The High Contracting Parties are agreed that, subject to the amendment for which Article 2 of the present Treaty provides, the following documents shall be deemed valid and binding, that is to say:

(*a*) The Turco-Persian Delimitation Protocol signed at Constantinople, November 4th, 1913;

(*b*) The Minutes of the meetings of the 1914 Frontier Delimitation Commission.

In virtue of the present Article, the frontier between the two States shall be as defined and traced by the Commission aforesaid, save in so far as otherwise provided in Article 2 hereinafter following.

ARTICLE 2.

At the extreme point of the island of Choteit (being approximately latitude 30° 17′ 25″ North, longitude 48° 19′ 28″ East), the frontier shall run perpendicularly from low water mark to the thalweg of the Shatt-el-Arab, and shall follow the same as far as a point opposite the present Jetty No. 1 at Abadan (being approximately latitude 30° 20′ 8.4″ North, longitude 48° 16′ 13″ East). From this point, it shall return to low water mark, and follow the frontier line indicated in the 1914 Minutes.

[1] *Source*: *League of Nations Treaty Series*, 189–190 (1938) No. 4423, p. 241, at p. 256.

ARTICLE 3.

Upon the signature of the present Treaty, the High Contracting Parties shall appoint forthwith a commission to erect frontier marks at the points determined by the commission to which Article I, paragraph *(b)*, of the Treaty relates, and to erect such further marks as it shall deem desirable.

The composition of the commission and its programme of work shall be determined by special arrangement between the two High Contracting Parties.

ARTICLE 4.

The provisions hereinafter following shall apply to the Shatt-el-Arab from the point at which the land frontier of the two States enters the said river to the high seas:

(*a*) The Shatt-el-Arab shall remain open on equal terms to the trading vessels of all countries. All dues levied shall be in the nature of payments for services rendered and shall be devoted exclusively to meeting in equitable manner the cost of upkeep, maintenance of navigability or improvement of the navigable channel and the approach to the Shatt-el-Arab from the sea, or to expenditure incurred in the interests of navigation. The said dues shall be calculated on the basis of the official tonnage of vessels or their displacement or both.

(*b*) The Shatt-el-Arab shall remain open for the passage of vessels of war and other vessels of the two High Contracting Parties not engaged in trade.

(*c*) The circumstance that the frontier in the Shatt-el-Arab sometimes follows the low water mark and sometimes the thalweg or *medium filum aquae* shall not in any way affect the two High Contracting Parties' right of user along the whole length of the river.

ARTICLE 5.

The two High Contracting Parties, having a common interest in the navigation of the Shatt-el-Arab as defined in Article 4 of the present Treaty, undertake to conclude a Convention for the maintenance and improvement of the navigable channel, and for dredging, pilotage, collection of dues, health measures, measures for preventing smuggling, and all other questions concerning navigation in the Shatt-el-Arab as defined in Article 4 of the present Treaty.

ARTICLE 6.

The present Treaty shall be ratified and the instruments of ratification shall be exchanged at Baghdad as soon as possible. It shall come into force as from the date of such exchange.

In faith whereof the Plenipotentiaries of the two High Contracting Parties have signed the present Treaty.

Done at Teheran, in the Arabic, Persian and French languages; in case of disagreement, the French text shall prevail.

This fourth day of July, one thousand nine hundred and thirty-seven.

NAJI AL ASIL.
SAMIY.

Annexe 4

PROTOCOL.

At the moment of signing the Frontier Treaty between Iraq and Iran, the two High Contracting Parties are agreed as follows:

I.

The geographical co-ordinates designated approximately in Article 2 of the Treaty aforesaid shall be definitively determined by a commission of experts consisting of an equal number of members appointed by each of the High Contracting Parties.

The geographical co-ordinates thus definitively determined within the limits fixed in the Article aforesaid shall be recorded in Minutes, the which, after signature by the members of the said commission, shall form an integral part of the Frontier Treaty.

II.

The High Contracting Parties undertake to conclude the Convention to which Article 5 of the Treaty relates within one year from the entry into force of the Treaty.

In the event of the said Convention not being concluded within the year despite their utmost efforts, the said time-limit may be extended by the High Contracting Parties by common accord.

The Imperial Government of Iran agrees that, during the period of one year to which the first paragraph of the present Article relates or the extension (if any) of such period, the Royal Government of Iraq shall be responsible as at present for all questions to be settled under the said Convention. The Royal Government of Iraq shall notify the Imperial Government of Iran every six months as to the works executed, dues collected, expenditure incurred or any other measures undertaken.

III.

Permission granted by either of the High Contracting Parties to a vessel of war or other public service vessel not engaged in trade, belonging to a third State, to enter its own harbours on the Shatt-el-Arab shall be deemed to have been granted by the other High Contracting Party in such sort that the vessels in question shall be entitled to use the waters of the latter for the purpose of navigating the Shatt-el-Arab.

The High Contracting Party granting such permission shall immediately notify the other High Contracting Party accordingly.

Annexe 4

IV.

It is clearly understood, without prejudice to the rights of Iran in respect of the Shatt-el-Arab, that nothing in this Treaty shall affect the rights of Iraq and the contractual obligations of the same *vis-à-vis* the British Government in respect of the Shatt-el-Arab under Article 4 of the Treaty of June 30th, 1930, and paragraph 7 of the Annex thereto signed on the same date.

V.

The present Protocol shall be ratified at the same time as the Frontier Treaty, of which it shall form an Annex and integral part. It shall come into force at the same time as the Treaty.

The present Protocol is drawn up in Arabic, Persian and French; in case of difference, the French text shall prevail.

Done at Teheran, in duplicate, the fourth day of July, one thousand nine hundred and thirty seven.

NAJI AL ASIL.
SAMIY.

ANNEXE 5

Joint Iranian-Iraqi Communiqué[1]
[The Algiers Protocol] of 6 March 1975

During the holding at Algiers of the Summit Conference of the States members of OPEC and on the initiative of President Boumediene, His Majesty the Shahinshah of Iran and His Excellency Mr. Saddam Hussein, Deputy Chairman of the Revolutionary Command Council of Iraq, met twice and held long talks on the subject of relations between Iran and Iraq.

These talks, which took place in the presence of President Boumediene, were marked by great frankness and were characterized by the sincere desire of the two Parties to achieve a final and lasting solution to all the problems pending between the two countries.

In accordance with the principles of territorial integrity, the inviolability of frontiers and non-interference in internal affairs, the High Contracting Parties took the following decisions:

1. They will proceed with the definitive demarcation of their land frontiers on the basis of the Constantinople Protocol of 1913 and the minutes of the Frontier Delimitation Commission of 1914;
2. They will delimit their river frontiers along the thalweg;
3. By so doing, they will restore mutual security and trust throughout the length of their common frontiers. They thus undertake to exercise strict and effective control over the frontiers with a view to the complete cessation of all subversive infiltration from either side;
4. The two Parties agreed to regard the above provisions as indivisible elements of an overall settlement and, accordingly, a breach of any of its component parts would clearly be incompatible with the spirit of the Algiers Agreement.

The two Parties will remain in constant contact with President Boumediene, who will, should the need arise, give Algeria's brotherly assistance in the implementation of the decisions reached.

The High Parties decided to renew the traditional bonds of good neighbourliness and friendship by, *inter alia*, eliminating all negative factors in their relations, by continually exchanging views on matters of common interest and by promoting mutual co-operation.

The two Parties solemnly declare that the region should remain free from any outside interference.

The Ministers for Foreign Affairs of Iran and Iraq will meet, in the presence of the Minister for Foreign Affairs of Algeria, on 15 March 1975 at Tehran in order to

[1] *Source: United Nations Treaty Series*, 1017, No. 14903.

Annexe 5

determine the methods of work of the Mixed Iranian-Iraqi Commission established by mutual agreement for the purpose of implementing the above decisions.

In accordance with the wish of the two Parties, Algeria will be invited to all meetings of the Mixed Iranian-Iraqi Commission.

The Mixed Commission will determine its timetable and methods of work and will meet, as necessary, alternately at Baghdad and Tehran.

His Majesty the Shahinshah accepted with pleasure the invitation addressed to him, on behalf of His Excellency President Ahmed Hassan El-Bakr, to make an official visit to Iraq; the date of this visit is to be agreed on.

His Excellency Mr. Saddam Hussein also agreed to make an official visit to Iran on a date to be agreed on by the two Parties.

His Majesty the Shahinshah and His Excellency the Deputy Chairman, Saddam Hussein, wished to address warm thanks in particular to President Houari Boumediene, who, inspired by brotherly and disinterested feelings, facilitated the establishment of direct contacts between the eminent leaders of the two countries and thereby contributed to the inauguration of a new era in relations between Iran and Iraq, in the higher interest of the future of the region concerned.

Algiers, 6 March 1975.

ANNEXE 6
[TRANSLATION]

Treaty Concerning the State Frontier and Neighbourly Relations between Iran and Iraq[1] Signed at Baghdad on 13 June 1975

His Imperial Majesty the Shahinshah of Iran.

His Excellency the President of the Republic of Iraq.

Considering the sincere desire of the two Parties as expressed in the Algiers Communiqué of 6 March 1975, to achieve a final and lasting solution to all the problems pending between the two countries,

Considering that the two Parties have carried out the definitive redemarcation of their land frontier on the basis of the Constantinople Protocol of 1913 and the minutes of the meetings of the Frontier Delimitation Commission of 1914 and have delimited their river frontier along the thalweg,

Considering their desire to restore security and mutual trust throughout the length of their common frontier,

Considering the ties of geographical proximity, history, religion, culture and civilization which bind the peoples of Iran and Iraq,

Desirous of strengthening their bonds of friendship and good neighbourliness, expanding their economic and cultural relations and promoting exchanges and human relations between their peoples on the basis of the principles of territorial integrity, the inviolability of frontiers and non-interference in internal affairs,

Resolved to work towards the introduction of a new era in friendly relations between Iran and Iraq based on full respect for the national independence and sovereign equality of States,

Convinced that they are helping thereby to implement the principles and achieve the purposes and objectives of the Charter of the United Nations,

Have decided to conclude this Treaty and have appointed as their plenipotentiaries:

His Imperial Majesty the Shahinshah of Iran: His Excellency Abbas Ali Khalatbary,

Minister for Foreign Affairs of Iran:

His Excellency the President of the Republic of Iraq: His Excellency Saadoun Hamadi,

Minister for Foreign Affairs of Iraq.

who, having exchanged their full powers, found to be in good and due form, have agreed as follows:

[1] *Source: United Nations Treaty Series*, 1017, No. 14903.

Annexe 6

ARTICLE 1.

The High Contracting Parties confirm that the State land frontier between Iraq and Iran shall be that which has been redemarcated on the basis of and in accordance with the provisions of the Protocol concerning the redemarcation of the land frontier, and the annexes thereto, attached to this Treaty.

ARTICLE 2.

The High Contracting Parties confirm that the State frontier in the Shatt al'Arab shall be that which has been delimited on the basis of and in accordance with the provisions of the Protocol concerning the delimitation of the river frontier, and the annexes thereto, attached to this Treaty.

ARTICLE 3.

The High Contracting Parties undertake to exercise strict and effective permanent control over the frontier in order to put an end to any infiltration of a subversive nature from any source, on the basis of and in accordance with the provisions of the Protocol concerning frontier security, and the annex thereto, attached to this Treaty.

ARTICLE 4.

The High Contracting Parties confirm that the provisions of the three Protocols, and the annexes thereto, referred to in articles 1, 2 and 3 above and attached to this Treaty as an integral part thereof shall be final and permanent. They shall not be infringed under any circumstances and shall constitute the indivisible elements of an over-all settlement. Accordingly, a breach of any of the components of this over-all settlement shall clearly be incompatible with the spirit of the Algiers Agreement.

ARTICLE 5.

In keeping with the inviolability of the frontiers of the two States and strict respect for their territorial integrity, the High Contracting Parties confirm that the course of their land and river frontiers shall be inviolable, permanent and final.

ARTICLE 6.

1. In the event of a dispute regarding the interpretation or implementation of this Treaty, the three Protocols or the annexes thereto, any solution to such a dispute shall strictly respect the course of the Iraqi-Iranian frontier referred to in articles 1 and 2 above and shall take into account the need to maintain security on the Iraqi-Iranian frontier in accordance with article 3 above.

2. Such disputes shall be resolved in the first instance by the High Contracting Parties by means of direct bilateral negotiations to be held within two months after the date on which one of the Parties so requested.

3. If no agreement is reached, the High Contracting Parties shall have recourse, within a three-month period, to the good offices of a friendly third State.

4. Should one of the two Parties refuse to have recourse to the good offices or should the good-offices procedure fail, the dispute shall be settled by arbitration within a period of not more than one month after the date of such refusal or failure.

5. Should the High Contracting Parties disagree as to the arbitration procedure, one of the High Contracting Parties may have recourse, within 15 days after such disagreement was recorded, to a court of arbitration.

With a view to establishing such court of arbitration each of the High Contracting Parties shall, in respect of each dispute to be resolved, appoint one of its nationals as arbitrators and the two arbitrators shall choose an umpire. Should the High Contracting Parties fail to appoint their arbitrators within one month after the date on which one of the Parties received a request for arbitration from the other Party, or should the arbitrators fail to reach agreement on the choice of the umpire before that time-limit expires, the High Contracting Party which requested arbitration shall be entitled to request the President of the International Court of Justice to appoint the arbitrators or the umpire, in accordance with the procedures of the Permanent Court of Arbitration.

6. The decision of the court of arbitration shall be binding on and enforceable by the High Contracting Parties;

7. The High Contracting Parties shall each defray half the costs of arbitration.

ARTICLE 7.

This Treaty, the three Protocols and the annexes thereto shall be registered in accordance with Article 102 of the Charter of the United Nations.

ARTICLE 8.

This Treaty, the three Protocols and the annexes thereto shall be ratified by each of the High Contracting Parties in accordance with its domestic law.

This Treaty, the three Protocols and the annexes thereto shall enter into force on the date of the exchange of the instruments of ratification in Tehran.

IN WITNESS WHEREOF the Plenipotentiaries of the High Contracting Parties have signed this Treaty, the three Protocols and the annexes thereto.

DONE at Baghdad, on 13 June 1975.

[Signed]	[Signed]
ABBAS-ALI KHALATBARY	SAADOUN HAMADI
Minister for Foreign Affairs	Minister for Foreign Affairs
of Iran	of Iraq

This Treaty, the three Protocols and the annexes thereto were signed in the presence of His Excellency Abdel-Aziz Bouteflika, Member of the Council of the Revolution and Minister for Foreign Affairs of Algeria.

[Signed]

ANNEXE 7

Protocol Concerning the Delimitation of the River Frontier between Iran and Iraq, Baghdad, 13 June 1975[1]

Pursuant to the decisions taken in the Algiers Communiqué of 6 March 1975,
The two Contracting Parties have agreed as follows:

ARTICLE 1.

The two Contracting Parties hereby declare and recognize that the State river frontier between Iran and Iraq in the Shatt al'Arab has been delimited along the thalweg by the Mixed Iraqi-Iranian-Algerian Committee on the basis of the following:

1. the Tehran Protocol of 17 March 1975;
2. the record of the Meeting of Ministers for Foreign Affairs, signed at Baghdad on 20 April 1975, approving, *inter alia*, the record of the Committee to Delimit the River Frontier, signed on 16 April 1975 on board the Iraqi ship *El Thawra* in the Shatt al'Arab;
3. common hydrographic charts, which have been verified on the spot and corrected and on which the geographical co-ordinates of the 1975 frontier crossing points have been indicated; these charts have been signed by the hydrographic experts of the Mixed Technical Commission and countersigned by the heads of the Iranian, Iraqi and Algerian delegations to the Committee. The said charts, listed hereinafter, are annexed to this Protocol and form an integral part thereof:

—Chart No. 1, Entrance to Shatt al'Arab, No. 3842, published by the British Admiralty;
—Chart No. 2, Inner Bar to Kabda Point, No. 3843, published by the British Admiralty;
—Chart No. 3, Kabda Point to Abadan, No. 3844, published by the British Admiralty;
—Chart No. 4, Abadan to Jazirat Ummat Tuwaylah, No. 3845, published by the British Admiralty.

ARTICLE 2.

1. The frontier line in the Shatt al'Arab shall follow the thalweg, i.e., the median line of the main navigable channel at the lowest navigable level, starting from the point at which the land frontier between Iran and Iraq enters the Shatt al'Arab and continuing to the sea.

[1] *Source: United Nations Treaty Series*, 1017, No. 14903.

2. The frontier line, as defined in paragraph 1 above, shall vary with changes brought about by natural causes in the main navigable channel. The frontier line shall not be affected by other changes unless the two Contracting Parties conclude a special agreement to that effect.

3. The occurrence of any of the changes referred to in paragraph 2 above shall be attested jointly by the competent technical authorities of the two Contracting Parties.

4. Any change in the bed of the Shatt al'Arab brought about by natural causes which would involve a change in the national character of the two States' respective territory or of landed property, constructions, or technical or other installations shall not change the course of the frontier line, which shall continue to follow the thalweg in accordance with the provisions of paragraph 1 above.

5. Unless an agreement is reached between the two Contracting Parties concerning the transfer of the frontier line to the new bed, the water shall be re-directed at the joint expense of both Parties to the bed existing in 1975—as marked on the four common charts listed in article 1, paragraph 3, above—should one of the Parties so request within two years after the date on which the occurrence of the change was attested by either of the two Parties. Until such time, both Parties shall retain their previous rights of navigation and of user over the water of the new bed.

ARTICLE 3.

1. The river frontier between Iran and Iraq in the Shatt al'Arab, as defined in article 2 above, is represented by the relevant line drawn on the common charts referred to in article 1, paragraph 3, above.

2. The two Contracting Parties have agreed to consider that the river frontier shall end at the straight line connecting the two banks of the Shatt al'Arab, at its mouth, at the astronomical lowest low-water mark. This straight line has been indicated on the common hydrographic charts referred to in article 1, paragraph 3, above.

ARTICLE 4.

The frontier line as defined in articles 1, 2 and 3 of this Protocol shall also divide vertically the air space and the subsoil.

ARTICLE 5.

With a view to eliminating any source of controversy, the two Contracting Parties shall establish a Mixed Iraqi-Iranian Commission to settle, within two months, any questions concerning the status of landed property, constructions, or technical or other installations, the national character of which may be affected by the delimitation of the Iranian-Iraqi river frontier, either through repurchase or compensation or any other suitable arrangement.

ARTICLE 6.

Since the task of surveying the Shatt al'Arab has been completed and the common hydrographic chart referred to in article 1, paragraph 3, above has been drawn up, the two Contracting Parties have agreed that a new survey of the Shatt al'Arab shall be carried out jointly, once every 10 years, with effect from the date of signature of this Protocol. However, each of the two Parties shall have the right to request new surveys, to be carried out jointly, before the expiry of the 10-year period.

The two Contracting Parties shall each defray half the cost of such surveys.

ARTICLE 7.

1. Merchant vessels, State vessels and warships of the two Contracting Parties shall enjoy freedom of navigation in the Shatt al'Arab and in any part of the navigable channels in the territorial sea which lead to the mouth of the Shatt al'Arab, irrespective of the line delimiting the territorial sea of each of the two countries.

2. Vessels of third countries used for purposes of trade shall enjoy freedom of navigation, on an equal and non-discriminatory basis, in the Shatt al'Arab and in any part of the navigable channels in the territorial sea which lead to the mouth of the Shatt al'Arab irrespective of the line delimiting the territorial sea of each of the two countries.

3. Either of the two Contracting Parties may authorize foreign warships visiting its ports to enter the Shatt al'Arab, provided such vessels do not belong to a country in a state of belligerency, armed conflict or war with either of the two Contracting Parties and provided the other Party is so notified no less than 72 hours in advance.

4. The two Contracting Parties shall in every case refrain from authorizing the entry to the Shatt al'Arab of merchant vessels belonging to a country in a state of belligerency, armed conflict or war with either of the two Parties.

ARTICLE 8.

1. Rules governing navigation in the Shatt al'Arab shall be drawn up by a mixed Iranian-Iraqi Commission, in accordance with the principle of equal rights of navigation for both States.

2. The two Contracting Parties shall establish a commission to draw up rules governing the prevention and control of pollution in the Shatt al'Arab.

3. The two Contracting Parties undertake to conclude subsequent agreements on the questions referred to in paragraphs 1 and 2 of this article.

ARTICLE 9.

The two Contracting Parties recognize that the Shatt al'Arab is primarily an international waterway, and undertake to refrain from any operation that might hinder navigation in the Shatt al'Arab or in any part of those navigable channels in the territorial sea of either of the two countries that lead to the mouth of the Shatt al'Arab.

DONE at Baghdad, on 13 June 1975.

<table>
<tr><td align="center">[Signed]
ABBAS-ALI KHALATBARY
Minister for Foreign Affairs
of Iran</td><td align="center">[Signed]
SAADOUN HAMADI
Minister for Foreign Affairs
of Iraq</td></tr>
</table>

Signed in the presence of
His Excellency ABDEL-AZIZ BOUTEFLIKA
Member of the Council of the Revolution
and Minister for Foreign Affairs of Algeria

[Signed]

Bibliography

A. UNPUBLISHED SOURCE MATERIALS

India House Library and Records (a Department of the British Library Reference Division)

(i) *Letters, Political and Secret: Departmental Papers, Political and Secret Separate (or Subject) Files: L/P&S/10*

L/P&S/10/132: File 345/1908, Part 1: Mohammarah Situation (1904–10)
L/P&S/10/266: File 1356/1912, Part 1: Turco-Persian Frontier (1912)
L/P&S/10/267: File 1356/1912, Part 2: Turco-Persian Frontier (1912–13)
L/P&S/10/291: File 3154/1912, Parts 1, 2: Turco-Persian Frontier (1912)
L/P&S/10/430: File 4880/1913, Parts 1, 2: Turco-Persian Frontier (1913–15)
L/P&S/10/522: File 5094/1914, Parts 1, 2: Turco-Persian Frontier Commission (1914–17)
L/P&S/10/932: File 7173/1920, Iraq–Persia Boundary (1920–3)
L/P&S/10/1098: File 4480/1923, Part 1: Persian Gulf: Ownership of Shatt-al-Arab (1928–31)
L/P&S/10/1229: File 41/1928, Parts 1, 2: Perso-Iraq Relations (1922–30)

(ii) *Letters, Political and Secret: Political and Secret Annual Files: L/P&S/11*

L/P&S/11/9: Files 901–1050 (Political and Scret Files) (1912)
L/P&S/11/16: Files 1741–1982 (Political and Secret Files) (1912)

(iii) *Letters, Political and Secret: Political (External) Files and Collections: L/P&S/12*

L/P&S/12/43: File PZ6689/31: Iraq: Persian Government's attitude towards Turco-Persian Frontier Settlement (1914). 22 Oct. 1931—29 Oct. 1931
L/P&S/12/1201: Ext. 1133/47: FO Print: Persian Frontiers (with Map) (20 May 1947–22 May 1947)
L/P&S/12/1822: Coll. 3/214: Anglo-Afghan Treaty of 1921: Legal Factors for Substantiation of the rights of transborder Afghans; Mr Fitzmaurice's note on the effect on its validity of the independence of India and Pakistan. Attached to F4010/29SA. Pakistan's Succession to the Anglo-Afghan Treaty of 1921 (4 June 1947–22 May 1950) File now withdrawn.
L/P&S/12/2869: Coll. 17/15(1): Relations with Persia: Persia–Iraq Frontier; Persia's Claim in the Shatt-al-Arab (1 May 1933–15 Mar. 1935)
L/P&S/12/2870: Coll. 17/15(2): ibid. (21 Feb. 1935–15 Jan. 1936)
L/P&S/12/3802: Coll. 30/86(1): Persian Relations with Iraq: Internationalization

144 Bibliography

of the Shatt-al-Arab and Establishment of Conservancy Board (10 Sept. 1932–10 Jan. 1936)

L/P&S/12/3803: Coll. 30/86(2): ibid. (31 Dec. 1935–22 Apr. 1937)

L/P&S/12/3804: Coll. 30/86(3): Persian Relations with Iraq: Shatt-al-Arab; Establishment of an International Conservancy Board (17 Apr. 1937–5 Mar. 1946)

(iv) *Political and Secret Memoranda: L/P&S/18*

L/P&S/18/B236: Statement [on the Expedition to Mesopotamia] Sir F. A. Hirtzel, 30 Aug. 1916

B. OFFICIAL PUBLICATIONS: GOVERNMENTAL AND UNITED NATIONS

(i) *Governmental Publications*

Government of Iran: *A Review of the Imposed War by the Iraqi Regime upon the Islamic Republic of Iran.* Legal Department, Ministry of Foreign Affairs, Iran, 1983

Government of Iraq: *Facts Concerning the Iraqi-Iranian Frontier.* Ministry of Foreign Affairs, Baghdad, 1960. *Comment on the Iranian Claims concerning the Iraqi-Iranian Frontier Treaty of 1937, and the Legal Status of the Frontier between the Two Countries in the Shatt-al-Arab.* Ministry of Foreign Affairs, Baghdad 1969. *The Iraqi-Iranian Dispute: Facts and Allegations,* Ministry of Foreign Affairs, Baghdad, 1981

(ii) *United Nations*

(*a*) General

UN Conference on the Law of Treaties

Official Records of the United Nations Conference on the Law of Treaties, first session, Summary Records of the plenary meetings of the Committee of the Whole: A/CONF.39/11

Official Records of the United Nations Conference on the Law of Treaties, second session, Summary Records of the plenary meetings of the Committee of the Whole: A/CONF.39/11/ Add. 1

Official Records of the United Nations Conference on the Law of Treaties (first and second sessions), Documents of the Conference: A/CONF.39/11/ Add. 2

Vienna Convention on the Law of Treaties: A/CONF. 39/27

UN Legislative Series: *Materials on Succession of States:* ST/LEG/SER.B/14, New York, 1967

UN Monthly Chronicle: 6 (1969), 8 (1971)

UN Treaty Series (*UNTS*): 1017, Nos. 14903, 14904, 14905, 14906, and 14907

UN Yearbook (*Yearbook of the United Nations*): 23 (1969), 28 (1974), 34 (1980)

Vienna Convention on the Succession of States in respect of Treaties: A/CONF.80/ 31 (22 Aug. 1978)

Bibliography

(b) General Assembly

General Assembly Official Records

[Deliberation of the] Sixth Committee at the Eighteenth Session, 792nd Meeting, Oct. 1963, on the Report of the International Law Commission on the Work of its Fifteenth Session (Document: A/C.6/SR.792)

General Assembly Declaration [and Annexe] on Principles of International Law Concerning Friendly Relations and Co-operation among States in accordance with the Charter of the United Nations, 24 Oct. 1970: 25th Session, Supplement No. 28 (A/8028). Resolution No. 2625 (XXV) (Document: A/8082)

Report of the Sixth Committee at the Twenty-Fifth Session, 19 Nov. 1970 on the Question of Defining Aggression. (Document: A/8171)

Report of the Sixth Committee at its Twenty-Ninth Session, Dec. 1974 on the Question of Defining Aggression. (Document A/9890)

Resolution of the General Assembly on the Definition of Aggression at its 2319th Plenary Meeting, 14 Dec. 1974, Resolution No. 3314 (XXXIX), Twenty-Ninth Session, Supplement No. 31 (A/9631). (Document: A:9890)

Reports of the Special Committee of the General Assembly on the definition of Aggression: No. 19, A/8019 (July–Aug. 1970); No. 19, A/8419 Feb.–Mar. 1971); No. 19, A/8719 (Jan.–Mar. 1972); No. 19, A/9019 (Apr.–May 1973)

(c) Security Council

Letters from the governments of Iran and Iraq to the President of the Security Council and Annexes

S/9185: 29 Apr. 1969; S/9190: 1 May 1969;
S/9200: 9 May 1969; S/9200 and Add. 1: 15 May 1969; S/9205: 13 May 1969;
S/9323 and Corr. 1: 11 July 1969;
S/9425: 2 Sept. 1969; A/35/268: 21 May 1980;
S/14020: 20 June 1980; S/14070: 23 July 1980;
S/14191: 22 Sept. 1980; S/14192: 24 Sept. 1980;
S/14206: 1 Oct. 1980;
S/14249: 10 Nov. 1980; S/14272: 25 Nov. 1980.

Statement of Israeli Representative in the Security Council: 9 July 1970 S/PV 1939, of 9 July 1970.

C. PUBLISHED SOURCES: LEGAL AND HISTORICAL

ADAMI, V., *National Frontiers in Relation to International Law*. Oxford, 1927

AKHTAR, S., 'The Iraqi-Iranian Dispute over the Shatt-al-Arab', *Pakistan Horizon*, 22 (1969), p. 213

AL-IZZI, K., *The Shatt-al-Arab River Dispute in Terms of Law*. Baghdad, 1972
—— *The Shatt-al-Arab Dispute: A Legal Study*. London, 1981

AL-MUKHTAR, S., 'The Iraqi Position' in Dessouki (ed.), *The Iraq–Iran War* (q.v), p. 7

AL-RAWI, J., *International Borders*. Cairo, 1970 (Arabic language)

AMERICAN LAW INSTITUTE, *Restatement of the Law: Foreign Relations Law of the United States*. 2nd edn., St Paul, 1965

AMIN, S. H., *International and Legal Problems of the Gulf*. London, 1981
—— 'The Iran–Iraq Conflict: Legal Implications', *ICLQ* 31 (1982), p. 167
ANDERSON, L., *The Belize Question: Continuation of White Book: Controversy between Guatemala and Great Britain relative to the Convention of 1859 on Territorial Matters*, Ministry of Foreign Affairs, Guatemala, 1940
BERNHARDT, R., *Encyclopaedia of Public International Law*. Vols. iii, iv, v, Amsterdam, 1982
BLACK, C. and R. A. FALK, *The Future of International Legal Order*. Princeton, 1971
BLOOMFIELD, L. M., *The British Honduras–Guatemala Dispute*. Toronto, 1953
BOUCHEZ, L. J., 'The Fixing of Boundaries in International Boundary Rivers', *ICLQ* 12 (1963), p. 789
—— 'The Netherlands and the Law of International Rivers', in Panhuys (ed.), *International Law in the Netherlands* (q.v.)
BOWETT, D. W., *Self-Defence in International Law*. Manchester, 1958
—— 'Reprisals involving Recourse to Armed Force', *AJIL* 66 (1972), p. 1
BRIERLY, J. L. *The Law of Nations*. 6th. edn., Oxford, 1963
BRIGGS, H. W., 'Non-Recognition of Title by Conquest and Limitations on the Doctrine', *Proceedings of the American Society of International Law*, 34 (1940), p. 72
—— 'Unilateral Denunciation of Treaties: The Vienna Convention and the International Court of Justice', *AJIL* 68 (1974), p. 51
British and Foreign Papers. 45 (1854–5), 89 (1896–7), 92 (1899–1900), 105 (1912), 141 (1937)
British Parliamentary Papers. Persia No. 1 (1919), 53 (1919); Cmd. 300
BROWNLIE, I., 'The Use of Force in Self-Defence', *BYIL* 37 (1961), p. 183
—— *International Law and the Use of Force by States*. Oxford, 1963
—— *Basic Documents on African Affairs*. Oxford, 1971
—— *African Boundaries: A Legal and Diplomatic Encyclopaedia*. London, 1979
—— *Principles of Public International Law*. 3rd edn., Oxford, 1979
—— *Basic Documents in International Law*. 3rd edn., Oxford, 1983
CASTREN, E., *The Present Law of War and Neutrality*. Helsinki, 1954
CHATTERJEE, S. K., 'Some Legal Problems of Support Role in International Law: Tanzania and Uganda', *ICLQ* 30 (1981), p. 755
CUKWURAH, A. O., *The Settlement of Boundary Disputes in International Law*. Manchester, 1967
DAY, A. J. (ed.), *Borders and Territorial Disputes*. London, 1982
DE ARECHAGA, E. J., 'General Course in International Law', *Recueil des Cours*, 159 (1978–I), p. 1
DELBRÜCK, J., 'Effect of War on Treaties', in Bernhardt (ed.), *Encyclopaedia of Public International Law* 4 (q.v.), p. 310
DESSOUKI, A. E. H., *The Iraq–Iran War: Issues of Conflict and Prospects for Settlement*. Princeton, 1981
DETTER, I. D., 'The Problem of Unequal Treaties', *ICLQ* 15 (1966)
DE VISSCHER, C., *Theory and Reality in Public International Law*. Rev. edn. trans. P. E. Corbett, Princeton, 1968

Digest of the United States' Practice in International Law. Vols. 1974, p. 700; 1976, p. 700

DIXON, H. and M. KHADDURI. 'Passage through International Waterways', in Khadduri (ed.), *Major Middle Eastern Problems in International Law* (q.v.) p. 65

DUGARD, C. J. R., 'The OAU and Colonialism: An Inquiry into the Plea of Self-Defence as a Justification, for the Use of Force in the Eradication of Colonialism', *ICLQ* 16 (1967), p. 157

EDMONDS, C. J., *Kurds, Turks, and Arabs*. Oxford, 1957

—— The Iraqi-Persian Frontier, 1639–1938, *Asian Affairs*, 62 (1975), p. 147

EL-AZHARY, M. S. (ed.), *The Iran-Iraq War*. London, 1984

FALK. R. A., 'The Legal Control of Force in the International Community', in Falk and Mendlovitz (eds.), *The Strategy of World Order*, (q.v.), Vol. ii

—— 'The New States and the International Legal Order', *Recueil Des Cours*, 118 (1966-II), p. 2

—— and C. E. BLACK, *The Future of International Legal Order*. Princeton, 1971

—— and S. H. MENDLOVITZ, *The Strategy of World Order*. Vols. i and ii, New York, 1966

FARER, T. J., 'Law and War', in Falk and Black, *The Future of International Legal Order* (q.v.), iii. 15

FERENCZ, B. B., *Defining International Aggression, The Search for World Peace: A Documentary History and Analysis*. Vols. i and ii, New York, 1975

FISCHER-WILLIAMS, J., 'The Permanence of Treaties', *AJIL* 22 (1928), p. 89

FITZMAURICE, G., 'The Juridical Clauses of the Peace Treaties', *Recueil des Cours*, 73 (1948-II), p. 259

—— 'Second Report on the Law of Treaties', *YILC*, 1957, ii. 16. Document A/CN.4/107

—— 'Third Report on the Law of Treaties', *YILC*, 1958, ii. 1. Document A/CN.4/113

—— 'The Contribution of the Institute of International Law to the Development of International Law', *Recueil des Cours*, 138 (1973-I), p. 203

FONTEYNE, J.-P., 'Forcible Self-help by States to Protect Human Rights', in Lillich (ed.), *Humanitarian Intervention and the United Nations* (q.v.), p. 197

GARNER, J. W., 'Non-Recognition of Illegal Territorial Annexation and Claims to Sovereignty', *AJIL* 30 (1936), p. 679

—— 'The Doctrine of the Thalweg as a Rule of International Law', *AJIL* 29 (1935), p. 309

—— and V. JOBST, 'Unilateral Denunciation of Treaties by One Party Because of Alleged Non-Performance of Another Party or Parties', *AJIL* 29 (1935), p. 569

GREIG, D. W., *International Law*. 2nd edn., London, 1976

GREWE, W. G., 'Peace Treaties', in Bernhardt (ed.), *Encyclopaedia of Public International Law*, (q.v.), iv. 102

GROTIUS, H., *De Jure Belli Ac Pacis Libri Tres*, 1625, trans. F. W. Kelsey, 1925. Carnegie Endowment for International Peace, Washington, DC, 1964

HACKWORTH, G. H., *A Digest of International Law*. Washington, DC, Vols. i (1940), ii (1941), and v. (1943)

HALL, W. E., *International Law*. 8th edn. London, 1934

HANSARD, *House of Commons Debates*. 466, 549, and 558: 5th Series

HANSARD, *House of Lords Debates*. 212: 5th series

HARASZTI, G., 'Treaties and the Fundamental Change of Circumstances', *Recueil des Cours*, 146 (1975-III), p. 1

—— 'Reflections on the Invalidity of Treaties', in Haraszti (ed.), *Questions of International Law*. Budapest, 1977, p. 59

Harvard Draft Convention on the Law of Treaties, *AJIL* 29 (1935), Supplement, p. 657

HEIKAL, M., *Iran: The Untold Story*. New York, 1982

HIGGINS, R., *The Development of International Law through the Political Organs of the United Nations*. London, 1963

HUNSELER, P., 'The Historical Antecedents of the Shatt al Arab Dispute', in El-Azhary, *The Iran–Iraq War* (q.v.), p. 8

HURST, C., 'The Effect of War on Treaties', *BYIL* 2 (1921–2), p. 37

HYDE, C. C., *International Law Chiefly as Interpreted and Applied by the United States*, Washington, DC, 1947, Vols. i, ii, and iii

Indian Journal of International Law, 4 (1964)

International Law Association, Report of the 48th Conference at New York, 1958

—— Report of the 53rd Conference at Buenos Aires, 1968

—— *The Effect of Independence on Treaties*, London, 1965

International Legal Materials, 9 (1970), 11 (1972), 13 (1974), 14 (1975), 15 (1976), 17 (1978)

ISMAEL, T. Y., *Iraq and Iran: Roots of Conflict*. Syracuse, 1982

JENNINGS, R. Y., *The Acquisition of Territory in International Law*, Manchester, 1963

JONES, S. B., *Boundary Making*, Washington, DC., 1945

KAIKOBAD, K. H., 'Some Observations on the Doctrine of Continuity and Finality of Boundaries', *BYIL* 54 (1983), p. 119

KEELEY, J. R., 'The Effect of End of War on Pre-War Treaties between the Belligerents', *Transactions of the Grotius Society*, 12 (1927), pp. 7

KEETON. G. W., 'Extraterritoriality', *Recueil des Cours*, 72 (1948-I), p. 287

KELSEN. H., 'The Draft Declaration on Rights and Duties of States', *AJIL* 44 (1950), p. 259

—— *Principles of International Law*, 2nd edn., New York, 1966

KHADDURI, M. (ed.), *Major Middle Eastern Problems in International Law*, Washington, DC, 1972

LA PRADELLE, A., 'The Effect of War on Private Treaties', *International Law Quarterly*, 2 (1948), p. 555

LAUTERPACHT, E., 'The Contemporary Practice of the United Kingdom in the Field of International Law', *ICLQ* (1956), 6 (1957), and 8 (1959)

—— *The Contemporary Practice of the United Kingdom in the Field of International Law*, 1962, Part II, London, 1962

—— 'River Boundaries: Legal Aspects of the Shatt-al-Arab Frontier', *International and Comparative Law Quarterly*, 9 (1960), p. 208.

LAUTERPACHT, H., *The Function of Law in the International Community*. Oxford, 1933

—— 'Report on the Law of Treaties', *YILC*, 1953, ii. 90. Document A/CN.4/63

League of Nations, *Report of the Committee of the Council of the League of Nations*: 5 Oct. 1935: *The Dispute between Ethiopia and Italy*: VII, Political. 1935. VII. 16. Official No: C411(1). M.207(1). 1935. VII. in *American Journal of International Law*, 30 (1936), Supplement, p. 1

—— *Report of the Work of the League of Nations since the Fifteenth Session*, 1935, Part 1. (A.6. 1935).

League of Nations Official Journal, 16 (1935)

League of Nations Treaty Series, 90, No. 4423, p. 241

LEIGH, M., 'Memorandum on Israeli-Occupied Territories', *Digest of the United States Practice in International Law*, 1976, p. 700

LESTER, A. P., 'State Succession to Treaties in the Commonwealth', *ICLQ* 12 (1963), p. 475

LILLICH, R. B., (ed.), *Humanitarian Intervention and the United Nations*. Charlottesville, 1973

LINDLEY, M. F., *The Acquisition and Government of Backward Territory in International Law*. London, 1926

LISSITYZN, O. J., 'Treaties and Changed Circumstances (*Rebus Sic Stantibus*)', *AJIL* 61 (1967), p. 895

McEWEN, I., *International Boundaries of East Africa*. Oxford, 1971

McNAIR, A., 'The Functions and Differing Legal Character of Treaties', *BYIL* 11 (1930), p. 100

—— *The Law of Treaties*. Oxford, 1961

MARTENS, G. F., *The Law of Nations*, trans. Cobbett. 4th edn., London, 1829

MEEKER, L. C., *The Legality of US Participation in the Defence of Vietnam*, Legal Memorandum of the Legal Adviser to the United Nations Department of State, *AJIL* 60 (1966), p. 700

MELAMID, A., 'The Shatt-al-Arab Boundary Dispute', *Middle East Journal*, 22 (1968), p. 351

MENDOZA, J. L., *Britain and her Treaties on Belize* . . . . Ministry of Foreign Affairs, Guatemala, 1946

MENON, P. K., 'International Boundaries: A Case Study of the Guyana–Surinam Boundary', *ICLQ* 27 (1978), p. 738

MOORE, J. B., *A Digest of International Law*. Washington, DC, 1906

—— *History and Digest of the International Arbitrations to which the United States has been a Party*, ii, Washington, DC, 1898

MOVCHAN, A., 'Problems of Boundaries and Security in the Helsinki Declaration', *Recueil des Cours*, 154 (1977-I), p. 1

NAHLIK, S. E., 'The Grounds of Invalidity and Termination of Treaties', *AJIL* 65 (1971), p. 736

NAVAL INTELLIGENCE DIVISION (UK), *Iraq and the Persian Gulf*, 1944

O'CONNELL, D. P., *State Succession in Municipal Law and International Law*. Vols. i and ii, Cambridge, 1967
—— *International Law*. 2nd edn. Vols. i and ii, London, 1970
OPPENHEIM, L., *International Law*. 7th edn. (H. Lauterpacht), Vols. i and ii: 'Peace' and 'War', London, 1952
PANHUYS, H. F. VAN (ed.), *International Law in the Netherlands*. The Hague, 1978
PARRY, C., *Consolidated Treaty Series*, 101 (1847), 139 (1869), and 215 (1911–12)
PHILLIMORE, R., *Commentaries upon International Law*. 2nd edn., London, 1873
PHILLIPSON, C., *Termination of War and Treaties of Peace*. New York, 1916
PIPES, D., 'A Border Adrift: Origins of the [Iran–Iraq] Conflict', in Tahir-Kheli, (ed.), *The Iran–Iraq War*, (q.v.), p. 3
PUFENDORF, S., *De Jure Naturae et Gentium Libri Octo*, 1688, trans. Oldfather, 1934. Carnegie Endowment for International Peace, New York, 1964
RAMAZANI, R. K., 'Iran's Search for Regional Cooperation', *Middle East Journal*, 30 (1976), p. 173
RANK, R., 'Modern War and the Validity of Treaties', *Cornell Law Quarterly*, 38 (1952–3), p. 321
RYDER, C. H. D., 'The Demarcation of the Turco-Persian Boundary in 1913–1914', *Geographical Journal*, 66 (1925), p.227
SCHINDLER, D., 'The Administration of Justice in the Swiss Federal Court in International Disputes', *AJIL* 15 (1921), p. 149
SCHWARZENBERGER, G., *International Law as Applied by International Courts and Tribunals*. Vol. ii: *The Law of Armed Conflict*. London, 1968
SCHWEBEL, S. M., 'What Weight to Conquest?' *AJIL* 64 (1970), p. 344
SHIHATA, I. F. I., 'Destination Embargo of Arab Oil: Its Legality under International Law', *AJIL* 68 (1974), p. 591
SINHA, B. P., *Unilateral Denunciation of Treaty Because of Prior Violations of Obligations by Other Party*. The Hague, 1966
STONE, J., *Legal Controls of International Conflict*. New York, 1954
—— *Conflict through Consensus*. Baltimore, 1977
TAHIR-KHELI, S., *The Iran–Iraq War: New Weapons, Old Conflicts*. New York, 1983
TREVIRANUS, H.-D., 'Boundary Settlements between Germany and her Western Neighbours after the Second World War', in Bernhardt (ed.), *Encyclopaedia of Public International Law* (q.v.), iii. 71
TWISS, T., *The Law of Nations*. Oxford, 1884
TYRANOWSKI, J., 'State Succession: Boundaries and Boundary Treaties', *Polish Yearbook of International Law*, 10 (1979–80), p. 115
UDOKANG, O., *Succession of New States to International Treaties*. New York, 1972
United Kingdom Treaty Series, No. 29 (1929): Cmd. 3410; No. 58 (1980): Cmnd. 7964
VALLAT, F., 'First Report on the Succession of States in respect of Treaties', *YILC*, 1974, Vol. ii, Part One, p. 1. Document A./CN.4/278
VAN DER MOLEN, G. H. J., 'The Present Crisis in the Law of Nations', in *Symbolae Verzijl*. The Hague, 1958, p. 238
VATTEL, E. DE, *The Law of Nations*, 1773, trans. J. Chitty. London, 1834

VERZIJL, J. H. W., *International Law in Historical Perspective*. Leyden, Vols. iii (1971), vi (1973)
WALDOCK C. H. M., 'The Regulation of the Use of Force by Individual States', *Recueil des Cours*, 81 (1952-II), p. 455
—— 'Second Report on the Law of Treaties', *YILC*, 1963, ii. 36. (Document A/CN.4/156 and Add. 1–3)
—— 'Sixth Report on the Law of Treaties', *YILC*, 1966, ii. 51. (Document A/CN.4/186 and Add. 1–7)
—— 'First Report on Succession of States and Governments in respect of Treaties', *YILC*, 1968, ii. 86. (Document A/CN.4/202)
—— Fifth Report on Succession in respect of Treaties, *YILC*, 1972. ii. 1. (Document A/CN.4/256 and Add. 1–4)
WESTLAKE, J., *International Law*, Parts I and II: 'Peace' and 'War'. Cambridge, 1904 and 1907
WHARTON, F., *A Digest of the International Law of the United States*. Washington, DC, 1887
WHEATON, H., *Elements of International Law*. 6th edn. by Keith, London, 1929
WHITEMAN, R., *A Digest of International Law*. Washington, DC, iii (1964), v (1965), xiv (1970)
WIDDOWS, K., 'The Unilateral Denunciation of Treaties Containing no Denunciation Clause', *BYIL* 53 (1982), p. 83
WRIGHT, Q., 'The Goa Incident', *AJIL* 56 (1962), p. 617
—— 'The Legal Aspects of the Vietnam Situation', *AJIL* 60 (1966), p. 750
—— 'The Termination and Suspension of Treaties', *AJIL* 61 (1967), p. 1000
Yearbook of the International Law Commission. Years 1949, 1953, 1957, 1963, 1966, 1968, 1972, 1974, Vols. i and ii.
Yearbook of the United Nations. 23 (1969), 28 (1974), 34 (1980)

Index

Abadan; Abadan Anchorage (Al Khizr) 6, 8, 13, 17–20, 24, 29, 34, 54–9, 62–3, 66–7, 70, 72, 85, 92, 95
  cession of 17–19
  lease of 58
Abadan Marakat 57 n., 58, 66
Abdullah Marakat 57 n., 58, 66
Abrogation of Boundary Treaties, *see* unilateral abrogation
Abu Jidiyeh (Djudei) 20, 22, 26, 29
accretion 81
acquiescence, *see also* recognition 69–72, 83, 88 n., 104, 118
Acts of Renunciation 102
acquired rights 82
Adams, J.Q. 101
Adami, V. 83 n., 84 n., 72
Afghanistan 73–4
Afghanistan–Pakistan Frontier, *see* Durand Line
aggression, *see* war and self defence 2, 49, 108 n., 110 n.
Akhtar 4 n., 94 n.
Algiers Protocol 64–5, 93, 96–7
Al Izzi 4 n., 8 n., 17 n., 31 n., 50 n., 63 n., 76 n., 83 n.
Al Khizr: *see* Abadan
allocation of territory, *see also* successive recognition of title to territory
  by treaty, validity of 70–5
  and successive recognition 70–5
Aloisi, Baron 56
Alvarez Tabio 89 n.
Alverstone 79
Amin 4 n., 64 n., 65 n., 67, 118 n.
Ammoun 85 n.
annexation of territory, *see* war
Anglo-American War of 1815 101–2
Anglo-Persian Oil Company 41, 43, 46
anticipatory self-defence, *see also* self defence and war 143 n.
Arabs 9, 53 n., 68, 94–5
Ararat (Mount) 8, 25, 34, 52
armed attack, *see* war
Austria–Hungary 113
Avulsion 81

Baghdad 41, 55, 58, 63, 65
Baghdad Treaty of 1975 64–7, 93–115
  abrogation of 67, 93–9
  allocation of territory 94–5, 99, 103–6, 108–18
  effects of material breach and countervailing circumstances 95–9
  frontier security and territorial integrity as material breach 95–8
  interpretation of 94–9
  permanence of 97–9
  spirit of 96–7
Balkan States 76
Bamishere River 6, 12–13, 16, 19
  navigation of 16
Basra (Busrah) 5, 9–10, 12–15, 22, 29, 53, 58
Basra Port Authority 53, 56, 62
Bathurst, Lord 101
Belgium 104–5
Belize (British Settlement in the Bay of Honduras) 91
Beni Salih 29
Beni Sukain 29, 40
Beni Turuf 29, 40
Black 109–10, 109–10 n.
Bouchez 76 n., 78 n., 84 n.
boundaries, excluding boundary cases, *see also* frontiers
  Germany–Belgium 104–5
  Germany–France 104–5
  Germany–Luxembourg 104–5
  Germany–Netherlands 104–5
  Guatemala–Belize 91
  India–Pakistan 105
  Iraq–Turkey 54
  Liberia–Ivory Coast 84
  Pakistan–Afghanistan 73–4
  Peru–Ecuador 91–2
  Uganda–Tanzania 105
  United States–Canada 77 n.
  Venezuela–Guiana 92 n.
  Vietnam–Cambodia 104
boundaries
  finality and continuity of, *see* finality and stability
  local, historical and ethnological factors, *see also* fundamental changes 3, 29–31, 40–8, 101, 104–5
  modifications and revisions 50–4, 67, 72–4, 104–5, 112
  requests for mutual rectification 93, 118
boundary
  allocation and attribution, preclusion of subsequent examination and irrelevance of ethnicity in valid delimitation, *see also* finality and stability of boundaries 94–5

boundary—*cont*
　Commission of 1914 51–2, 65
　　and of 1937–38 63–4
　disputes, political and factual aspects 70, 92–4, 99–100, 116–18
　　and genuine interests of States 117–18
　　and rigidity of law 118
　Mark No. 2 51
　Pillar No. 2 66
　treaties, *see also* abrogation, *rebus sic stantibus*, war
　　and *rebus sic stantibus* 85–9
　　as evidence of transfer of territory 86, 103
　　as mutual conveyance and transfer of title 103–4
　　as sources of title to territory 74, 86, 99
　　existence of rights independent of 103–4
　　extinction after execution 103–4
　　finality, continuity and permanence 85–92
　　lapse and abrogation and breach of obligations 94–9
　　rule against abrogation 87–93
　　supersession of boundary treaty by delimitation 86–7
　　survival in war, *see* war
　　valid conclusion of 103
　Boundary Protocol of 1913 23–56, 58, 65, 69–70, 74, 85, 95
　　validity of 53–4
Bowett 106 n., 109 n., 111 n.
Brierly 88 n., 97 n., 113 n.
Britain/British Government 3, 11, 35, 40, 47, 49, 52, 54–5, 63, 71, 74, 78–80, 91–2, 101, 102
　Britain as mandatory power 52
　British ambassadors 22, 46–50, 55
　Foreign Office 13–14, 25–6, 28–9, 52, 58, 62–3, 74–5, 83
　Foreign Secretary, *see also under individual name* 31, 48, 50, 53, 83
　interests in frontier location 23–51, 52–64
　Joint Parliamentary Under Secretary for Foreign Affairs, *see* Marquess of Lansdowne
　policy in the Gulf and Shatt 23–51, 52–64
　Secretary for Commonwealth Relations, *see* Noel-Baker
　Secretary for War and Colonies, *see* Lord Bathurst
　sector of boundary 25, 52
　shipping in the Shatt 54 n.
Brownlie 73 n., 78 n., 82 n., 83 n., 84 n., 90 n., 106 n., 107 n., 109 n., 111 n., 112 n.

Canada, Supreme Court of 103
Cañas–Jerez Treaty 90
Cairo Resolution of 1964 73
Canning, Sir Stratford 16–17, 19
Castren 106, 143, 113 n.
ceasefire lines as boundaries 92 n.
Central American Court of Justice 90
cession
　of Abadan, *see* Mohammerah
　of the Shatt, *see* Shatt al Arab, cession
　of Mohammerah, *see* Mohammerah
　of Shia lands 40–8
　of territory 88, 91–2, 94–5, 101–2
Chaab 3, 9–14, 16, 22
change and the law 116–18
changed circumstances, *see rebus sic stantibus*
Chatterjee 105 n.
Clausa Rebus Sic Stantibus, *see rebus sic stantibus*
clear state principle, *see* state succession
Cleveland Award 90
Clive, Sir Robert 54
codification of international law 89 n.
Coleman Philipson 100 n., 113 n.
Confederate Award of 1555 82
Conference of Erzeroum, *see* Erzeroum, Conferences of
Conservancy Board, *see* Shatt al Arab Conservancy Board
Constantinople 16, 22–4, 31, 43, 46–7, 49–50
Cordozo 103 n.
Council of the League of Nations, *see* League of Nations
counter-insurgency operations 96
Cox, Sir Percy 23, 25–6, 28–31, 40, 52–3
Cox-Wilson Alignment 35, 40
Cukwurah 76 n., 78 n., 83 n., 84 n.
Curzon 16

Davidson, Sir E 83
Day 85 n.
de Aréchaga 87, 106 n.
de Castro 72 n.
de facto territorial situations 111
de Giers 43
Delbrück 100 n.
De Luna 87 n.
demarcation of boundaries 18–23, 51–2, 63–4, 66–7, 73–4, 86
Dessouki 4 n., 94 n.
Detter 113 n.
de Visscher 110, 112 n.
Dezful 6, 30
Diaji (Di'aiji) 23, 26, 28–9, 31, 34
distribution of power, effects of 117

Index

Draft Declaration on Rights and Duties of States 106 n.
Dugard 109–10 n.
Durand Line 73–4

Earl Curzon of Kedleston 53
Earl of Crewe 26
El-Azhary 4 n., 96 n.
Elvand 41–3, 46–8
enforcement of international law 111
equity 118
Erzeroum, Conferences 12, 14, 16–19, 22
Erzeroum, First Treaty of, *see* First Treaty of Erzeroum
Erzeroum, Second Treaty of (1847), *see* Second Treaty of Erzeroum
essential validity of treaty, *see* treaties
estoppel 118
Euphrates 5, 9, 12–14
ex iniuria jus non oritur 106
explanatory note 17–19, 31

Falliyeh 20, 22, 26, 28–9, 40
Falk 106 n., 109–10 n.
Farer 109–10 n.
Fellaliyeh 6, 10
Fellaliyeh, Sheikh of 9
Ferencz 110 n.
feudal law 82
Field, Justice 79
finality and stability of boundaries and boundary treaties, doctrine of, *see also* abrogation of treaties, termination of treaties and war 72–5, 85–9, 94–6, 98–9, 104–5, 117–18
  and state succession to boundary treaties 90
Finlay, Sir Robert 79
First Treaty of Erzeroum 8
Fischer Williams 86 n.
Fitzmaurice, Sir Gerald 71 n., 74, 88 n., 99 n., 100 n. 106 n.
Fonteyne 110 n.
force, unlawful use of, *see* war
France/French government, *see also* treaties 71, 73, 80, 84, 104–5
frontier customs post 28
frontier incidents 23–4, 55–6, 64–5
frontier instability, rule against 111
frontier security 94, 98, 104
  and relationship with Baghdad Treaty 94
  and abrogation 96
fundamental boundary changes 72
fundamental change of circumstances, *see rebus sic stantibus*
Fuller 80

Garner 80 n., 97 n., 106 n.
Germany/German government 102, 104–5, 110 n., 113

Hawizeh 6, 13–15, 19–20, 26, 29–31, 34–5, 40, 43, 50
Heikal 67
Helsinki 107
Higgins 109 n.
Holy Roman Empire 76
Hungary 101
Hurst, Sir Cecil 83, 87 n., 100 n., 103
Hunseler 96 n.
Hyde 77 n., 78 n.
hydrographic charts 67

Identic Map 22–3, 52
indemnity 11
India/Indian States 71, 105
India office 52
Indo-China 104
inequality of states 64, 117
International Court of Justice 70, 72–3
international disputes, final and conclusive settlement of 85–93
International Law Association 86
International Law Commission 87
  preparatory work on the Law of State Succession to Treaties 90
  preparatory work on the Law of Treaties 87–90
International Military Tribunal 110 n.
interpretation of treaties
  of Erzeroum (1847) 15–16, 18–22, 51, 68 *passim*
  of 1937 68 *passim*
invalid and void treaties 53–4, 75, 85–92, 94–5, 99, 112–15
inviolability of frontiers 66, 98, 104, 106–7
Iran (Persia)
  traditional limits of 7–16, 25–51
  tribes of 9–12
Iranian
  Foreign Minister 50, 53, 55, 59, 65, 75
  police and custom 55
  Prime Minister 49–50
  revolution 67
Iraqi
  Foreign Minister 56, 59, 62–3, 65
  Iranian-Algerian Committee 66–7
  Kurdish rebellion 94
  national waters 53
  Turkish frontier 54

Japan 92
Jennings 106 n., 108 n., 109 n., 110 n., 114.
Jetty No. 1 58

156 *Index*

Jeyhani Maps 12
Jobst 97 n.
Jones 76 n.
jurisdiction of states regarding rivers 75–85

Kaab, *see* Chaab
Kaikobad 72 n.
Kampala 105
Karun 5–6, 12–15, 19, 34
Kasr-i-Shirin 6, 41, 43, 47
Keeley 103 n.
Keeton 113 n.
Kelsen 106 n., 110 n., 159
Khaiyin Canal 26, 31, 34–5, 51, 56, 64, 66
Khanaqin 6, 41, 64
Khizr, *see* Abadan
Khomeni, Ayatollah 67
Kinneir 14
Kornah 5, 13–15, 20
Kurdish rebellion 64–5, 67, 94–9
  abandonment of support of as *quid pro quo* 94
  and Article 3 of the Baghdad Treaty 94–9
  counter-insurgency operations 96
  effects on Iraq 96
  formenting and support of by Iran 94
Kuretu river and town 41–3, 46, 48
Kutch 71

Lachs 89 n.
Lagergren 71
Lake Geneva 84
La Morge 84
La Pradelle 100 n.
Lauterpacht, E. 4 n., 74 n., 76 n., 78 n., 92 n., 110 n.
Lauterpacht, H. 100 n., 106 n., 109 n., 112 n.
Law of Treaties, *see* Vienna Convention on the Law of Treaties
Layard 114
League of Nations, Council of 56–7, 75
Leigh 109
Lester 86 n.
Liberia 84
Lindley 83 n., 84 n.
Line of Convenience 78
Lillich 109 n.
Lissityzn 87 n.
Lowther 46, 48
Luxembourg 104–5

main navigable channel, *see* Thalweg
Mamishan 41
Mahdali 6, 41–3, 46–8, 52
Mankoli (Manquli) 29, 51
maps 13, 16, 35, 52, 67, 70–1, 104

Marling 49
Marquess of Lansdowne 92
marshland/marshes 30–1, 35, 40
Martinez Caro 89 n.
McEwen 76 n., 78 n., 84 n.
McNair 86 n., 88 n., 97 n., 100 n.
median line in navigable rivers as a principle of law *see also* Thalweg 64, 75–85
mediating commissioners, British and Russian 15–16, 18–19, 23, 25, 30, 69
mediating powers, *see also* Britain and Russia 12, 18, 25, 46, 48–9, 68
mediation 98
Medieval Grants, *see also* Thalweg 76
medium filum acquae, see median line in navigable rivers
Meeker 110 n.
Melamid 4 n., 75 n.
Mendoza 91 n.
Menon 84 n., 85 n.
Mesopotamia 5, 7, 52–3, 94
Mixed Technical Commission 66–7
Mohammara 5–11, 13–24, 28, 34, 40, 53, 55, 66–7, 72, 85, 92, 95
  as enclave 19
  cession of 16–20
  rights of access to 16–17
  Sheikh of, *see* Sheikh of Mohammara
Moore 73 n., 77 n., 78 n., 83 n., 100 n.
Morocco 72 n.
Movchan 107 n.
multilateral agreements 70
municipal instruments, *see* recognition by official documentation
Murdos Armistice 52
Myslil 89 n.

Nahlik 88 n., 97 n.
Nahr Abul Arabid 31, 51
Nahr Al Khaiyin, *see* Khayin Canal
Nahr Diaji (Di'aiji), *see* Diaji
Nahr Nazaliyeh 31, 34, 51
navigable rivers, *see* Thalweg
Netherlands 78, 83–4, 104–5
Newfoundland 101
Nicaragua 90
Noel-Baker 74
No Man's Land 76
non-recognition of boundary, *see* successive recognition; allocation of territory
North Ship Channel 81
Norway 70
nul et non avenu 18

O'Beirne 49
occupation, *see* War
occupation rights, *see also* war 109

Index

O'Connell 86 n., 100 n., 106 n., 109–110 n., 111 n.
O'Conor, Sir Nicholas 24
oil bearing regions, fields and wells 41–3, 46, 53
oil refinery (British) 53
Oppenheim 100 n., 106 n.
Organisation of African Unity 73
Organisation of Petroleum Exporting Countries 65
Orlof 41, 48
Ottoman Empire and Government, *see* Turkey

pacta sunt servanda 89 n.
Pakistan 73–4, 105
Palmerston 19
Panhuys 84 n.
Parker 9 n., 10, 13, 24, 26, 34
Parry 8 n., 23 n., 31 n.
peace treaties 89–90 n., 101, 112–15
 and relevance of nature of force 112–15
 earlier rationale for 112–13
 later view, difficulties with 113–14
 role of multilateral and regional recognition and justification for role 114–15
Permanent Court of Arbitration 79, 102
Permanent Court of International Justice 70, 101
Persian Gulf, *see* British Policy in the Gulf & Shatt
Persian Boundary Commissioners 15, 18–19, 23
Phillimore 101
Pipes 65 n., 67 n.
Poland 101
Portland Channel 78–9
possession, long undisturbed, *see also* sovereignty 34
preclusion and prescription 68–70, 72–5, 81–2, 94–5, 98, 104
 and the thalweg rule, *see* Thalweg
Procès verbaux of 1914 58, 65–6, 69
Protocol Concerning Security on the Frontier between Iran and Iraq 65 n., 96 n.
Protocol Concerning the Delimitation of the River Frontier 66, 93, 96 n.
Protocol Concerning the Redemarcation of the Land Frontier 66, 96 n.

quid pro quo 34, 57, 65, 96–7

Ramazani 65
Rank 100 n.
Rawlinson 9–13

Rawlinson Line 13, 16
Raza Shah 53, 55, 64
rebus sic stantibus 85–9
 and exception for boundary treaties 86–7
 rationale for exception 86–7
recognition of boundaries and boundary treaties, *see also* succession of boundaries
 by official documentation 70–5
repute 69
revision of boundary treaties, *see* boundaries and modifications
revision of treaties, presumption against, *see* boundary modifications
Riparian States, territorial rights of medieval 76
River Co-dominion, Principle of 77
River Condominium 77
Robson 101 n.
Rooka Channel 57 n.
Rostow 109–10 n.
Rush 109–10 n.
Russia/Russian empire and government 8, 11, 14, 17–18, 20, 22, 25, 29, 34–5, 41, 43 46–9, 50, 76
 frontier with Persia 8
 sector 25, 34, 40–1, 43
 Vice-Chancellor 17

Schaffhausen, Swiss Canton of 82
Schindler 82 n., 89 n., 91 n.
Schwarzenberger 106 n.
Schwebel 109 n.
Scott, J.B. 73 n., 77 n., 78 n., 79 n., 82 n.
Scott, Sir William 83
Second Treaty of Erzeroum 8, 15–18, 28, 31, 43, 68, 74–5, 83, 85, 93, 95
Security Council, *see* United Nations
self-defence, *see also* war
 abuse of plea 109–11, 113
 and consent to treaties 112–14
 and disputed title 111, 113
 and United Nations Charter 109
 individual and collective 111 n.
 priority principle 110 n.
Senjabi 41–2, 46–7
Serkala 41, 46
Shah of Persia, *see also* Raza Shah 15, 64–5
Shatt al Arab
 as general frontier between Ottoman and Persian Empires 12–16
 cession of part of river, *see also* Abadan Anchorage 17–18, 31, 34, 50, 58–9, 62, 66, 95
 Conservancy Board 57
 conservancy measures and questions 55–9, 62–4

Shatt al Arab—cont.
  control of by parties during war 100
  droit d'usage 62–3
  equality of interest in 62–3
  Iranian control and claims over 13–15,
    18–22, 25–6, 28–9, 50–1, 54–64,
    68–70
  Iranian freedom of navigation in 16–18,
    26, 28, 51, 58–9, 62
  Left bank line 8, 12–18, 20, 26, 34–5, 50–2,
    54, 56–9, 65, 68–85, 92–3, 95, 117
    abandonment of 65–7
    as ground for invalidity 75, 85
    entrenchment of 69–75
    impracticable nature of 117
  levying of dues on shipping in 24, 53–4,
    58–9
  lighting, buoying and dredging of 53, 58–9,
    62
  midline boundary in 20, 26, 28–9, 31, 34–5,
    50, 54, 56–8, 62, 63, 66–9, 75–85,
    92–3, 98
  midline local boundary, abandonment of
    by Persia 69–70
  navigation in, *see also* Iranian freedom of
    navigation 13, 22, 24, 53, 55, 57–9, 62
  navigation of warships in 58–9, 62
  Thalweg boundary in 7, 34, 54, 56, 58–9,
    62–7, 70, 75–85, 92–9, 115–16
  traditional control over 12–22, 23, 25–6,
    28–9, 31, 34, 50
  Turkish/Iraqi sovereignty over 9–22, 23–7,
    28–9, 31, 34–5, 50–2, 54–9, 62–7,
    69–70
Shatt-Hawizeh Sector 29–30, 35–40
Sheikh of Mohammara
  and British policy 24
  territorial and proprietorial control of
    28–9
Sheil 14
Shia lands & tribes, *see also* Senjabi 41, 46,
  48
Shihata 106 n.
Sinha 88 n., 97 n.
Soane 41–2
Soane–Orlof Proposition No. 1 41–3
  Proposition No. 2 42–6, 48
  Proposition No. 3 42
Southern Terminus of Boundary 51, 57
sovereignty 18, 76, 82, 91–3, 101
Spain 80
state practice
  and finality of boundaries 73–4, 91–2
  and the principles of the thalweg and
    medium filum acquae 76–8, 84–5
Stimson Doctrine 106
stratae regiae, *see also* Thalweg 76

succession of states 73
  clean slate principle 90
  exception to the principle 90
  rationale for 90
  Vienna Convention on Succession of
    States in Respect of Treaties: Article
    11 73, 90
successive recognition
  by municipal documentation 71–2
  by treaty 70–2
  of boundaries and boundary treaties 70–5
  of left bank boundary 70
Sunni tribes 43, 46
Swiss Federal Court 82

tableau descriptif 52
Tahir-Kheli 4 n., 65 n.
Tanzania 105
Taiwan 92
Tehran 14, 23, 31, 49, 52, 54–5, 63, 65–6
Tehran Protocol of 1911 23, 30–1
territorial integrity 106–7
Thalweg
  as grounds for invalidity in treaty 95
  as presumption and principle 77–85
  claims to the whole river 76–7, 80–5
  different meanings of 75–6
  evolution in Europe of 76–8
  identification of 78–9, 93, 98
  in international jurisprudence 78–9, 82
  in national courts 79–81
  in the context of State practice 83–5
  rationale 76–8
  stratae regiae 76
Tigris 5, 9, 12–13
title to territory, *see also* cession and
    successive recognition
  acquisition by cession 69–70, 74, 86, 88,
    91–2, 94–5, 99, 103–4
  acquisition by treaty by victorious State
    112–15
  disputed title and self-defence, *see*
    self-defence
  ethnicity and transfer of 93–5
  permanence of, *see* finality and stability
  recognition of, *see* successive recognition
  rule against transfer in war 105–15
Townley 49–50
transferred territories 6, 40–8
Treaty of 1937 15, 52–64, 70, 72, 74, 85–93,
  95
treaties
  consent to treaties and use of force 112–17
  rationale 113
  collective or regional recognition of
    peace treaty 114, 117
  essential validity of 112

Index

suspension of 97, 101, 103–4
termination by material breach 94–99
Treviranus 104 n., 105 n.
tribal allegiances 9–12, 21, 24, 29–30, 40–3, 46–8
Turco-Persian Joint Delimitation Commission 14
Turco-Persian Frontier Commission 49
Turco-Persian Joint Commission 31
Turkish Boundary Commission 15, 19, 23
Turkish Minister for Foreign Affairs 19, 22, 43, 47–8
Turkish Mudirs 26
Tuwaijat 34–5, 51, 56
Twiss 77 n., 83 n.
Tyranowski 86 n.

Udokang 86 n.
Uganda 105
une acte de presence 51
Unilateral Abrogation of Treaties 85–93, 95–99
  and *rebus sic stantibus* 85–89
  and state succession to treaties 90
  expressio unius est exclusio alterius 98
  finality and stability as rationale 86, 88, 99
  frontier security and Baghdad Treaty 94–7
  investiture of territorial rights 86, 88, 90, 99
  material breach 97–9
  mutuality in abrogation and revision 93, 118
    and right to request 93, 118
  pacta sunt servanda 89 n.
  State practice 91–2
unilateral changes during war, *see* war
United Nations 92 n., 111 n., 109, 112, 114–15
  General Assembly 75 n., 89 n., 107–8, 114, 117
    Fourth Committee, General Assembly 92 n.
    Special Committee 108
    Sixth Committee 87 n.
  Security Council 65, 75 n., 109–10 n., 111 n., 112 n., 114
United States 78, 81, 101–2, 107, 109
  boundaries with Canada 77 n., 78–9, 101–2
  Thalweg principle in national courts 79–82
  war and boundary treaties in national courts, *see* war
usucapio 82 n.
uti possidetis 17, 28

Vallat 86 n., 90
Van der Molen 113 n.

Vattel 77 n., 101 n.
Venezuela 82 n., 92 n.
Verdross 87
Verzijl 76, 77 n., 83 n., 84 n., 100 n.
Vienna Convention on Succession of States in Respect of Treaties
  Article 11 90
Vienna Convention on the Law of Treaties
  Article 4 87 n.
  Article 52 112
  Article 60 97, 99
  Article 62 87
  Article 65 99
  Article 66 99 n.
  Article 70 99
  Article 75 112
  Draft Article 28 89 n.
  Draft Article 39 89 n.
  Draft Article 57 99
  Draft Article 62 99 n.
Vietnam 104
  War 110 n.

war
  and the Baghdad Treaty 99–115
  as an instrument of national policy 106–8, 116–17
    non-recognition 106
    State practice 106–8
  change of status during or after war 106–15
    rationale 108–11
    recognition (international) 114–15, 117
  effects of war on territories and boundary treaties 99–105, 114–15
    abrogation of bilateral treaties 100
    survival of boundary treaties 100–5, 114–17
    rationale 103–4
  limitations of military occupation 107, 109
  relevance of nature of force used 108–15
  suspension of boundary treaties during 101, 103–4
Ward 59 n.
Waldock 86–9, 97 n., 106 n., 109 n., 112 n.
Westlake 77 n., 83 n., 100 n.
Wharton 78 n.
Wheaton 83 n., 100 n., 103 n., 113 n.
Whiteman 91 n., 92 n., 100 n., 105 n., 107 n.
Widdows 88 n., 89–90 n.
Williams 16, 19–20, 22
Wilson 25–6, 29, 31, 66
Wright 92 n., 110 n., 111 n.

Zagros mountains 5
Zohab 6, 18–19, 35, 40–8
Zohab Sector 40–8
Zurich 82